A Path to Self Remembering

A Path to Self Remembering

Debby Edgerton

Valle Publishing

Table of Contents

Introduction

This is a book about how to grow in human consciousness. It has two parts. The first part of the book lays out the spiritual principles necessary for growth in consciousness. It looks at the topic of oneness, models for aspects of the soul and aspects of the human psyche, and defines the terms that will be used in the second part of the book. It sets the stage for what is to follow.

The second part of the book is a "how to" guide for work on being. It systematically lays out exercises that, if practiced, will lead to growth in consciousness. It looks at ideals and right attitude, and outlines processes for letting go of attachment to thoughts, limiting emotions, and limiting beliefs. It examines the role of the will and the forgiveness process.

In the end, there is nothing new here. Sages have been telling us for thousands of years what it takes to find our way home. The intent of this book is to create an easily understandable summary of the basics of the process in the hope that it will make the path easier for others to follow.

The intended audience is those at the beginner to intermediate level who have a sincere desire to know the God within. Although the first part of the book sets the stage and outlines the metaphysical basis for what will follow, it does *not* go into great detail about philosophy. Its intent is simply to create enough of a foundation to begin the inner work that supports growth in consciousness. In that sense, while setting a platform, it has intentionally avoided debate about philosophical issues or in depth exploration of topics such as reincarnation. That stems from the author's observation that it is easy to get sidetracked in the spiritual arena, and that it is focus on the basics that leads to the greatest growth.

The book can be read individually or in small study groups. At the end of each chapter are reflection questions and exercises and, in some chapters, meditations. If the book is read individually, the questions can be used for self-reflection. If read as a group, they can be used as discussion questions. There is opportunity whether read individually or as a group. Using them as self-reflection questions enables one to go deeper into the self. Working in a group offers various perspectives and the synergy that being part of a group brings.

Chapter 1 - Oneness

Have you ever wondered how two scientists on opposite sides of the world can have the same realization at the same time, how the answer you have been seeking appears in the next book you pick up, or how the person you were hoping to speak to shows up in an unexpected location?

The answer lies in the fact that there is just one being, one energy, one Source, one Divine Intelligence that permeates all that is. There is divine wisdom underlying everything. There is no separation between each of us and life itself.

The concept of oneness is difficult to comprehend precisely because it is difficult to put into words what can only be understood through experiencing it. And yet, openness to the concept of oneness is the fundamental principle underlying spiritual growth.

This excerpt from the Edgar Cayce readings emphasizes the importance of oneness:

The first lesson for SIX MONTHS should be ONE - One - One - ONE; Oneness of God, oneness of man's relation, oneness of force, oneness of time, oneness of purpose, ONENESS in every effort - Oneness - Oneness! (Edgar Cayce Reading 900-429)

This chapter is thus an attempt to create some understanding of the concept of oneness and of the implications that result from it.

Perennial Philosophy

If we look at the world's great religions and distill the core wisdom that underlies them, we find a common set of truths described as the perennial philosophy. This philosophy has been consistent across cultures and across the ages. It cuts across time to the heart of what it means to be human. Its central themes are the following:

- There is a single Divine Source that animates all that is. The world and all that is in it depends on this Source for its very being.
- Man possesses a double nature, an ego (small self) and an eternal Self, and it is this eternal Self that makes it possible for man to recognize his oneness with the Divine.
- We can come to know this reality through intuition, which is more encompassing than reason. This direct knowledge unites the knower with that which is known.

From a spiritual perspective, recognition (or remembrance) of our true nature as divine beings is the goal of human existence. The intellectual mind alone cannot reach this recognition. It is only through setting aside the intellectual mind and entering a state of inner knowing that union with our Source can be realized.

Symbols

Across time many symbols have reflected this understanding that all is one. Edgar Cayce suggested the use of a multipoint star as a way to depict the oneness of humanity.

When we are incarnate in the world of matter and perceive ourselves to be separate individuals, we are as a point on the star. When we are operating from the conscious mind, we see ourselves as separate from other conscious minds, just as each tip in the star appears separate from the perspective of any other tip in the star.

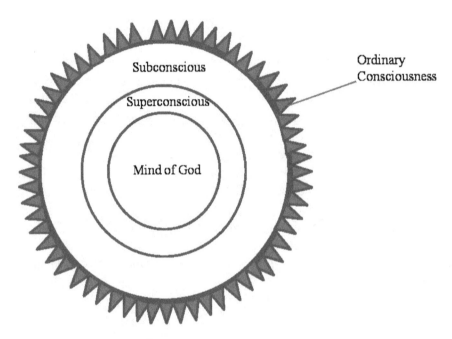

Diagram
Multipoint Star - The One Human Consciousness

The subconscious is the next layer in from the conscious. From the diagram, we see that each subconscious mind has a connection to every other subconscious mind. Telepathy occurs at the level of the subconscious, as do many of our experiences of subtly picking up what another person is thinking or feeling.

The third level in is what may be termed the superconscious mind. Clairvoyance and intuition operate from the level of the superconscious. Some authors like to make a distinction between the superconscious (the higher spiritual mind at the soul level, the Higher Self) and the universal consciousness (the Mind of God).

Use of the star allows us to picture in a visual way the one mind that is shared by all. Although we perceive ourselves as individuals, in fact, we are all connected at the level of the subconscious and again at the superconscious where we all connect to a higher universal mind. As we grow in consciousness and step further into the circle, we begin to realize our oneness with others until ultimately, we come to realize our true nature as one with the Source of all that is.

There are other symbols that show that the world of matter and the world of spirit are one. The trinity is a symbolic attempt to describe the aspects of God (pure spirit, creative force, and manifestation). As the aspects of God move through this cycle from potential to creation to manifestation, there is an ever expanding spiral of growth in consciousness. As the Father (the creative force) extends, so all of his creations continue to extend, creating a continuous extension of ever expanding love. God could also be described as an ever expanding consciousness coming to know itself. Likewise, the yin yang symbol shows that the seen and the unseen, the manifest and the un-manifest, are part of the same one reality.

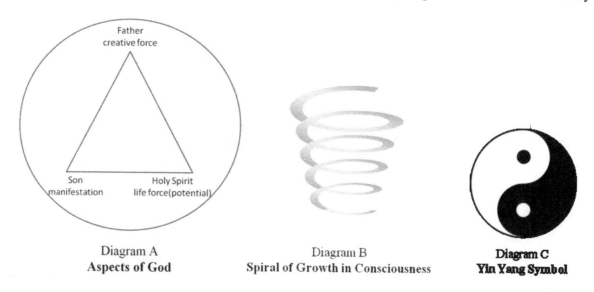

Diagram A
Aspects of God

Diagram B
Spiral of Growth in Consciousness

Diagram C
Yin Yang Symbol

Separation From God

Every culture has some form of a separation story that attempts to explain how man came to be separate from God. There are two primary schools of thought on how humanity came to have this perceived separation. The first suggests that the separation was a necessary step to further growth in human consciousness. It suggests that while God and "man" are one, man was not aware of this oneness, much as animals today are not fully aware. In other words, to develop more awareness, man needed the illusion of separation. The second suggests that man separated from God through error. It does not matter, in terms of how we go forward, which of these is reality; there is probably some element of truth to both.

While these two schools of thought differ on whether the "fall" was necessary, they are in agreement on the key points:

- Man has never really been separate from God, as nothing lives that is not animated by Source.
- The sense of separation was created by man and not by God.
- Returning to the Divine is a remembering of who we really are.

In a later chapter, we will look at how man perceives God as his level of consciousness rises. For now, it is sufficient to equate God with love, which can be defined as that which is life affirming. The fundamental nature of reality is spirit or pure conscious awareness, sometimes described as the "Mind of God." This fundamental reality also manifests itself as the universe. Matter then becomes love made manifest. It is the same energy or life force that permeates all that is - animate and inanimate. That life force is unlimited, pure potential.

Involution/Evolution

If we accept the premise that there is one life force that permeates all that is and that we have somehow come to see ourselves as separate beings, life in this three dimensional world becomes an opportunity to remove this illusion of separateness and thus reunite with the reality of who we truly are. Pictorially, this separation and return are described by the following picture.

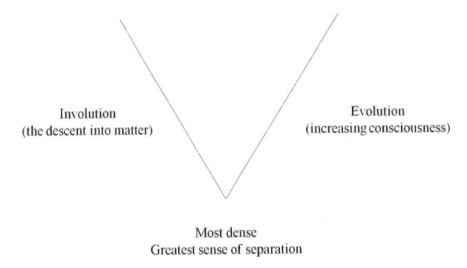

Involution
(the descent into matter)

Evolution
(increasing consciousness)

Most dense
Greatest sense of separation

In spiritual circles, the general belief is that consciousness is rising and humanity is beginning to awaken. Why is it important for humanity to understand this now? There are many who believe that humanity has had the opportunity to awaken at multiple points in the past and has regressed again to the lowest point. We are once again on the upward slope of the curve, but not so far along that we may not slip back. Each day is then, for each of us, an opportunity to see that perceiving from a sense of separation leads to suffering, while perceiving from a sense of oneness leads to joy.

All human suffering comes from this sense of separation - from God, from each other, and from the world around us. While we are under this illusion we cannot feel the sincere love that surrounds us. There are times when the veil becomes thin, at moments of intensity (birth, death, danger, near death experiences, etc.) or in moments of stillness (deep meditation, in the midst of nature, etc.) where we get glimpses in the form of mystical experiences. When these occur, they provide a strength of assurance that provides motivation to stay on the spiritual path.

What Does Oneness Mean?

If we look at the world from a position of oneness instead of separation, everything changes. The following chart summarizes some of the differences between approaching the world from separation versus oneness.

Separation	Oneness
Focus	*Focus*
Past and future	Present moment
Ways of Knowing	*Ways of Knowing*
Logical thinking and reasoning	Contemplation and internal knowing
Content	Context and the whole
Goal of Life	*Goal of Life*
To have, to do, to make money, to be in control	To be, to seek the truth, to grow in consciousness, equal pleasure in all circumstances

A Path to Self Remembering

Separation	Oneness
Measures of Success	***Measures of Success***
Power over	Being with
Net worth	Good of all
Social Order Maintained By	***Social Order Maintained By***
Domination and top down control	Reverence for life
Rigid roles	Respect for diversity
Rules	Golden Rule
Mind Control – shaming, comparison, religious and social righteousness, messages that we are unacceptable unless we conform	Trust of inner guidance
Symbols of Compliance	***Symbols of Compliance***
Loyalty to authority	Respect for diversity
Willingness to betray others in the name of competition	Cooperation & reciprocity
Willingness to accept the status quo	Willingness to embrace change
Motivation	***Motivation***
Extrinsic	Intrinsic
Self-preservation	Common good
Outlook on Life	***Outlook on Life***
Lack	Abundance
Life is suffering	Life is joy
Systems exist to maintain top-down order	Systems are here to enrich our lives
Blame	There is a bigger picture - things happen as they should
Expectations of others	Inner guidance
System needs first	Good of all
Healing	***Healing***
Healing is applied from the outside	Healing is the restoration of the memory of wholeness
Disease just happens	Disease is a call to recognize that things are not right
Apply fixes to the problem, mask the symptoms	Healing involves removing the obstructions to one's natural state of wholeness
Science	***Science***
Separate objects	Each part reflects the whole
Measurement in isolation, compartmental thinking	Systems thinking
Matter only	Interconnected fields
Emphasis on rational reasoning	Integrated head and heart
Form	Essence
Separation and duality	Integrated whole
Psychology	***Psychology***
Ego-separateness, many separate minds	A single mind, connectedness

Separation	Oneness
Reality is external	Reality is internal
Finance	*Finance*
Concentrate wealth	Support for all of life
Government	*Government*
Serve those in power	Serve the common good
Religion	*Religion*
Dogma	Inner guidance
Results	*Results*
Conceals	Reveals
Involution	Evolution
Irresponsibility	Responsibility
Stagnation	Growth
Conformity	Creativity

Implications of Oneness

The implications of this oneness are profound and include the following:
- There is no separation between each of us and life itself. Life will, by definition, sustain us.
- We are never alone in that we are connected to everyone and to everything.
- There is no death, simply changing of form. Incarnations are much like the changing of clothes. As pure conscious awareness, we always have and always will exist.
- There is - within each of us - that spark of the Divine obscured by what we, through misunderstanding, created. We are God stuff: pure awareness becoming more and more conscious. That Divine aspect goes by many names, including the Higher Self, Christ Consciousness, the Buddha Nature, etc.
- We are each an equally valuable aspect of the Divine, a unique and necessary expression of the one life force. No part is any more or less special than any other part. That implies that we are of the same fabric as Jesus and other enlightened masters who have preceded us in coming to an understanding of who they really are.
- What we do to another, we are doing to the self. In giving, we receive. As we forgive (see another as a pure and holy child of God), we are forgiven (see the self as a pure and holy child of God).
- We are all in this together and will return home together. When we grow, we are doing it for all of humanity.
- As an indispensable part of the Whole, none of us can ultimately be lost.
- Because we are one consciousness, unaddressed separation in any part of the Whole is also present within each of us.
- There is only one Will, the Will of the one Whole, the All That Is. Our sense of an individual will is illusion.
- There is only one Mind, one consciousness that permeates All That Is.
- As an extension of God and God's love, we are all creative beings.
- Because there is one universal consciousness, all knowledge is available to everyone all of the time.

Perceived separation leads to suffering and is a sign that we have lost sight of oneness. What serves the whole is always life affirming. The test for what comes from misperception versus spirit is the question, "Is this for the good of all?" It is the Will of God that all should live in harmony.

There are multiple ways to realize and express this oneness. We have a oneness with all of humanity. There is Divine wisdom in everything that happens, whether we understand it at the time or not. Everyone who comes into our lives is there for a reason. We have a oneness with each human as a fellow traveler making choices and working on growth just as we are. Less obvious is our oneness with our family tree and souls on the other side of the veil. It is through relationships that we come to know ourselves.

We have a oneness with the physical world. We have a symbiotic relationship with the Earth, the whole Universe, and all that is. We need each other to grow, to learn, and to develop. The same life force permeates everything.

We are one with God, the All That Is. This is, ultimately, a quest to remember who we really are. It is only by recognizing our true nature as God beings, sparks of the Divine, that we perceive ourselves as one with our Source.

Summary

- There is a single Divine Source that animates all that is.
- Man, either intentionally or through error, has come to see himself as separate from this Source. The spiritual journey is thus one of remembering our true nature as spirit.
- It is perceived separation that leads to suffering.
- As we begin to recognize our oneness with God, with each other, and with the environment in which we reside, human consciousness rises until, ultimately, we perceive our true nature as one with our Source (All That Is).
- While three dimensional existence makes it more difficult to perceive our true nature as spirit, it is an environment of high contrast that also allows us to more easily perceive the results of our thoughts and actions.

Reflections/Exercises/Practices

For Reflection/Discussion:

1. In what ways are all people alike?
2. To whom do natural resources belong?
3. How does nationalism fit with the idea of oneness?
4. What do you perceive if you look at history as the story of growth in human consciousness instead of a listing of conflicts?
5. If the education system was designed to foster oneness, how would it differ from what we have today? What would be its goals and objectives?
6. Where on the involution/evolution curve do you see humanity at this time?
7. If the involution and evolution of humankind has been cyclic (we grew in consciousness and then fell back again), what factors led to the regression? How might a graph of this involution/evolution process look across time?
8. What are some of the human behaviors (societal conventions) that were once accepted that have fallen aside as consciousness has increased?

Exercises:

1. Before eating, mentally review all of the steps and people involved in getting the food to your table. Give thanks for everyone involved in the process.
2. As people pass by on the street, resist the urge to pass judgment and instead feel for the gift each person brings to the world.
3. The next time you have to make a decision that involves other people, ask the question "Is this for the good of all?" Look for the win-win solution.

Meditative Practices:

1. Feel yourself in the heart of God. Let that part of you that is God sit with the Creator.
2. Allow your awareness to gently expand out from your body until it fills the entire universe.
3. Feel your connection to the plants and animals, to the Earth itself, and extend a deep respect and gratitude to them.
4. Choose someone with whom you have a close relationship. Feel your own heart. Feel the heart of the other person. Feel the connection between you. Sit in oneness with that other person. Do the same with someone you have difficulty being around. If necessary, separate the surface personality and actions from the core of who that person really is. Continue working with this until you can feel the heart to heart connection.
5. Feel the connection to your family tree. See if anything emerges from the silence that can be healed by you on behalf of your family.

Chapter 2 - Growth in Consciousness

The Nature of Consciousness

To further understand oneness, we look at the writings of Morton Blumenthal based on the readings of Edgar Cayce. He suggests that while we are operating under three dimensional perception, we are unable to perceive the true nature of our being.

Even what we perceive as inanimate matter has life and a form of consciousness. But for the mineral and animal kingdoms, that life force is only a section or a part of the universal life force. He further says that even inanimate matter is connected with certain wholes described as the noumenon or life essence of that particular thing. An individual tree, for example, is a manifestation or instance of the "mind" or "intelligence" or "section of the life force" that is the essence of tree. Although it *cannot* be experienced via the five external senses, there are other ways of "knowing" the essence of something.

The consciousness of humanity has developed to where we are self aware while the mineral, plant and animal kingdoms are not, although they are still animated by the same universal life force. When man incarnates, there is "... made manifest in physical form not only a sectional representation of the operation of this one force or essence, but also in the mind or soul of man, the universal forces themselves" (Report of Cayce Reading 254-107, Morton Blumenthal). Because we have the whole of the universal forces within us, we are capable of being co-creators with the Divine. A Course in Miracles[1] (ACIM) describes man as being an "extension" of God. "To extend is a fundamental aspect of God which He gave to His Son. In the creation, God extended Himself to His creations and imbued them with the same loving Will to create" (ACIM, T-2,.I.1.2).

ACIM also says that there is only one Son. If we see the essence of humanity and our individual three dimensional bodies as instances of this same "mind of man," it becomes easier to see how we are all One, and how raising what we perceive to be our individual consciousness raises the consciousness of humanity as a whole.

Edgar Cayce said that this consciousness occurs at all levels. In other words, while each tree has its own consciousness, the forest also has a consciousness of its own. The same applies to humanity, where groups of people - such as a nation - have developed a consciousness. From the Cayce readings:

Hence you speak of the spirit of America, of Germany, of the Nordic people, of the Mayan, of the Celtic, or what not. These are influences that have taken shape in the realms beyond matter, yet

---

[1] *A Course in Miracles* (also referred to as ACIM or the Course) is a book written and edited by Helen Schucman, with portions transcribed and edited by William Thetford, containing a self-study curriculum to bring about what it calls a "spiritual transformation." Schucman believed that an "inner voice", which she identified as Jesus, guided her writing.

influence same [matter], *with as much of a body as the mind (the builder) has builded* (Edgar Cayce Reading 254-95).

To further increase understanding of what it means to be a higher-dimensional being living in a three-dimensional world, think of a two dimensional being living in a three dimensional world. When a three-dimensional object enters the world of this two-dimensional being, he sees only the intersection of that object with the flat (two-dimensional) plane. For example, if he comes into contact with a three-dimensional hand, he first sees it as the five circles at the tip of the fingers. Later, he might perceive it as two ovals of different sizes as the palm of the hand reaches his plane and still later as a single larger oval when the final portion of the hand passes through his plane of existence.

We are higher-dimensional beings having a three-dimensional experience and just like our two-dimensional friend, if we perceive only with our outer three-dimensional senses, then we are aware of only what intersects our three-dimensional plane. Just as the five fingers are part of a whole hand, the projection of our individual human bodies is part of an interconnected whole that lies outside our sense of perception.

This analogy also helps with the understanding that there is no time. Changes to the hand as it passes through the two-dimensional plane seemingly appear to a two-dimensional being as the passage of time, while in fact, the full hand is always present.

The Blumenthal article goes on to talk about the change of mind from its physical form to its elemental state at death.

"If not blocked while in physical form, the mind or soul of man changes at death to become of the fourth, higher dimensional elemental kind that this life essence possesses in its elemental state, and also becomes self aware of being that. In other words, man changes from being the Created, and knowing himself to be that, to the Creator, and becomes aware of himself being that." (Edgar Cayce Reading 254-107)

Key points from the remainder of the article include the following:
- While incarnate, the mind of the Creator is that side of man's mind called the universal subconscious.
- The subconscious is the seat of memory and retains previous development of personality and character tendencies, likes and dislikes, as well as knowledge gathered in previous lifetimes and in other realms.
- Whereas return to the physical is automatic for animals, it is a choice for man.
- Although we are all heirs to this higher state, what we will be able to do with life and ourselves in this changed higher state will depend on what we learn to do with it in this three-dimensional world. (Consciousness goes with us.)
- We are this higher or more universal kind of being with a higher than three-dimensional viewpoint, and may, even while in physical form, understand ourselves to be that.

Reincarnation, then, occurs so that man may know himself to be himself and yet one with the Whole. The contrast is greater in three dimensions than in four where the love and pure essence of all is more visible. That contrast makes it easier for us to learn lessons more deeply and rapidly here than on the other side. Each lifetime provides the opportunity to raise human consciousness even higher, not for the self alone, but for the good of the Whole. It is, in that sense, a gift not to be squandered.

(Note: Although the concept of reincarnation will be taken as a given within this book, a belief in reincarnation is not essential to the concepts that will be presented here. Once the groundwork has been laid, this book will look at various methods for making spiritual progress. These methods are independent of the need for belief in reincarnation.)

Stages of Awakening

Growth in consciousness can be thought of as occurring in stages. As one moves along the path, there is an increase in understanding of how interconnected everything is. What is understood at lower levels becomes the basis for the more subtle levels of understanding. As one progresses, there is an increase in unity within the self, a greater understanding of one's true identity, a more inclusive context to everything that occurs, and a greater sense of oneness with all that is.

For example, let us say that an individual was a king in a previous lifetime who treated his subjects cruelly and held a strong sense of entitlement or specialness. In this lifetime, that soul has chosen to enter into the persecuted class. Initially, this could be perceived as karma in the sense of atonement for past deeds. If the unresolved issue of entitlement is still present, and without awareness of previous lifetimes, this person might feel a strong sense of unfair treatment and expect compensation to correct perceived wrongs of the past. As life progresses, this person will get constant opportunities to change the incorrect perception of entitlement, and in a sense forgive himself, through interactions with other people, through his own dreams, etc. Assuming that progress is made, that person may eventually come to a realization that no one deserves special treatment, letting go of the misperception of specialness or entitlement. With continued awareness, this person might recognize that as a member of the oppressed class, he is in the best position to help other others in the same situation, thus moving from karma as atonement to karma as the opportunity to help bring back into balance what was previously put out of balance.

This story demonstrates the imbalance (specialness or entitlement) which the individual has come to recognize and resolve, and the larger context that becomes apparent with growth in consciousness (all are equally valued parts of the whole, karma as the opportunity to restore balance as opposed to atonement for past deeds). In so doing, the individual recognizes an increased oneness with others. (Note that racism, sexism, and religious intolerance are current examples of specialness and entitlement that still abound in our world today.)

Charts of Growth in Consciousness

Many over time have attempted to describe what it means to progress along this path, including some authors currently popular in the marketplace. Their charts are worth obtaining and reviewing as they are readily accessible, easy to understand, and reflect key understandings of how the growth process progresses.

Although the charts in these sources appear hierarchical, it is important to assign no judgment to the levels. We are all on a journey. Think of multiple children in a family. While the younger children are less capable of certain understandings due to their age, they are equally loved by their parents who know that in time all of their children will mature into adults.

The similarity of these charts shows that this is a progression and the path is one we can all undertake. Later we will look at elements of what it takes to succeed on this path, but for now the most important criteria are an openness to new ideas, a belief that this higher reality is one that all can obtain, and acceptance that there is a workable process that will lead to growth in consciousness.

Abraham Hicks - The first chart is the "Emotional Guidance Scale" put forth by Abraham Hicks. Abraham is a group consciousness that comes through Esther Hicks. The following brief synopsis of this work is based on the book The Amazing Power of Deliberate Intent[1] by Esther and Jerry Hicks.

The basic premise of the Abraham information is that by paying attention to your emotions, you can literally feel your way to vibrational alignment with Source (God)[2]. The better you feel, the more you are allowing your connection to Source and conversely, the worse you feel, the *less* you are allowing your connection to Source. "A good feeling emotion indicates vibrational alignment between the perspective of your Inner Being and you [your personality self] and a bad feeling emotion indicates vibrational *mis*alignment between your Inner Being and you [your personality self]."[3]

The Abraham work involves an awareness of both thoughts (head) and emotions (heart). In addition to choosing a subject of attention and focusing on it, you must also feel for the vibrational content of your thought. The key to deliberate creating is "to choose the subjects of your thoughts intentionally while paying close attention to how each thought feels."[4] What you are looking for is control of your own attention. You are free, but the only way you will ever perceive that freedom is by understanding that you have the ability to feel good, no matter what happens in the outside world.

What Abraham suggests is that the way to joy and alignment with who we really are is to deliberately choose better feeling thoughts. We do this in the various areas of our life until finally we are free of our own limiting beliefs. This work also suggests that this is a process. One does not jump from despair to joy, but rather by replacing a despair thought with a thought that is a little better feeling, and so on, one gradually moves up the scale over a period of time.

Dr. David R. Hawkins - The second chart is the "Map of Consciousness®" put forth by Dr. David R. Hawkins M.D., Ph.D,. a medical doctor and psychiatrist who reached high states of consciousness during his lifetime. After a period of withdrawal from society, he returned to write and teach in the area of spiritual development. He is known for his work in the area of kinesiology, a tool used to determine truth from falsehood.

The Hawkins Map is logarithmic, so a jump of even a few points over a lifetime is significant.

There are two critical transition points:

- "The first is at 200, the initial level of empowerment: Here, the willingness to stop blaming and accept responsibility for one's own actions, feelings, and beliefs arises ...
- The second is at the 500 level, which is reached by accepting love and nonjudgmental forgiveness as a lifestyle ..."[5]

Dr. Deepak Chopra - The third set of charts is from the book How to Know God[6] by Deepak Chopra. Deepak Chopra is a well-known medical doctor, author, and spiritual teacher. This book suggests that we come to know God in stages and that understanding these stages can assist in the growth process. It is not God who changes, but our understanding of God as we grow in awareness. While, at times, we regress to lower stages just as we regress to lower emotional stages, in general, this is an upward trend until we reach full unification with the Divine.

Are there exactly seven stages to growth in consciousness as suggested by Deepak Chopra? Are these the exact emotions we grow through on the path? Maybe, maybe not. The value of charts like these is that they provide a model that the conscious mind can use to increase understanding.

All three sets of charts show the parallel between emotional state and level of consciousness. All three show a progression that ranges from the baser emotions of fear, blame, and shame to the higher emotions of joy and happiness. They suggest that happiness and joy are internal states that are under our own control and that nothing outside of us can give us happiness.

It is the natural state of man to live in peace, joy, and happiness. It is separation (blame, judgment, etc.) that leads to the lower emotions, and taking responsibility for our thoughts, feelings, and actions that frees us. Although only the Chopra charts speak in terms of God, all of the charts are a reflection of what it means to come to know the Divine within. This is the path we are meant to follow; one of increasing awareness of the Divine within.

All three authors agree that this is inner work and involves an awareness of thoughts and feelings, and ultimately, a letting go of limiting beliefs. The oft used saying "line upon line, precept upon precept" applies. This is a progression and all three charts show a consistent pattern of movement through stages of growth. This is a progression that all are capable of following with the presence of understanding and willingness.

Our understanding of reality changes as we move through the stages. Everyone is doing the best they can from their own level of consciousness. When acting from lower levels of consciousness, man primarily acts out of ignorance. Wrongdoing is in that sense involuntary, and it is far better to see habitual reactions as misguided rather than stemming from an evil motive. Ultimately, we must see the internal goodness that resides within ourselves and each other.

Reflections/Exercises/Practices

For Reflection/Discussion:

1. Why does humanity start out fearing God?
2. Where would you place yourself on each of these scales?
3. If happiness is an inside job, why do we continue to blame others for our mental and emotional states?
4. If people have the opportunity to gain or lose consciousness in a given lifetime, what factors influence that gain or loss?
5. Think back to an event in your own life that you have re-contextualized. This might be an event from your childhood that you understood one way as a child, but now understand more fully as an adult.

Chapter 3 - Aspects of the Soul

This chapter will be devoted to increasing understanding of the metaphysics of human consciousness. Again, models like these should always be approached as tools to aid understanding rather than hard and fast representations of reality. Several ways of looking at the topic of consciousness are presented in this book because the conscious or rational mind needs a framework on which to build understanding and to which one can relate experiences.

Soul/Mind

The soul is the bridge between the realm of spirit and the world of physical reality. A famous Cayce saying is that "the spirit is life, mind is the builder, and the physical is the result" (Edgar Cayce Reading 349-4). Energy is patterned by the mind and becomes manifest in the physical world. A simple way to draw the diagram that reflects the creative ability of the mind is below:

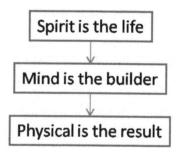

Edgar Cayce described three attributes of the soul:
- The spiritual life energy, which is eternal and limitless
- The mind, the creative force
- The will, which gives us an independent identity and freedom of choice

It should be noted here that what Cayce refers to as the soul, in some literature, will be referred to as the mind. Pictorially, another way to draw the relationship with the universal mind might be as follows:

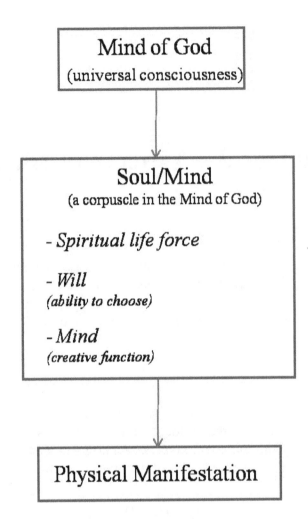

Diagram of Aspects of the Soul

Edgar Cayce described the soul as a corpuscle in the body of God.[7] That description makes it understandable that, as a bit of God, we are endowed with the same creative abilities as that of which we are a part (God), and at the same time are each an indispensable part of the whole.

While we are asked to give up the personality self that stands in the way of perceiving who we really are, God is not asking us to give up our true individuality, that unique aspect of the greater whole. As Cayce says, we are here that "we may come to know ourselves to be ourselves, and yet one with the Creative Forces" (Edgar Cayce Reading 2021-1). It is not the small personality self but the Higher Self that is God.

Superconscious (Spiritual Mind)

As an integral part of the Whole, we each have access to information from the non-physical realm. The same superconscious mind is present in each of us. All knowledge is there all of the time; it is simply that we are unable to perceive it because the mist that is the ego is obscuring our perception. The message is pure; it is the receiver that is cloudy.

The love of God is absolute and unconditional and has always been there for us. Love is our natural state of being and it is seen once the clouds of misperception are removed. Everyone is already one with

God; the Self is already present or life and existence could not be. It is our connection with the Divine that sustains us every minute of every day. Nothing needs to be "done" to achieve higher states, it is more a matter of removing what is in the way. Self realization is therefore not a gain or accomplishment; it is a matter of perceiving who you already are.

Recalling the multipoint star diagram again, it is possible to see how new ideas appear to multiple people at once. When the time has arrived for an idea to come into human awareness, it is there at the level of shared consciousness where multiple people can tap into it. In addition, it appears that once an idea resonates in one brain, it becomes easier for that idea to resonate in other brains. The work of Rupert Sheldrake, author, speaker, and researcher in the field of parapsychology, has increasingly confirmed what he calls "morphic resonance."[8]

Conscious Versus Subconscious Mind

The conscious mind operates through the five senses and the intellect, which are focused on details. Separation is the creation of the conscious mind. In a sense, the conscious mind suppresses or holds back the subconscious and the superconscious aspects of the mind. If, however, the body relaxes (meditation, sleep, etc) and we ignore information from our external senses, the conscious mind begins to loosen its hold on these other aspects.

The subconscious mind functions through intuition and is founded in oneness. If we were to prepare a chart of differences between the conscious mind and the subconscious mind it might look something like this:

Conscious Mind	Subconscious Mind
Thinking	Intuition
Objective	Subjective
Focused on details	Picks up everything
Content	Context
Uses words	Uses pictures and symbols
External	Internal
Local	Non-local
Separation	Oneness
Imperfect memory	Perfect memory

What distinguishes the conscious mind from the subconscious mind is the focus of attention. While the conscious mind is good at detail, the subconscious is better at perceiving patterns, particularly patterns of meaning. The subconscious notices and remembers what we miss with ordinary consciousness.

It is at the level of the subconscious that the power of thought becomes important. We pick up the thoughts of others, and conversely, our thoughts affect others. Although we are not consciously aware of what others are thinking, their thoughts nevertheless affect us and vice versa.

Will

While the mind generates many patterns, the choice of which to focus attention on is the job of the will. The will is the chooser, an active principle within the soul. It can be thought of as a form of self-discipline: the ability to direct attention where we want it and to act, inhibit, or redirect action in a particular manner. Choosing to do nothing can be an act of the will.

When we are not aware of our beliefs, perceptions, and values, we choose unconsciously. Attention and behavior follow the path of habits. This is what spiritual literature describes as the state of being "asleep." To regain the use of will, we must become consciously aware of what we have been choosing out of habit. Allowing the events of the outside world to control one's inner state is an indication that one is acting out of habit. For example, immediately going to anger when one is cut off on the road is an example of habitual and uncontrolled behavior.

The will can be thought of as having two parts: one that is associated with the personality self and one that is associated with the Higher Self. We lose wholeness when we give reign to the lower will, and return to wholeness when we shift allegiance to the higher or Spiritual Will. Use of self will has the feeling of effort. In contrast, use of Spiritual Will has the feeling of determination, like voluntary surrender to a meaningful choice. The will can be thought of as a muscle that is strengthened through use. Choices made in accord with God's Will bring one closer to the Creative Forces, while choices made in support of separation move one away from one's true identity. Within the mind are both freedom (Higher Self) and attachment (ego); we make the choice which to attune to.

"self" will	Spiritual Will
Feels like effort	Feels like determination
Benefits the self	For the good of all

Many ask whether we really have free will if we must ultimately do God's Will in order to experience freedom and happiness. The answer lies in the definition of freedom. Is it chaos, free reign, and the ability to act with no limits? Or is it choosing that which is life affirming, that which benefits the whole? If we are all one, only choices that follow the Will of God, made for the benefit of all, can ultimately bring happiness.

One way to look at karma is as a way to experience what we are putting out into the world (what we do comes back to us). It is a way of testing different ways of thinking and acting, to see how we like the results. In this earth environment, we face constant choices each day as we live our lives. We each have the opportunity to see the results of our choices and to choose differently if we do not like the outcomes. What brings us peace and happiness? With free will, we have the opportunity to find the answer to that question. It is through our life experiences that we come to the understanding that our real will is the Will of God and employing it is the path to love, joy, and happiness. Obedience then becomes cooperation with that which is larger than the self through the use of free will (inner choice). To be obedient, one must understand what is desired, have the ability to make conscious decisions, learn to control one's own actions, and have both the skill and the psychological maturity to carry out those actions. Development of the will thus enables surrender to that which is larger than the self.

Proper use of the will might then be seen as acting in accordance with necessary constraints through one's own control. We must exercise our freedom of choice and in so doing grow in personal strength, but at the same time we must attune to, and surrender to, the Higher Will. The stream of energy that God is continuously sending must be channeled into creations patterned after the Divine Will. Each of us is intended to manifest a specific facet of the divine intent.

As beings of free will, the choice to defy Higher Will is always available. If we think of all that is as one large energy field, this defiance, however, creates waves of negativity in the energy field. Cayce said we can expect disturbances from nature (sun spots and earthquakes among them) until human beings start using their wills to choose love, justice, and truth.

Nothing, however, can limit our freedom to choose. We assume our role in the cosmic scheme by choice. Even the heavenly hosts must be petitioned, invited to intervene, before they are permitted to intercede on behalf of humanity. Consciousness and will cannot be given, they must be obtained through personal experience. This earth plane can be seen as the training ground for growth in consciousness and development of the will.

We cannot make use of this Higher Will until we are willing to give up self will. Self will means believing you have all the answers, preferring to be in control and acting from one's own interests rather than turning within, surrendering to a Higher Power, and acting for the good of all. In one who is not "awake", will is the result of desire and fluctuates as desires change.

If the will remains undeveloped, spiritual understanding isn't worth much. Growth of the will can also be seen as an expanding spiral alternating between inner work on the self and action in the world, where that which has been understood is put into practice. We will look, in a later chapter, at the importance of ideals. In developing the will, it is important to set a standard against which one can measure actions.

Will can be grown if one is willing to look inside, to work on oneself, and to make choices that are in accord with one's chosen ideal. We can never control the more difficult things if we do not learn to control the easy things. Eventually, using self observation, and addressing the conflicts that arise within, it is possible to move to the point where when one feels an attachment (to one's own opinions, the need to take control, etc.), it is possible to feel that attachment occur, to choose to stop it, and at the same time to be aware that one is stopping it.

Body, mind, and spirit are meant to function as an integrated whole. In the enlightened state, that is what occurs. Limiting beliefs, imbalances, and misperceptions no longer drive behavior. The individual spirit (the spark of the Divine within us) is in alignment with the Mind of God, the individual will is aligned with God's will, and the mind creates from a position of oneness in accord with the Will of God.

It is with the idea of separation and creation of the ego that the picture becomes more complex. Once the ego is present, the mind creates many patterns based on the values and beliefs we hold. The will now has to choose between that which originates in the Mind of God and that which is created through separation (the egoic mind). Most people choose unconsciously based on conditioning and habit patterns. Spiritual growth then can be seen as developing enough awareness and self-discipline to choose from a position of oneness rather than from a position of separation.

Summary

- Ordinary consciousness is the superficial layer of who we are and leads to the perception of separation.
- While the conscious mind is sharply focused on details (content), the subconscious mind absorbs everything in the environment (context).
- The will is an aspect of the soul that allows free choice. It is like a muscle in that it must be exercised and developed to be strengthened.
- Using the will, we try different ways of thinking and acting to see how we like the results. This earth plane can thus be seen as an environment to test which choices lead to the love and happiness that we seek.

Reflections/Exercises/Practices

For Reflection/Discussion:

1. Many of the early saints and even the Buddha early on practiced extreme physical deprivation. What purpose might this have served in that person's growth? In humanity's overall growth?
2. If physical manifestation is the result of patterning energy in the mind, what are the implications of this?
3. If there is synergy in groups with respect to the development of ideas, do you think the same is true for development of the will?

Exercises:

1. When you perceive that you have an opinion on a topic, stop. Instead of stating that opinion, explore the opposite.
2. Choose a situation that reoccurs in your life to which you react negatively. Define the behavior you would like to exhibit and resolve that the next time that situation occurs you will react differently. When the time comes, act from the intention you have set.
3. The next time you are in a room full of people, try focusing on context. Rather than focusing on a particular person or activity, or mentally commenting on what is going on, place your awareness on the entire room at once.
4. Begin to pay attention to your internal self talk. What messages do you give yourself on a regular basis?

Chapter 4 - Aspects of the Ego

One obstacle to man's further development is his lack of knowledge about the nature of consciousness itself. In this chapter, we move into understanding what happens within the individual that prevents the light of God that is always present from being fully perceived within us. We have already looked at charts of consciousness and understand that one's level of consciousness is tied to perception, but how is it that we each perceive things and how is it that two individuals can have such different perceptions of the same situation?

When an event occurs in the outside world, a sense impression is formed based on input from the five senses of hearing, sight, taste, smell, and feel. However, more and more, experiments are showing that the observer affects the observed. The very act of observing something changes it; there is no objective reality, only subjective experience. Our expectations, assumptions, beliefs, emotional state, and thought processes determine what we experience. Our senses don't inform us of the actual physical events, they give us subjective individualized sensations of what has occurred. To make sense of the world around us, we take what occurs, assign meaning to it, and organize it in ways that make sense based on previous events and experiences.

Before moving into the next topic, spend a few minutes with the following questions.

At what age were your parents old?

What illnesses afflict your family?

To what age would you like to live? Why?

What does it take to have good health?

What do you consider to be the best thing about being female? Male?

What do you consider the worst thing about being female? Male?

Would you choose to come in your next life as a man or as a woman? Why?

What do you consider to be the primary value of money (i.e., what is nice about having it)?

What would you have done differently to have more money in your life if you had it to do over again?

What is your biggest fear about money?

What belief patterns did you inherit from your family?

What is the strongest family message you received?

List the blessings that came from your family.

What is the most important thing you learned from your parents?

What would you like to have been better in your parents' relationship with each other?

What do you consider to be the most important thing your child (children) learned from you?

What role did you play in your family?

When you have finished, go through and highlight any recurring words or themes that stand out.

Beliefs

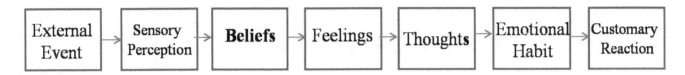

As shown above, beliefs can be seen to act as a filter for everything that follows. Sensory impressions filtered through our belief system generate emotions that are sometimes perceived, but often are suppressed or projected. Out of the beliefs and emotions come thoughts (evaluations, judgments, criticisms, resentments, regrets) and more decisions and beliefs.

A belief is something you hold onto because you think it is true. Generally, beliefs are unconscious although they have powerful impact over our lives. Unlike thoughts, beliefs are silent. What are beliefs? For the most part, they are conclusions we have drawn based on the events in our lives. Many come about during early childhood and are created to meet the expectations of others, to avoid pain, and to protect ourselves. It feels comfortable to be part of a group to whom we feel spiritually, emotionally, and physically connected. Later, we create beliefs based on interactions with teachers, friends, and society in general.

In addition to the early childhood and societal/cultural experiences that lead us to create beliefs, we include our own karmic inheritance and extended familial impacts. In a sense, karmic inheritance can be thought of as perceptions we have brought forward from previous lives and past experiences in this life, both individually and in groups. Although it is outside the scope of this book to talk at any length about epigenetics[2], there is increasing evidence that genetic markers are passed from generation to generation and that beliefs as well as a host of environmental factors are an element in the setting of these markers.

Core beliefs are the views that we hold about ourselves, other people, the world, and the future. They serve as guides to making sense of the world. Although beliefs can be helpful in interpreting what occurs in the world, some are limiting and no longer serve us well.

A key concept here is that beliefs were *created by us* in response to life events. They are not necessarily accurate. For example, when I was 4 or 5 years old, I attended a dance class. At the end of the class, there was a little recital that our parents attended. The teacher called students up two at a time and had them dance a brief segment. I kept waiting and waiting and was the last person called up and had to dance by myself because there was no one else left. As a young child, I felt like I had done something wrong, since I had to wait so long and had to dance by myself. About five years later, I was at an instrumental recital when I realized that the music teacher had put the participants on the program in order from beginners to the most advanced. But, that did *not* rewrite my previous memory with the dance experience. I was in my 40s before, I "resaw" that experience and realized that I must have been a good dancer. Beliefs make sense based on our experiences, but they are not always accurate. When a belief becomes conscious, it is much easier to change. In the example above, simply seeing the event again as an adult was enough to change it. With other beliefs, it may be necessary to test validity before choosing to make a change.

---

[2] the study of changes in organisms caused by modification of gene expression rather than alteration of the genetic code itself

Beliefs are, for the most part, transparent to us. A study done using magnetic resonance imaging (MRI) of the human head showed that volunteers offered cash to "sell out" beliefs found that "core" beliefs have no price - they are kept in a part of the brain that stores information on right and wrong.[9] Core beliefs lie dormant most of the time and only become activated when a "threatening" situation triggers them. We want to break free of beliefs that no longer serve our development. Growth in consciousness can be seen as a process of making our beliefs visible, then separating ourselves from those which limit us. When we change inwardly, we outgrow certain belief patterns and choose instead to strengthen others.

All of this matters because the environment around each of us is a reflection of our own beliefs. What one believes is true, is true for that person. In other words, one's consciousness is what creates one's reality. To take responsibility for that reality, it is necessary to reclaim the power of choice. The conscious mind acts based on what is rational, but the subconscious acts based on the beliefs stored in its memory. To reclaim the power of choice means bringing what is currently hidden into the light so choices can be made with fuller awareness. Even something we consider an "accident" may be unconsciously drawn by what we hold in the subconscious.

At the deepest level, it is the limiting beliefs about not being loveable and not being good enough that need to be exposed. The universal human journey is one of becoming conscious of how powerful we really are and reclaiming the choice to use that power wisely.

If beliefs are deeply entrenched, were created to protect ourselves, and for the most part are not visible to us, how is it that we work on changing beliefs? The first step is acknowledging that each of us is the source of our own beliefs; you created them and you have the power to change them. The second is to begin to expose what is occurring on the inside through self observation. By working with the diagram above in reverse order, starting with customary reactions, then with thoughts and emotions, it is possible to work into limiting beliefs. The remainder of this chapter will explore this process. Prayer and meditation which open one to higher aspects of the Self and expose the subconscious are also helpful. Study processes such as A Course In Miracles that question assumptions about unworthiness and not being loved can precipitate a sudden jump in consciousness through encouraging a total change of perception. An attitude of openness and willingness to question everything are also helpful.

Feelings/Emotions

Feelings (emotions) are driven by beliefs and in turn drive thoughts. We are meant to fully feel at the time an event occurs, and then to release that response and move on. Rather than fully feeling a given emotion, we often choose to suppress it and pretend it is not there. The problem is that these suppressed emotions are standing in the way of experiencing the higher emotions of peace, love, and joy. We can*not* selectively suppress emotions. So in suppressing the lower emotions, we also suppress joy, gratitude, and happiness. I like to think of suppressed emotions as a wall around the heart. It does not matter how thick or thin the wall, the presence of the wall prevents love from getting in or out.

Diagram
The wall around the heart

Eckhart Tolle refers to these suppressed negative emotions as the "pain body"[10] and there is an increasing body of research that shows that suppressed emotions do create physical changes in the body that lead to health problems. When an emotion is suppressed, we keep our attachment to it and only shut down the external expression. The elimination of suppressed emotions, in turn, removes impediments to the flow of energy in the body and sets the stage for better health.

Again, what is going on inside gets reflected in the outer world. If you believe that you are not loveable or are not good enough, then that is what gets reflected back to you. Conversely, those who know their own value find that reflected back to them. As positive feelings increase, relationships improve and self sabotaging behavior decreases.

In the charts of consciousness, we saw that there is a parallel between emotional state and level of consciousness. Another way to say this is that there is a parallel between emotional state and how far one has come in getting in touch with one's own spirit. Emotions and feelings are a deeper aspect of one's being (sense of self) that must be looked at if one is to move forward. They are a window to what is hidden. When limiting emotions are present, there is an unmet need somewhere; something is out of balance. Extremes of emotion are a good indication that a core belief is at work.

Emotions are stronger and quicker than thoughts. When thought goes one way and feelings go another, it is feelings that will win out. Eventually, one can learn to observe emotions just as one can learn to observe thoughts. Initially, however, this is not possible. Since emotions are quicker than thought, it is not possible to "catch" emotions using the intellect. It is for that reason that we start by observing thoughts and work back into emotions. Working with the intellect can only take us so far and then it becomes necessary to work with feelings to make further progress. Ultimately, this is about letting go of the mind and moving to the heart. We are heart-centered beings and that is where wisdom, power, and love reside. Thus the saying: "you cannot think your way to God."

Peace, love, and joy are our natural state. The mind and the heart are meant to work together, but that is not possible until limiting emotions are addressed. It is important to realize that emotions also are part of the egoic structure and are made up; they are *not* who we really are. Beneath the emotional roller coaster there is peace and the realization of who we really are. In living life, we get to explore this arena of emotions and learn to be successful at creating our reality with love.

How does one go about releasing this emotional charge? Awareness is the first step. Once you can see it, you have a choice. Ask yourself, "Do I want to go with this emotion or would I rather be at peace?" It always comes down to choice. We will explore this process further in a later chapter.

Thoughts

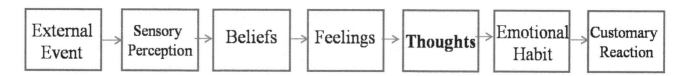

Thoughts are things. They are of the fourth dimension and not visible to the human eye, but they nonetheless shape the physical world according to their patterns. Abraham says: "every circumstance, every event, and every meeting of every person, everything that you live - is because of what you have been thinking about, wondering about, pondering, remembering, observing, considering, and imagining ... You are literally thinking your life into being."[11] The more energy we give to our thoughts, the more they have the power to manifest physically.

The mind directs and shapes the body. The mind plays a role in the creation of disease and the mind heals. When we are sick, we often say "I am so sick," instead of "my body is temporarily feeling sickness," "I am and have always been radiantly healthy," or "show me where the imbalance is so I can change this." Many body functions are controlled by the subconscious, which is amenable to suggestion. The impressions we take in from the environment and what we say to ourselves matter. However, when we say we want one thing and constantly reinforce its opposite by careless thoughts, we confuse the subconscious. The way to change our bodies is to change our thoughts and feelings.

The same is true for relationships. We routinely and without understanding affect others by our emotional state and thoughts; we transmit them to those around us. What we think and what we feel affect others, and vice versa. The world, then, can only see us as we see ourselves. People are not responding to our physical form; they are responding to our internal state of being. When we change our inner world, the relationship changes.

The same is true for manifestation of our physical surroundings. What we focus our energy on is what we draw to us. The Cayce readings frequently reinforce the concept that spirit is the life force, mind is the builder, and the physical is the result.

For remember, MIND is the Builder between the things spiritual (from which all emanate) and that which is material (which is the manifestation that Mind seeks to bring ever into the experience of all). (Edgar Cayce Reading 1999-1)

For the activity is first in spirit, then in mind, and THEN it may become a MATERIAL manifestation. One is the projection as it were of the other into materialization, as we see about us in the earth. (Edgar Cayce Reading 1597-1)

Great changes, then, have come. Again and again the entity has found itself determining in itself to correct physical and mental errors, as it has become aware of same. (Edgar Cayce Reading 3394-2)

Thoughts are so real that in looking at the akashic records[3] for an individual, Cayce described that it was sometimes difficult to differentiate between thoughts and actions.

---

[3] The akashic records are the records written on the skeins of time and space, the cosmic record of all that has ever occurred.

As thoughts are deeds in the mental world, as are the activities of a physical being as related to the associations, the relations, the words, the activity in a material world, so do they leave their impressions and the titles and the activities of each entity are thus written upon the skein between time and space, that may be indeed a record ever for the entity to meet, to experience throughout its activity in whatever consciousness the entity may be. (Edgar Cayce Reading 752-1)

Hence often there is confusion in the experiences of those interpreting for individuals their activities through any given period, in differentiating between that which was the thought of an individual and that which was the actual activity. (Edgar Cayce Reading 1562-1)

Habit and Reaction

When we are not consciously aware of what is going on internally, we tend to follow set patterns in how we respond to the world around us. How we react follows how we have reacted in the past. It is not that the past causes the present, but rather that the same level of consciousness, with its underlying beliefs, emotions, and thoughts, leads to the same reaction. It is almost as if unconscious grooves form in the psyche.

Once awareness increases, one of the ways to know that something still needs work is that one will react to a situation as they would have in the past, or will see someone else react in that manner and will realize that the other's way of responding still bothers them. Eventually, there will be a moment of choice when one can choose to react or to let it go. Just as with emotions, pretending not to react is not effective and only masks the issue. This must be a true "letting go."

The Egoic Cycle Versus Our True Reality

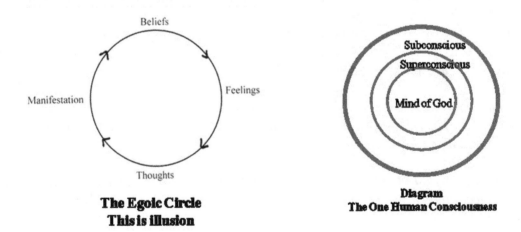

The Egoic Circle
This is illusion

Diagram
The One Human Consciousness

The egoic cycle is like a self-perpetuating circle. Because we operate under incorrect beliefs and assumptions, we generate negative emotions that feed negative thoughts and result in outcomes (manifestation) that are a reflection of our incorrect beliefs. We then see what occurred as confirmation that our beliefs are correct, which further strengthens them and perpetuates the cycle.

Various sources state that thoughts drive emotions, and vice versa. Similarly, various sources state that thoughts create beliefs, and vice versa. This is a reflection of the circular nature of the whole process. It is a self-confirming, although illusionary, loop that continues to perpetuate itself until one steps outside the circle and begins to question the validity of this perception.

In contrast, the one human consciousness is our true nature. Our true nature is that of pure conscious awareness - the spark of the divine that is within each of us.

Summary

- Our beliefs, feelings, and thoughts color perception. Our senses do not give us what occurs in the world around us; they give us subjective, individualized sensations of what occurs.
- For the most part, beliefs are unconscious and were created by us to facilitate our understanding of the world around us.
- Our true nature is that of heart-centered beings.
- Negativity creates a wall around the heart that prevents us from experiencing the peace, joy, and love that are our true nature.
- Thoughts and beliefs create our reality. The mind directs and shapes the body and the circumstances around us. When we change internally, the world around us changes.
- The egoic cycle is an illusionary self-perpetuating circle that, until interrupted, continues to feed itself. In deconstructing this illusion, one must cultivate the skill of self-observation. This is inner work.
- Since emotions are quicker than thoughts, it is necessary to begin with the realm of thought and work back into emotions and then beliefs.
- Eventually, one will come to see the whole egoic circle as illusion and will be able to act from one's true divine nature.

Reflections/Exercises/Practices

For Reflection/Discussion:

1. Think back to a time in your life when you misperceived an event. This may be an event from your childhood or a more recent event.
2. Review the chart at the start of the chapter. What common themes run through your beliefs? Reflect on what you might need to let go of to grow in consciousness.
3. If the environment around us is a reflection of our beliefs, what happens when we go to fear?
4. If each of us creates our own beliefs, what is required to release a limiting belief?
5. If we are constantly transmitting our thoughts and picking up the thoughts of others at the subconscious level, how important is the company we keep? What are the implications of keeping our own thoughts pure?

Exercises:

1. Make a list of the various roles you play in your life. Write down the characteristics you display in each role. Identify inconsistencies between how you behave in one role versus another.

Chapter 5 - Terminology and General Principles

One of the issues in looking at the area of human consciousness is that the same term can vary in meaning across different authors and speakers. The following definitions are provided to set a common understanding for this book.

Terminology

Consciousness

Consciousness can be defined as the life force. It is the awareness that lies at the root of our being. It is the primary source behind all that is. It can be thought of as a universal energy field, the underlying essence of the capacity to know or experience. In meditation, thoughts can be seen to arise from this underlying awareness.

As the universal energy field, consciousness is the source of all information available in the universe. It is beyond time and space, non-local (i.e., everywhere at once) and is by its very nature beyond duality. While nothing earthly goes with us when we die, level or degree of consciousness does go with us. The true nature we will eventually remember ourselves to be is that of pure conscious awareness.

Ego

In psychological terms, having a "healthy" ego is seen as a good thing and denotes the coping and survival skills needed to deal effectively with the world. From a spiritual perspective, it is seen more as a cloud or mist that obscures the reality of who we truly are.

The ego is self-created and family, society, and the culture in which we grow up all play a role in its formation. The human infant constructs his personality and egoic mind from the environment in which he lives. If we look at what is known about early child development, it is possible to see how the ego is formed.

Those who have observed early childhood development - such as Rudolph Steiner (philosopher, educator, founder of anthroposophy, and originator of the Waldorf method of schooling) and Maria Montessori (physician, educator, and founder of the Montessori method of schooling) - explain that there are unconscious psychic powers available in early childhood that are not available later in life. The child has two roles: to create and build up his mental faculties *and* to adapt to the culture and time in which he is born. The absorbent mind of the young child takes knowledge directly into the psyche and those impressions form the mind. In other words, the child creates his mind using what he absorbs from the world around him. There is no choice; what is there is absorbed instantaneously. Language, customs, and values become a part of who the child is. It is as if the environment has come to live in the child. Montessori likened the absorbent mind to a camera[12] where every nuance is captured and recorded. This self-identity is initially imposed by others; we learn to be whom we are told to be.

All aspects of our being (body, mind, and spirit) are meant to function as an integrated whole. It is conditioning that keeps us from this integration. We are conditioned by civilization from the moment we are born. Society (parents, family, the education system) creates fragmentation or disharmony by over-emphasizing some faculties at the expense of others and it is spirit that has been de-emphasized in the current culture. The human psyche is like the hardware of a computer in that it accepts any software with which it has been programmed. Once these thought patterns are in place, they are constantly reinforced by the environment around us. In time, we come to believe that we are this set of adopted beliefs and habit patterns and our sense of identity moves away from the integrated whole to a limited sense of the self as the physical body and the thinking mind.

The mind will believe any software program that society has programmed and is incapable of discerning what is really true. It believes that because multiple people "share" a belief system, that makes it true. The mind is constantly seeking to confirm what it already believes. The basic premise of the spiritual path is that egoic thoughts are of little value; there is another way of "knowing" that will lead to truth.

Identification with the ego prevents us from knowing our deeper reality as pure conscious awareness. Identification with the mind obstructs the recognition of wholeness. Language itself further reinforces this sense of a separate self through use of the words "I," "me," and "mine."

To further increase understanding, we look at some of the characteristics of the ego. The ego was created through misunderstanding primarily as a protective mechanism. Because it perceives everything external as separate from the self and resources as limited, it chooses dominance and control as the means for protection of the self.

The ego is blind to its own limitations and has no mechanism for self-correction. Rather than recognize something distasteful within the self, the ego will repress it (place it in the subconscious), project it (place it on someone else), or deny it. That inability to correct is what leads to the extreme cases of choosing "being dead" over "being wrong." Criticism, judgment, guilt, fear, and shame all strengthen this sense of a separate self.

The ego buys into the concept of being a victim, sees pain as "other inflicted," and suffering as confirmation of the need for its existence. The ego is always looking to confirm its own worth, whether that be through feeling better than another, exerting control, or playing the victim.

The ego does not experience the world as it is, only its own perception of it. When something is perceived via the five senses, it is immediately filtered based on the beliefs and values the ego holds.

Self

The Self or Higher Self is our true nature and can be thought of as the divine within us. It is the part of us that is pure and holy, that has always existed, and that always will exist.

Karma

Karma can be thought of as imbalances in the energy field that must be brought back into balance. Habits, patterns, or tendencies that do not serve the greater whole must be released and actions must be taken to bring any distortions back into alignment. Karma incurred in this lifetime or an earlier lifetime remains with the soul until it is released via forgiveness.

If level of consciousness goes with us when we leave this earth plane, and imbalances are retained from lifetime to lifetime until they are resolved, then we need to be open to the possibility that we choose life situations (birth family, a particular culture, etc.) that best positions us to work on those imbalances.

Enlightenment

Enlightenment occurs when karmic patterns have been released and consciousness is free of habitual ways of acting, feeling, thinking, and believing. It is a state where allegiance has moved from the self to the Self. One is still capable of using the rational mind when needed, but the primary presence is that of the Higher Self. In the state of enlightenment, the inner voice of the ego is silent and one is at peace with what is.

Because our true nature is that of pure conscious awareness (spirit, a spark of the Divine), which is masked by the presence of the ego, we will all ultimately come to realize our true nature. Evolution is thus seen as a remembering of who we truly are.

Attachment/Identification

To aid in understanding the concept of attachment or identification, use the following exercise. Before reading this list, get centered and assume the position of observer so that you are simultaneously reading the items and observing your internal reaction. Below is the list:
- Climate change
- Managed health care
- The Social Security debate
- Child sexual abuse
- The effectiveness of government
- Spiritual opportunities in your country of origin
- Immigration laws
- The education system

If you are honest, it is likely that some portion of this list triggered a reaction within you. That inclination to form an opinion, to react emotionally, and to grab onto those reactions are what is called attachment or identification. This is how our day goes: we let the events of the day take us up and down an emotional roller coaster based on our reaction to those events. Letting go of identification is similar to the Buddhist concept of non-attachment; it is an acceptance of things as they are. This exercise was intentional in that it demonstrates that the state of identification does not apply simply to material things, but also to ideas, opinions, perceptions, thoughts, and emotions.

Liking or disliking something is an indication that attachment has come into play. We focus our attention on something but rather than see it as it is, we choose to see it as what we want it to be. Simply "being with" allows energy to flow freely while latching on in either a positive or negative way creates an attachment and impedes the flow of energy. Joy is our natural state and comes from being with what is *just as it is* without judgment. It is the judgment - "this is good, this is bad" - that blocks the joy. It is identification that is the destructive force. Diagrammatically, we might draw the distinction like this:

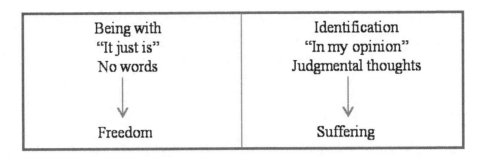

Being with "It just is" No words ↓ Freedom	Identification "In my opinion" Judgmental thoughts ↓ Suffering

Ultimately, we must give up all attachment and act based on what comes through us. Once we have released all identification (clinging, attachment to our opinions, defense mechanisms, etc.) our natural intuition is able to operate freely and we know things as they really are, which is to say we know their true essence.

Self Remembering

This topic of Self remembering warrants further understanding because of its importance to growth in consciousness. I like to think of it as remembering who I really am (a pure and holy child of the Light) who is able to rise above a situation using the Will, and dedication to my higher ideals. It is a change of allegiance from the self to the Self.

Subconscious

The terms unconscious or subconscious mean that something is below conscious awareness. One of the points of confusion in spiritual literature is that the same term is used to describe two different aspects of our inner world. We have seen that Cayce used the term subconscious to describe the outer ring of the circle of oneness, an aspect of the Higher Self.

The terms conscious and subconscious are also used with the egoic circle. That which has been suppressed or has become habitual is considered to be subconscious. In the case of the egoic circle, suppressed thoughts, emotions, and limiting beliefs are illusion. It is desirable to "make them known" so they no longer unconsciously control behavior. The diagram below is an attempt to reflect this relationship. The ego is shown as a cloud or mist hiding the true reality of the Higher Self. In both cases, by making known what is hidden, we are able to choose with greater awareness.

Inner

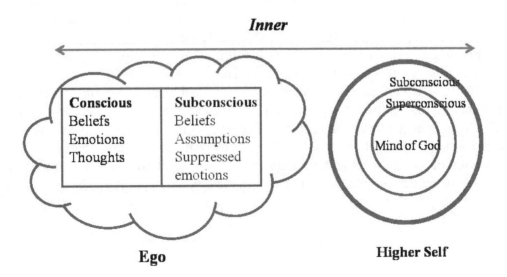

General Principles

This section is devoted to outlining general principles or understandings that facilitate spiritual growth. They are an integration of what has been derived from spiritual teachings and personal experience. They are placed early in the book because they form a platform for what will follow.

Personal Responsibility - Accepting responsibility for what you have created is a basic principle of spiritual growth. It means giving up both blame and playing the role of victim. It means looking within every time you are unhappy with someone or something in the outside world and looking at your own actions, thoughts, feelings, and beliefs. The famous phrase "if only..." is an indication that you are looking for the problem outside yourself, when in fact, it is within. As long as you are blaming someone or something, you are disempowered because you are saying the other has power over you. It isn't life's events but how one reacts to them that determines whether events have a positive or negative effect on one's life. Another way of saying this is that the presence of painful thoughts and emotions (disharmony) indicates that there is something within yourself that needs to be looked at. Growth in consciousness demands that we look at these imbalances within the self without creating guilt or judgment of self or others. With both past memories and new interactions, it is better to simply acknowledge what was, to accept that you did the best you were able to do at the time, and to resolve to do better in the future.

You don't get to fix others - A corollary to personal responsibility is the fact that you cannot "fix" another. Just as you are the only one responsible for your own growth, so is everyone else. In assuming self-responsibility, you not only teach by example, but also change the nature of the relationship between you and another. As tempting as it is to want to help another, especially when the other is a close family member, sending love and offering a deep respect for that person is more effective than any attempts to "fix." Rescue implies that you know what is best for someone. Loving support, conversely, is empowering. It honors the other person's path, his or her own connection to the Divine, and the right to use his or her own free will.

This is inner work - Change takes place on the inside. Progression on the spiritual path means becoming as aware of what is going on inside as one is of what is going on in the outside world. It means learning to pay attention to thoughts and feelings, and ultimately to letting go of limiting beliefs, and recognizing the pure awareness that lies behind all of these. The expression "know thyself" is sometimes understood to mean knowing the contents of the ego in greater detail. In fact, knowing oneself means observing everything that arises within. Becoming the observer of what is occurring within oneself is a major step towards recognition of our true nature as pure conscious awareness.

Inner Honesty - Inner honesty is required to do this work. You cannot make progress if you continue to deny that certain thoughts, feelings, behaviors, and beliefs are present. When we refuse to take responsibility, the problem repeats itself later in time. Denial and suppression simply mean that the issues continue to grow larger until they cannot be denied. A part of this inner honesty is the willingness to admit that your life is not what it could be. This is a bit like Alcoholics Anonymous in that you do not begin to make progress until you recognize that you have a problem. It is not enough to admit this intellectually; one must feel its truth at a deeper level.

Not about "fixing" the ego - Spiritual growth is not about perfecting the ego. It is about realizing who you really are. One does not need to work on the ego, or attempt to eliminate it. The task is to let go of identification with it, and to recognize that it is not who you really are. Identification with the ego is a mistake that everyone on this Earth has made.

You are not your story - Everyone has a story, but you are not your story. Your story is comfortable and familiar and there has been much invested in it. But ultimately you have to realize that is not who you are and let go of it. Past lives are also stories. All of these are what have brought you to the point you are currently at, but they are not who you are. The sooner you are able to become an observer of the story and let go of attachment to it, the sooner you will find peace.

You are not your thoughts, your feelings, your body, or your beliefs - Your true Self is the pure conscious awareness that lies behind all of these. God cannot be found in the mind or the emotions, only in the realm of spirit. As a God being, your true Self also resides in the realm of Spirit.

We learn experientially - Spiritual growth comes from doing something with these ideas, not just hearing them or talking about them. We learn and develop through a process of application and testing. The best approach to all of this is to test it; experiment, and see what happens. Spiritual growth is a constant process that can be thought of as a spiral of going within and then applying what is learned in the world outside, a path of knowledge and action.

Change occurs at the level of mind - We are creative beings and what we hold in our minds is what gets reflected in the physical world around us. Thus, for change to occur in the body, and in the world at large, it is necessary for that change to first occur at the level of mind. There is increasing evidence that sickness is the result of imbalances held in the mind that are reflected in the physical body. When those imbalances are corrected at the level of mind, the physical body also heals.

A similar philosophy applies to social issues such as addiction or war. Until the underlying origins have been understood and healed at the level of mind, it is not possible for the physical manifestation to change. That is why traditional wisdom tells us not to fear evil or fight it, but merely to avoid it. To fear it or to fight it gives it energy and makes it more real. The statement "to see peace, be peace" is also rooted in the understanding that change occurs at the level of mind. For peace to occur it must first be patterned, and the *only* place you have to begin is in your own mind.

God can be experientially known - It is possible to experience God directly. Mystics across time have reported experiences that share similar characteristics. Because one must be in a state beyond that of the intellectual mind to experience them, they are sometimes difficult to put into words and are not possible to "scientifically" prove. There are multiple states of awareness and to properly understand what is occurring, one must be in that same state of consciousness. Higher states are so powerful that once they have been experienced, they are never forgotten, and motivate one to continue on the spiritual path.

All knowledge is available all of the time - We have a direct connection to universal consciousness. The ability to perceive what is available evolves with one's level of consciousness. The words "insight" and "inspiration" are used to describe that which comes from within by accessing these higher levels. The term "discernment" is the ability to distinguish between that which comes from the ego and that which comes from the Higher Self and it also is a skill that is developed over time. While intellectual facts are accumulated by effort, what comes from these higher levels comes with grace and ease.

A Path to Self Remembering

It's easy to get sidetracked - When one first starts working in the spiritual arena, it is easy to become fascinated with all that is out there. In the end, this is internal work and it is about letting go of what is in your way and turning to the light that is already within you. It is important to keep the focus there. Becoming fascinated by all the interesting topics available could be described as horizontal versus vertical growth. One needs to know enough to understand what is required and how to make progress but then it is application that moves one forward. Continuing to accumulate intellectual knowledge and terminology may be fun, but it can get in the way of the real work.

There are no shortcuts - This is slow steady work. The adage "line upon line, precept upon precept" applies here. While quantum leaps in understanding and full enlightenment can occur in an instant, it is because of the groundwork that has preceded them.

Drugs and mind-altering techniques - The effect of drugs is to temporarily suppress the lower energy fields. While it is possible to experience higher states through the use of mind altering drugs, breathing techniques, etc., if one is not simultaneously working on raising one's consciousness, the impact will be short term and may even be harmful (one is opening to forces that the level of consciousness is not ready to support). It is safer and more effective to have these experiences through internal growth rather than by artificial means.

Summary
- Consciousness is the life force, the universal energy field, and the underlying essence of the capacity to know or experience.
- The personality and ego are formed after birth from the environment in which a child is raised.
- The ego is a self-created and self-sustaining illusion reinforced by the family, society, and culture in which one resides.
- Higher Self is our true nature and can be thought of as the divine within us.
- In the enlightened state, one is free of habitual ways of acting, feeling, thinking, and believing.
- Growth in human consciousness can be seen as moving past habits, patterns, and tendencies that are standing in the way of full awareness.
- Taking responsibility for what we have created is a fundamental principle of spiritual growth.
- This is inner work that requires self honesty and a commitment to do the work required.
- The ultimate objective is to move allegiance from the ego to the Higher Self.
- Change occurs at the level of the mind; the physical is simply a reflection of what is held in the mind.
- This is a process of understanding and application. We are experiential beings and we learn by putting into practice what we have come to understand.
- Focus on the core principles of spiritual development provides the surest path to growth in consciousness.

Reflections/Exercises/Practices

For Reflection/Discussion:

1. What are the implications of one universal energy field?
2. If reality is filtered by the ego, how do we undo this veil of perception?
3. One of the concepts coming out of Montessori's work is that if we want to change society, we need to start with the child. What does this statement mean?
4. In what areas of your life have you chosen to give up responsibility and instead blame others?
5. In what ways have you been dishonest with yourself?
6. What physical skills have you learned experientially? What are the implications of this for the use of spiritual tools?
7. Is it possible to think your way to God?
8. Is it possible for a war on drugs to succeed?

Exercises:

1. As you interact with people throughout the day, watch what is occurring inside of you. Do not judge it, simply observe.
2. Make a list of the people you find to be the most difficult to be around. What about those people bothers you? Reflect on whether those are issues you need to look at within yourself.
3. Make a list of the people in your life that you are trying to "fix." Practice giving up the urge to "fix" and replace it with "sending love" and "trust" that the Divine is working its purposes out in this person just as it is in you. How does this feel as opposed to attempting to fix that person?
4. Instead of using the word "I" today, use your name.
5. Write your own story but use "he" or "she" instead of "I." When you have finished look at your story from the perspective of another person who is reading it.
6. Choose one spiritual tool from what you have read so far and begin using it.

Chapter 6 - Attitudes and Ideals

Since it is just as easy to pick up and continue to cultivate a negative pattern of behavior as a positive one, the readings frequently advised individuals to set an ideal - purposeful, positive intent against which they could measure their potential thoughts and actions in the present. This method of weighing daily life against a spiritual ideal was called, "the most important experience of this or any individual entity ..." ---(Edgar Cayce Reading 357-13)

*****

This chapter will look at what it means to have a growth mindset and will work with the Cayce concept of ideals.

Willingness to Learn and Change

The attitude with which we approach this work is key. As we saw in Chapter 1, the holistic viewpoint is a totally different way of looking at the world that will by definition come into conflict with previous conditioning and societal expectations. It is an open mind, a willingness to question everything, and a willingness to be open to a new way of being that will lead to the greatest growth.

Because there can be discomfort from starting any new process, and particularly one that calls into question core beliefs, it is important to recognize that discomfort is an acceptable part of the process. While it is not easy to let go of something that has been one's "self" for many years and that has given one a sense of self esteem, it is important to have the openness to embrace all aspects of one's self, especially those that feel threatening. At times, because we are working with such deep-rooted conditioning, it will seem as if the spiritual path takes one step back for every two steps forward. As we bring things up from the subconscious and make known what was previously unknown, it tends to feel as if we are not making progress when, in fact, it is simply that what was previously unknown is now visible. When we consider that we are undoing conditioning that has been in place for many years and that feels like who we are, we should expect resistance and setbacks and know that it is persistent effort that will lead to success.

Just as with any new physical skill, it is practice that leads to success, and so it is in the spiritual arena. It is the willingness to make continuous effort, to view obstacles as opportunities, and to persist when the going gets tough - whether that be personal setbacks or clashes with societal expectations - that leads to growth.

We are being asked to accept that there is a Christ (Buddha, etc.) within each of us and that we are capable of remembering our true nature as that enlightened being. At heart, there needs to be an acceptance that "I am this", and that although it will take effort, this is a process that I am capable of

37

undertaking and completing. We have assurance from those who have persisted to enlightenment that the process is worth the effort. If peace can only come from within, there really is no other way out of the insanity of everyday existence.

What Is an Ideal?

The ideal is to be a guiding force in one's life, a beacon that shines ever bright, calling you to it. It can be thought of as a point in consciousness saying "come closer." Cayce defined the ideal as the highest spiritual quality we could hope to have motivating us.

The ideal then is a spiritual quality chosen by you because it calls to you at this point in your life. The ideal should be very personal, and something you feel the need to work with right now. Ideals are meant to change throughout life as we change and grow. There is within each of us a perfect pattern that in the Cayce work is called the "Christ Consciousness," as it was exhibited in the man Jesus. The phrase "Christ Consciousness," however, represents the universal pattern of perfection that is within each of us. The ideal could be thought of as a characteristic of the Christ Consciousness with which one chooses to work at this point in time - a building block to the universal higher ideal. It could be described as a stretch pattern for spiritual development.

Cayce talked about the importance of spending time defining this ideal and writing out how it will manifest in your life. Why did he place such emphasis on the concept of the ideal? First, this is about knowing where you are going. If you don't know where you are going, how can you ever get there? It is also about understanding what is important in your life. Where do you want to focus your energy? Are you a spiritual being having a physical experience, or did you come here to wander? Where you focus your energy is what you will get.

Life should be fun and a joy, but it is also a precious gift and an opportunity not to be wasted. We choose to come into the exact circumstances we need to grow and learn spiritually and yet most often we choose to squander that. Without ideals, and the corresponding attitudes and actions that flow from them, we are unfocused and wander aimlessly.

The power of intention also comes into play here. By setting the ideal and defining how it can manifest, the power of intention is available and *will* influence actions. By establishing and committing to the ideal, one allows it to begin to change who you are. It is almost as if, by going through the ideals process, we are choosing to align with the Higher Self, including the Higher Will. Once the life force is aligned with a higher ideal, it sets the stage to experience higher vibrations.

The process itself creates a consistency between body, mind, and spirit. If you wander from the ideal, in moments of calm, you again see the light and say, "I forgot about this. This is what is important in my life."

The remainder of this chapter will look at a process for defining a spiritual ideal and mapping it through attitudes (mental) into actions (physical). This process can be thought of as taking the spiritual and making it manifest. Body, mind, and spirit are meant to work together as one. By setting the ideal in the spiritual and mapping out what this means in the mental and physical, we put in place a process by which the spiritual can become manifest. As Kevin Todeschi says, "We'll know progress has been made with our spiritual ideal when the mental attitude on the ideals sheet becomes our usual state of mind and the physical activity listed becomes our automatic and natural response."[13] At that point, it is time to work with another ideal.

This table[14] demonstrates this concept of flowing the ideal through from spirit to mind into physical manifestation:

Ideal	Attitude	Action/Behavior
Love	Acceptance	Refrain from complaining about things I can't change
	Kindness	Find time to talk to my neighbor who is going through a hard time
	Forgiveness	Say a friendly word to (person's name) who insulted me yesterday
Spirit	**Mind**	**Body**

There is a distinction to be made between ideal and life purpose. Life purpose is something you came to accomplish in this lifetime. It could be an undertaking, a set of things to be accomplished, or lessons to be learned. The ideal, on the other hand, is the guiding force. In the following section, the emphasis will be on coming to know one's self with respect to defining an ideal, or motivating force. As you grow in consciousness, the ideal should grow with you.

Know Thyself

A good first step in defining an ideal is to become aware of your current motivations. Actions are always driven by motives, whether we are conscious of them or not. The following exercises and questions are designed to expose tendencies that currently exist in your psyche and the underlying motivations for them. For some, these exercises will be easy. For others, they may be difficult. In all cases, it will help to use whatever process you prefer (watching the breath, etc.) to move into a quiet, centered state before beginning this work.

In doing this inner work, it is important to be honest with yourself and to keep a hopeful growth mindset. This is ongoing work and it is expected that what you record will change over time as you dig deeper and as you change. As you start to do this work, more will come to you in moments of quiet as you go about your day. It is best to work with these questions over a period of days.

With all of these exercises it is best to write your responses. Writing seems to lead one to the inner depths more easily, but in this case, we will also be looking for patterns across the questions and it will be helpful to have written answers to refer to. If you have difficulty completing this worksheet, the sample worksheet at the end of this chapter, may provide some guidance on how deep to go in responding to these questions. When you have completed this worksheet, it will be used to create a table similar to the one above but tailored to your particular life situation..

* *

STOP and complete the Motivation and Tendencies Worksheet at the end of this chapter.

* *

When you have completed these questions, go back through the answers and make a list of items or areas that you think need work. What insights did you gain about what you brought forward from childhood? In reviewing this list, look for places where you do not have control of your own life's direction. These may be places where you are still acting from childhood defense mechanisms or where you have abdicated control based on societal expectations. Items that appear in multiple places are currently controlling your life, whether you were previously aware of them or not.

We have already talked about how other people are mirrors for us, and how they help us to see our own characteristics. What bothers you in other people may provide some insight on things you need to look at within yourself. Although there may be an inclination to blame other people or circumstances, working with an ideal is about what goes on within the self. It is helpful to remember that the same behavior(s) that bother you in another person often do not bother others.

Defining an Ideal

Defining an ideal is about taking control of the direction of your life; it is about taking decisions and interactions that previously occurred from habitual emotional patterns and making them conscious. It is about establishing a standard (guiding force) that will be used for future decision-making and interactions. It is about developing enough awareness to see a habitual reaction arise, to remember the desired response, and to choose differently. If others are mirrors, this is about putting out to others the relationship you would like to have returned to you. The *only* one we *can* change is the self. Working with and applying an ideal is the day-to-day work of making a new way of being become the natural response. We have previously looked at how what is patterned in the mind becomes manifest in the physical. Defining an ideal (and the desired attitudes and behaviors associated with it), and making slow steady progress through applying it in daily life, is a process that allows the spiritual to become manifest.

From the list you have prepared in the previous section, choose an item that you wish to use as your spiritual ideal, keeping in mind that the ideals work is ongoing, and that what you choose can be changed at a later date if that is appropriate. In choosing this ideal, free yourself from any outside expectations. For example, the person in the sample write-up who has a tendency to withdraw in the face of conflict might choose a spiritual ideal of openness.

The Cayce material recommended creating a table similar to that shown earlier in the chapter in the "*What Is an Ideal*" section. Ultimately, this is a nice format because it easily allows one to see how the spiritual ideal is reflected in one's mental attitudes and then in one's day-to-day activities. In working through the specifics of what each attitude means and how it applies, however, it may be beneficial to create smaller tables or even a mind map that will later be melded into the main table.

For example, if the person in the sample write-up knows that she is having trouble staying open when interacting with a specific person, she might create a table that looks like this:

Person	Spiritual Ideal	Attitudes	Behaviors
Emily	Openness	Acceptance	-See her as a kind and loving person
		Receptivity	-Say, "I respect what you are saying, but this is my perspective..." -Stay open rather than withdrawing and being frustrated during discussions
		Self Love	- Remind myself that I am only responsible for my

			reaction and not the other person's reaction

Or this:

Person	Desired Positive	How You Would Feel	Behaviors
Emily	React positively when she is in the room	At peace	-Catch any negative reaction to her presence immediately and breathe deeply -See her as a kind and loving person
	React to what is said and not the manner in which it is said	Would enjoy the environment without stress	-Say, "I respect what you are saying, but this is my perspective..." -Stay open rather than withdrawing and being frustrated
	Discuss changes without an emotional reaction on my part	Like I have made progress within myself	-Remind myself that I am only responsible for my reaction and not the other person's reaction

A helpful exercise, at this point, would be to write out the key people in your life and where you have difficulty manifesting the ideal you have chosen. If, on the other hand, you are having difficulty defining what an attitude means, you might do something like this:

Ideal	Attitude	What Does This Mean?	Behaviors
Openness	Acceptance	Of the past	When I am tempted to dwell on past events, I will: - See them in the larger context of that which has brought me to where I am now - Recognize that everyone does the best they can at their level of consciousness
		Of other people - Adopt a welcoming attitude toward everyone I encounter - Remain open in the face of negativity and undesirable behavior	- Greet others rather than waiting for them to greet me - Recognize that others have issues just as I do - Look for the goodness in the other person - Say something that indicates acceptance in spite of the negativity, like, "I respect your right to have that opinion, even though I disagree"

Ultimately, this person might prepare a summary table that looks like this:

Ideal	Attitude	Action/Behavior
Openness	Acceptance	When I am tempted to dwell on past events, I will: - Fully feel the related emotion and release it - See those events as that which has brought me to where I am now - Recognize that everyone did the best they could at their consciousness level - Choose to let go of the past and dwell in the present moment
		Adopt a positive attitude toward everyone I interact with
		Greet others first
		If I see that I am having negative or judgmental thoughts, I will remember my ideal and immediately turn them out as not who I am
		In the face of conflict, I will say something that indicates acceptance in spite of the negativity, like, "I respect your right to have that opinion, even though I disagree"
	Trust	When I am facing a new situation or person, I will assume a positive outcome
		When I feel inadequate in a situation, I will say: "God is with me, and all is well"
		When I am tempted to take something personally, I will question further to clarify understanding rather than assume self-serving behavior on the part of the other
		I will trust that everyone in my life is there for a purpose
	Self Confidence	I will believe my needs are important and will be met
		In decision-making, I will give my needs equal weight with the needs of others
		When I am tempted to minimize the value of my input, I will speak anyway
		I will: - Play with anger and conflict until I am convinced that they are not the threat I believe they are - Tell the other person what I am feeling when I am angry
		Stay open and express my opinions and feelings when I disagree rather than shut down and harbor resentment
		In quiet times, I will visualize myself: - Communicating freely and easily with everyone I come into contact with - Enjoying group interaction - Presenting to large groups with grace and ease, knowing my topic well, guided by the knowledge that this is the work I should be doing, confident in the knowledge that what needs to be said will be provided at just the right time
		In the face of what appears to be criticism, I will:

		- Resist the urge to withdraw - Clarify the meaning of what was said: "Can you explain more?" - Assess whether the criticism is valid (something I should own) - Reject what does not apply without getting upset: "I am not accepting that as appropriate" - Recognize that criticism that is accurate is a gift and criticism that is not accurate belongs to the other person

There are several things to note about this ideals chart:

- The ideal is tailored specifically to this person and will be of value to the extent this person has been honest with herself.
- Although this chart does contain some visualization, for the most part, the chart contains specific actions to be taken in everyday circumstances. They create a yardstick by which progress can be measured.
- The learning is in the doing. There may be times when this person will overreact in the opposite direction or says things that are inappropriate, but that is all part of learning to be guided by the ideal. When one falls short of the ideal, which we all do, it is important not to move into blame of self or others but simply to observe what has occurred and to resolve to do better.
- When these actions become the familiar way of being, there is a consistency between body, mind, and spirit.
- By doing this inner work and preparing the chart, this person has set a powerful intention and created a means to focus her energy in a very conscious way.
- For this individual, the ideal is a stretch pattern. It puts this individual outside her comfort zone and is a powerful motivation for change.

Role in Interrupting the Egoic Cycle

Know the spirit which ye do a thing is the spirit that will respond to thee.
(Edgar Cayce Reading 1688-9)
*****

Although emotion is quicker than thought, thought can be made "continuous." When emotion arises, it hits against this continuous thought and cannot manifest - thus, the need for right attitudes. Our attitudes determine the influence we receive from a given event. If a certain event currently influences us, this influence can be changed by our attitude. By putting the right attitude in place before-hand, one has resistance when the actual event occurs. By thinking rightly over a long period of time, that right thinking grows into a permanent attitude, which results in a changed reaction.

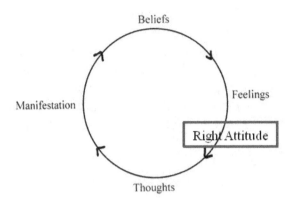

The Egoic Circle
Insertion of Right Attitude

If we return to the diagram of the egoic circle, it is as if we have inserted a correction between feelings and reaction. When feelings arise, they pass through this right attitude which influences thinking in the desired direction. Over time, with right thinking comes the capacity for a different reaction or manifestation.

As we see the change in impact on the people and the world around us, it leads to change in the previously held belief or misperception. It might be said that in living the desired behavior on a day-to-day basis, we become that change; it becomes a part of who we are. It is also possible to see that, over time, feelings change as the underlying belief changes.

It is in the application that we own these new attitudes. This is all to say that intellectual understanding of these topics is not enough. They must be lived on a daily basis to have an impact. The ideals process makes this "work on being" much more focused and tailored to individual personal growth needs.

A key point in the readings is the concept that we are constantly creating, and we do so either consciously or unconsciously. It is far better to consciously set an intent and choose where to focus our energy. Since we are already creating our own reality, often unconsciously based on limiting beliefs, the ideals process allows us a means to take conscious control of what we choose to create. It should be noted that this varies from cognitive-behavioral techniques in that the spiritual is driving both the mental (cognitive) and the physical (behavioral), giving a powerful spiritual dimension to the process.

Cayce made it clear that working with ideals should be an ongoing activity. While we all have within us that Christ Consciousness, choosing attitudes and ideals that address our own personal everyday struggles will take us further than choosing lofty ideals that are difficult to understand and put into practice.

Choice

Know that no influence surpasses the will of the entity. Make that will, then, one with that which is the entity's ideal. (Edgar Cayce Reading 1089-3)

One might think of the scenarios defined above regarding how to relate to the difficult people in your life as rehearsals for the opportunities you will have to exercise your will. In the end, it always comes down to choice. Will you choose to act in accord with the ideal you have set, or will you react from the smaller self and habit? The advantage of setting an ideal and mentally rehearsing the attitude(s) with which you would like to approach situations is that now you get to choose with increased awareness and motivation. Life becomes the opportunity to practice your ideal and make it a living thing.

Setting an ideal provides a spiritual standard for decision-making. When questions arise, decisions have to be made, and when unrehearsed opportunities arise in the moment, the ideal provides a standard to measure courses of action against.

The ideal also provides a certain resilience to outside expectations. Having an ideal makes decision-making spiritually directed from the inside out and provides a buffer to the "shoulds" of the outside world. There is a strength of conviction and higher power that comes from knowing that what one has set as the ideal is founded in spirit - that it comes from a place of oneness, and not from separation. "For, it is better to be right in self than to be thought of highly by others." (Edgar Cayce Reading 2995-1) This is not a puritan or self-centered rightness, but rather a knowing that is founded in the spirit within.

For those who are prone to take on the judgments and upsets of others, it provides a means to keep harmony within the self.

"So long as the activities of others are allowed to upset the body, this produces first inharmony within self. This does not necessarily mean to become indifferent, but in the physical and in the mental and in the spiritual, there is required first the surety within self. Know not only what ye believe but who is the author of same; not because, merely, this or that may have been said by this or that person, but - according to the true spiritual law - because "My spirit beareth witness with thy spirit..." (Edgar Cayce Reading 303-39)

Summary

- It is best to approach this work with an open mind - with the understanding that abilities are learned and that change is a matter of practicing the new way of being.
- The ideal is a personal stretch goal for spiritual improvement.
- An appropriate ideal is defined through an inner process of self-reflection and analysis, first by identifying existing motivations and tendencies, and then choosing an appropriate stretch pattern.
- The process of mapping the ideal through attitudes into behaviors acts as a mental rehearsal for the integration of body, mind, and spirit and a specific means to practice the concept of oneness.
- When right attitudes are employed, they enable change in the egoic circle.
- Although this process is a little time consuming, it provides the basis for work on being and is a key component to growth in consciousness.
- Setting an ideal provides a spiritual standard for conscious decision-making and a resilience to outside expectations.

Reflections/Exercises/Practices

For Reflection/Discussion:
1. Are there aspects of your life that you think cannot be changed?
2. Are good leaders born or made?
3. What opportunities did you reject along your life path because you believed them to be innate gifts as opposed to something you could learn?
4. In dreams, the car is sometimes a symbol for the self. Who is driving your car?

5. How does your personal ideal relate to your life's purpose?

Exercises:

1. Choose something you have always wanted to try and give it a go.
2. The next time you are having difficulty interacting with someone, change nothing but your attitude and observe the change in the other person's behavior.
3. Tie a piece of yarn around your wrist. Every time you notice the yarn, look at your motivation for whatever you are currently doing.
4. The following chart is provided for further practice with the ideals process. Complete the chart with specifics from your own life.

Ideal	Attitude	Action/Behavior	Specifics
Love my neighbor as myself	- Loving acceptance of everyone	- Service motivated by love - Treating all as equals in the eyes of God - Giving people space to be who they are - Self love	
Happiness	- Welcoming expectancy - Everything in life is an opportunity to express my inner happiness	- Patient understanding - Tolerance - Cooperation	
Truth always	- Willingness to look at everything - Trust that God is with me and will guide my every step	- Self introspection - Reading and investigation of spiritual literature - Empowered action/ willingness to speak	
Peace	- There is a win-win solution in every situation - We are all part of the same family of humanity - We all matter - I can be peace in my own world	- Looking for solutions that serve all equally - Recognition of how we are alike over how we are different - Tolerance for differences - Treating others as equals - Seeing every person as a gift to the world	
Spirit	**Mind**	**Body**	

5. When you see a negative reaction in another, think back to your attitude going into the interaction. Is there a correlation?

6. For a few days, try "giving up control" without going through the ideals process. Then, go through the ideals process. Note any differences in your ability to be successful at "giving up control."

7. Each evening, make a list of five events from the day. For each, ask, "In what spirit did I do this?" Keep these lists and observe how your responses change over time.

Meditative Practices:

1. Meditate on the phrase, "I listen to the voice of my spirit, and trust in the Lord with all my heart."

Motivation and Tendencies Worksheet

- *Childhood Tendencies*

1. Look at your entire life from childhood to the present. How did you think and act as a child? As a teenager? As a young adult? As you settled and found work, started a family? In what ways have you grown over the years? What tendencies have you brought forward from childhood to adulthood? What would you still like to change about yourself? Record any memories that come up during this questioning.
2. Write the story of your childhood. What issues (fears, emotional wounds, blockages) would someone who had your childhood be likely to have? What tendencies might someone who had your childhood be expected to exhibit?
3. What causes you unhappiness in life now? Was there anything in childhood that gave you a similar feeling?

- *Motivation*

1. Think about what occupies your time in a typical day. What is the motivation for each of your activities? Why do you do what you do? Is there a theme or pattern that is common to why you do what you do?
2. Choose a characteristic (examples: openness, rigidity, risk-taking) and describe how you behave related to that characteristic in the various roles you play (with significant other, with birth family, with subordinates, with boss, with strangers, with children, at church, etc.). What leads you to behave differently in different environments?
3. Who is making the decisions in your life - you, other people, or circumstances?
4. In general, what motivates you to do the things you do?
5. Complete this statement: "If I could change any pattern (or motivation) that has been operating in my life, it would be to... "
6. Complete this statement: "I think the one quality I like best about myself is my ability to... "
7. When you make decisions, how do you typically decide what to do? What factors into your decision?
8. Look back to the last difficult decision you had to make - one that really made you struggle. What made you decide to do what you did?

- *Interactions*

1. How do other people perceive you?
2. What bothers you about other people? What behaviors do you dislike in other people?
3. Think of a few people you admire. What traits do they exhibit that you admire? Which of these traits would you most like to take on for yourself?

Trait	Is Admirable Because...

4. Think of someone you have difficulty interacting with. What bothers you about this person and which of their traits irritate you? What traits do you find most disturbing?

Trait	Is Irritating Because...

5. The most important characteristics of a good relationship are ...

- Beliefs

1. Go back to Chapter 4 and see if there are any themes you would like to record from your response to the questions at the beginning of that chapter.
2. What personal beliefs would you most like to undo?

- Personal Behaviors/Traits

1. What five things about yourself would you least like to write about?
2. How do you react in stressful situations? What negative emotions do you harbor as a result?
3. Make a list of the 5 behaviors/ways of being you like best about yourself and then make a list of the 5 behaviors/ways of being you like least about yourself.

I like best	I like least

4. What would you like to change about yourself and in the environment around you?

Desired changes in me	Desired changes around me

5. What traits would you like to undo in yourself?

Motivation and Tendencies Worksheet

- Fears

    1.   What are your biggest fears?

-Dreams

    1.   What recurring dreams have you had?

Sample Writeup

- Childhood Tendencies

1. Look at your entire life from childhood to the present. How did you think and act as a child? As a teenager? As a young adult? As you settled and found work, started a family? In what ways have you grown over the years? What tendencies have you brought forward from childhood to adulthood? What would you still like to change about yourself? Record any memories that come up during this questioning.

Child - I loved to be outside. I was a pretty quiet child. People would ask me if I was an only child even though I grew up in a pack. I loved to read. I was always introspective. I was what might be described as a late bloomer. I never liked new situations. I had to be forced out the door to go to kindergarten. My parents put me in music so I would have to learn to be out in front of people. Even as a child, I could feel the truth or falsity of things but I wouldn't argue with what people said. I had to know how to do everything - how to cook, sew, embroider, knit, how to repair things. I always had the feeling that if I didn't learn how to do everything, that knowledge might be lost. I had a lot of freedom as a child; we were not closely supervised so we kind of "ran wild" during the summer. For 10 years, all of my siblings were male so ours was a very male-oriented household. There was little emphasis on emotions and expressing them. My mother wasn't around much. She worked afternoons, so she left for work right after we got home from school. When she was around, there was always so much to be done that she "didn't have time" for us.

My father believed that women were inferior to men. If my first brother- who is a year younger - and I messed up (like painting the basement wall with our hands instead of the brush), he would yell at me and tell me he shouldn't have trusted a girl. But he wouldn't fuss at my brother. For whatever reason, I never questioned that as a child, but by the time I was in 9th grade, I clearly remember an incident where his statement about the superiority of men was so blatant that I just shut down and never really related to him after that. Similar memory with my mother when I was about 4 or 5. I was crying and she told me she didn't want to hear it anymore. If I needed to cry, I should go into the bedroom and do it by myself. I clearly remember shutting down to her. She tells me now that I never got to be a baby because the first four of us were born within five years of each other and my first brother is only 13 months younger than me. When a cousin and I wrote stories one day, she wrote about a princess. I wrote the story of the ugly duckling. I was always the responsible one and spent a lot of time looking after my brothers and later my sister. When I was 9, I would watch the four boys for about 3 hours between the time my mother left for work and my father came home.

Teenager - As a teenager, I started to get out into the world a little more. For the first 2 years of High School, I took three buses to get back and forth to school each day. That meant my home and school life were pretty separate, so I didn't really have friends in the new neighborhood. I played on a basketball team, and a baseball team, and I took music lessons. I found the teenage years to be awkward. Although I enjoyed being in a female environment, I found the catty meanness of girls to be upsetting and so I was wary of getting really close with people. Now, I can see that I thought anger meant the relationship was over. I think I still have these lack of trust issues. One memory from this period was talking back to my father one day. He hauled off and slapped me right in the face which further confirmed my resolve to speak as little as possible to him and to get out of that crazy house as soon as possible.

Young adult - I went away from home alone for the first time at the age of 17 and worked at a resort hotel where I stayed in a dorm with other college students. The first summer was an overwhelming experience for me, but I stuck it out. This was my first real job and I clearly remember thinking "If this is all I have to do, I will never be without money again." I was a hard worker anyway, so the idea that I could be paid for that was awesome. My first job after college was the same. I was thrilled to be an independent person. I learned a lot of social skills and ways about the business world that I just didn't have exposure to growing up the way I did. I joined a ski club for social activities and bought a house where I lived alone. What I remember from that period of time is feeling a lot of freedom and independence like I had my whole life in front of me, and some loneliness.

Marriage and family - etc.

On re-reading, this is what I see:
I was emotionally abandoned as a child
There were no opportunities to practice expressing emotions
I was not valued for who I was
I was expected to be the responsible one (oldest child syndrome)
My needs were not met
I didn't understand that anger is OK
I developed a strong sense of independence and the feeling that I have to go it alone instead of asking for help
I am used to going it alone
My way of dealing with conflict has been to withdraw
There were times in childhood and later life when I felt a sense of hopelessness, that there was no way out
I learned not to trust other people
Financial security is synonymous with freedom in my mind

2. Write the story of your childhood. What issues (fears, emotional wounds, blockages) would someone who had your childhood be likely to have? What tendencies might someone who had your childhood be expected to exhibit?
3. What causes you unhappiness in life now? Was there anything in childhood that gave you a similar feeling?

Now - Being minimized and insulted by family members, feeling over-controlled, feeling frustrated when I am trying to get something done and things keep going wrong.

I still play out this sense of responsibility and put too much on myself. I get frustrated that others don't see what needs to be done.

- *Motivation*

1. Think about what occupies your time in a typical day. What is the motivation for each of your activities? Why do you do what you do? Is there a theme or pattern that is common to why you do what you do?

Themes - security and responsibility

2. Choose a characteristic (examples: openness, rigidity, risk-taking) and describe how you behave related to that characteristic in the various roles you play (with significant other, with birth family, with subordinates, with boss, with strangers, with children, at church, etc.). What leads you to behave differently in different environments?

Characteristic - openness

Husband - I have let him see who I am at pretty deep levels now. At times, I still withdraw when I feel like he is not really listening. I sometimes challenge what he says when he is totally off base, but mostly I just let it go.

Mother - etc.

Sister - etc.

Children - etc.

Friends - etc.

Service work - etc.

Group Interactions - etc.

3. Who is making the decisions in your life - you, other people, or circumstances?

As much as I enjoy being married (and value it more as time passes), I have not felt like my life is my own since I got married. There is always someone else's needs that have to be considered whether that be husband, children, or family expectations. I do things independently - travel, take classes, etc. - but I still sometimes feel like my life is not my own. I try to be more aware of motivations now because I know I do too many things out of a sense of responsibility.

4. In general, what motivates you to do the things you do?

I do them because I "should"

5. If I could change any pattern (or motivation) that has been operating in my life, it would be to...

Stay open instead of withdrawing

6. I think the one quality I like best about myself is my ability to...

Persist in the face of obstacles

7. When you make decisions, how do you typically decide what to do? What factors into your decision?

Other people's needs, logic, pros and cons, financial impact, my own needs

8. Look back to the last difficult decision you had to make - one that really made you struggle. What made you decide to do what you did?

- Interactions

1. How do other people perceive you?

Quiet and reserved. Sometimes, they act like I am not even present. Like I don't matter.

2. What bothers you about other people and how does that make you feel? What behaviors do you dislike in other people?

Bossiness in others - feel like I am being treated as stupid
Unfairness in any situation - to me or to others - feel like rights are being violated
Not being allowed to speak - people who monopolize conversation - feel minimized
Being told what to do - authority problem - feel over-supervised
Criticized - feel like I am not being appreciated for what I do

3. Think of a few people you admire. What traits do they exhibit that you admire? Which of these traits would you most like to take on for yourself?

Trait	Is Admirable Because...
Deeply spiritual	I consider this to be what life is about
Brave enough to do what called to do	Inner guided
Willing to let others see who they are	Takes inner strength to do this

Positive I most want - To be brave and let others see who I am

4. Think of someone you have difficulty interacting with. What bothers you about this person and which of their traits irritate you? What traits do you find most disturbing?

Trait	Is Irritating Because...
Speaks over me when I talk	Disrespectful
Condescending	Thinks she/he has all the answers and knows better
Lies to make self look good	Not looking at her/himself
Controlling	My needs don't seem to matter
Concerned about appearance	Priorities are in wrong place

Negative I least like - condescending and controlling

5. The most important characteristics of a good relationship are ...
Most important - kindness, understanding, commitment, ability to forgive, trust, gentleness

- Beliefs

1. Go back to Chapter 4 and see if there are any themes you would like to record from your response to those questions.
2. What personal beliefs would you most like to undo?

That I have to be perfect to be loved
That life is hard
That I am not good enough
That resources are limited - that there might not be enough (money, time, food, etc)

- Personal Behaviors/Traits

1. What five things about yourself would you least like to write about?
- About a past event - how painful that experience was, how abandoned I felt, how my needs did not matter, how negatively that event impacted a large part of my life
- How I can obsess about something trivial. How something that I know to be silly can take control of my mind.

- How emotionally immature I can be at times.
- How many times in the past I have incorrectly interpreted something someone has said and how I tend to take things personally.

2. How do you react in stressful situations? What negative emotions do you harbor as a result?
Withdraw, retrench and analyze / Anger and resentment
When too much to get done, I become bossy and intolerant/Frustration

3. Make a list of the 5 behaviors/ways of being you like best about yourself and then make a list of the 5 behaviors/ways of being you like least about yourself.

I like best	I like least
Good listener	Can be bossy/controlling under pressure
Organized	Worry too much
Intelligent	Obsess about trivial things
Hard worker	Have trouble letting go sometimes
Fair	Feelings of inadequacy

4. What would you like to change about yourself and in the environment around you?

Desired changes in me	Desired changes around me
Believe I am good enough	Respect from others for what I know
Stay open instead of withdrawing	Loved for being me just as I am
Act from love rather than responsibility	
Use intuition over intellect	
Give up the attitude of having to go it alone	
Quit taking things personally	

5. What traits would you like to undo in yourself?
Self doubt/ Lack of confidence/ Over-responsibility and perfectionism to compensate
Fear of speaking up/ Tendency to withdraw in face of conflict
Judgment and Intolerance
Worry
Lack of Trust

- Fears
1. What are your biggest fears?

-Dreams

2. What recurring dreams have you had? What do you think is the significance of each?
- As a child and into early adulthood, I would dream that I was lying in a ditch in the ground on a very dark night and I knew that if I lay very still, no one would know I was there and I would be safe
- As a child, I would have a dream that I was being chased and I could not scream

I have since been told that I had my tongue cut out in a previous lifetime for speaking the truth. I think these dreams are a flashback to that experience, but I also can see how they relate to my inclination to keep silent and withdraw in the face of conflict.

As an adult, I have had two recurring dreams:

- In one, I enter a cave and as I go further in, the cave gets tighter and tighter. So I am concerned about getting totally stuck, but I feel like I have no alternative but to keep going.

- In the other, I am driving a car from the back seat. I am concerned about crashing because I cannot react quickly enough from the back seat to control the car.

I see these dreams as related to letting other people run my life instead of taking control of my own choices and decisions.

Chapter 7 - Know Thyself - Directing Attention, Self Observation, and Uncovering the Personality

Awareness is inner work. This chapter is devoted to getting used to accessing the internal. In previous chapters, we have alluded to the importance of self observation or second attention, which is the ability to observe what is going on within as one observes what is going on without. A prerequisite to that skill is learning to focus attention. In this chapter, we will look at developing the skills of directing attention and of self observation along with other things that tend to make the masks we wear more obvious. These exercises are meant to be done on a regular basis over a long period of time, until you are consistently able to direct and hold your attention where you choose to place it.

Directing Attention

Even more basic than the skill of self observation is the skill of learning to direct or focus attention. It might be said that learning to control attention is the first step in development of the will. Attention is a silent alertness with no thoughts interfering. The following exercises are designed to aid in the development of focusing attention:

1. Select an object to serve as the center of your focus. Think about it exclusively for five minutes. Any thoughts related to the object are acceptable, including how it is used, how it came to be, its texture, its color, how it might feel, etc. Take time to focus on this object over several days to learn to focus your thoughts on a particular object.
2. Focus on a candle, a plant, or some other object and hold that focus for three minutes. Watch with no thoughts; simply observe what is in front of you. Keep your attention strictly on the object with no thoughts about it or anything else. Hold your focus until you can feel its essence or until you have a sense of merging with it.
3. Practice broad focus: For five minutes, keep your focus equally on everything in the room. If your focus is drawn to a particular object or you are distracted, return to observing the entire room at once.
4. Choose an object and look at it. Direct your energy to that object and wait silently for a moment until it (your energy) returns to you.
5. Go for a 20-minute walk outside. As you walk, place your attention on each of the following senses for five minutes:

- o *Sight* -For the first five minutes while walking, focus your attention strictly on what you see. Note textures, colors, distances, shading, heights, etc. At first, you may feel the need to state these mentally to keep focused. But as you practice, move to a place of stillness where you simply observe these things.
- o *Hearing* - For the second five minutes, focus strictly on hearing. Listen to the sounds of the birds or animals in the environment, and the sound of the leaves rustling in the wind. Listen for background noises you may have previously blocked out. Listen for the sounds of your own body as you walk. Listen to your own breathing. Again, eventually move to the point of doing this with no mental commentary.
- o *Feeling* - For the third five minutes, focus strictly on the sense of touch. Feel the clothes moving against your body. Feel your feet touching the ground. Feel the breeze and the sunlight on your face. Pick up a leaf or a stone and feel the texture.
- o *Smell* - For the last five minutes, focus on the sense of smell. As you walk, see if there are subtle changes in smell. Can you smell the earthy aroma of the soil? Can you smell your own body? Choose a few leaves or flowers to smell.

Do this for several days. Once you can use each sense without thinking, practice cycling through them more quickly to learn to direct attention at will.

6. Close your eyes and focus awareness on various parts of your body. (Initially you may also need to touch that part of your body to direct awareness there.) For example, you may start with your toes, gradually move along the foot, and then move up the body. What sensation do you feel in the body as you focus awareness there? Learn to do this without any thoughts or commentary. Once you have learned to move your awareness within the body with your eyes closed, practice doing the same thing with your eyes open.

7. Closing your eyes is one way to move from the external to the internal. Sit for a period of five or ten minutes and practice first observing externally with your eyes open for a time, then closing your eyes and changing your focus to what is occurring internally. Note the difference between observing what is occurring in the world around you versus what is occurring internally. What thoughts, emotions, images, and feelings are occurring inside? When you feel ready, practice changing your focus of attention from the external to the internal with your eyes open. You may want to create a phrase that goes with the change of focus, such as "...and now I sense with my inner senses." Eventually, simply saying that phrase may help move your focus.

8. Focus on the breath: With your eyes open, begin watching the breath and giving it your full attention. Notice every aspect of your breathing - the cool on the inhale, the warmth on the exhale. Notice the breath arise, as the chest and abdomen rise and fall. Some say that the universe breathes us. Be at peace with this natural rhythm. If you become distracted, return to the breath with no judgment.

9. From now on, if you are listening to or speaking with someone, give that person your full attention. If your mind begins to wander or you begin to formulate your response, return your awareness to the person speaking.

10. Practice changing focus. For example, look at a tree or plant and first observe the details. Then, change focus, empty the mind, and focus on the tree or plant as a whole. Let your vision soften. Silently observe it; feel its wholeness and perfection. Feel its essence and your oneness with it.

11. Choose or write a short phrase, mantra, or affirmation that is meaningful to you, and focus your attention on it for a few minutes. First do this with your eyes closed, and then do it with

your eyes open. The recitation of phrases like this helps calm the mind and aids in the development of concentration.

12. When you are performing a task, devote your full attention to it. If your mind begins to wander, pull your attention back to the task at hand.

Self Observation

It could be said that awakening is a shift in perspective. Identity shifts from association with the ego to that of the Higher Self. Self observation plays a role in making this shift.

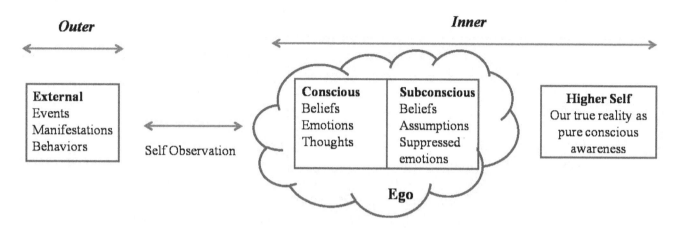

Diagram - Self Observation and the Shift in Perspective

Our true reality is that of pure conscious awareness, but for most, it is not possible to make this shift in perspective without the process of first learning to observe the self or ego. In a sense, the ego is nothing but a filter. With self observation, we learn to look at the filter and see it for what it is rather than looking through it. The goal of self observation is to see the ego arise (in the form of thoughts and feelings), but at the same time to view it as of no value; it is a cloud or mist, an illusion that is obstructing the presence of who we really are. Thus self-observation is the first step in awakening.

From the diagram, one can see that both the Higher Self and the self (ego) are part of the inner world. Once one has learned to focus attention, the next step is to begin this process of learning to observe what is occurring within as things occur in the outer world. Fortunately, self observation is a skill and can be learned just as it was possible to learn to focus attention.

Becoming the observer allows one to disassociate with the body, the mind, the personality, and the emotions. The ego is undone not by pushing against it, but simply by observing it and seeing it for what it really is. One way to think of the observer is as a positive aspect of the ego that has begun to crystallize around the ideal. Through self observation, using self will, one chooses to let go of those aspects of the self that are not consistent with the ideal.

This process of coming to know the self is a two-edged sword. From an enlightenment perspective, the role of psychology is to direct people inward - to familiarize them with the inner terrain, to expose aspects of the self - all in order to move beyond them. To let go of something, you need to know it is there. Self knowledge, in that sense, enables conscious choice. Once the shadow is made visible, one is no longer driven by what has been suppressed. One can make decisions from full awareness.

If, however, one continues to associate with the *self*, to define it as who one is, and loses sight of the intent to move beyond it, "fixing" the ego can become a never-ending project that stands in the way of enlightenment. What we really are has no beliefs, no emotions, and no thoughts. Spending time fixing these things rather than seeing them to release them is an exercise in fixing what is not real.

In "The Biggest Mistake Most Of Us Make On the Spiritual Path,"[15] Craig Hamilton clarifies the intent of this work:

"...rather than sending you on an endless and pointless archaeological dig into your psyche, we'd simply encourage you to face directly into the Truth of what you were seeing, to see the psychological tendency clearly, and the motivations that are driving it in the present. Most importantly, we'd encourage you to make direct effort in the opposite direction of your habitual response. So, in this example, when you see yourself preparing to put on a good face, we would encourage you to instead take the frightening leap to be transparent and vulnerable."

It is as if, by choosing to act in a non-habitual manner one comes to understand that there was nothing to the original motivation and the fear behind it. This concept of making direct effort in the opposite direction of the habitual response is exactly the work we were patterning with the Cayce ideals process in mapping the ideal through attitudes to desired response.

"But what happens when we let go of this compulsion to work out our problems, and instead begin to directly engage in a path of active transformation like the one I encourage, is that we find suddenly that we have access to a part of our self that is already free from our ego's limitations and issues."...

"Miraculously, what we find in doing this work is that when people awaken to and begin to act from this deeper, truer part of the self, then all of the psychological issues, blocks, wounds, complexes, and neuroses that would have taken years to work through suddenly seem to dissolve."

The following statements are from the work of author and spiritual teacher Jan Frazier. She was journaling during the time when her ego went silent and as she adapted to existence in this world without the presence of the voice in the head.

"...I eventually identified my primary spiritual practice: witnessing my reactions to events in my daily life. I began to notice my responses (inner and outer) to the contents of ordinary experience. This practice of witnessing helped me to explore the complex interplay between outer and inner reality".[16]

"Don't try to change your ego or cultivate a certain identity. Rather than judging the misdeeds of your mind-made self, simply become acquainted with how it operates. See the strength of identification with your history and beliefs. See how easily you get sucked into your thoughts, as if they were the truth. As if they were you."[17]

"It's the identification with ego that keeps the suffering going. That identification must occur first, before the familiar pattern of thought-induced suffering can continue to run. If you don't mistake the ego for what you are – if you don't take it seriously – it will unwind quite naturally. It will no longer so enthrall you. To linger in the ego itself, to focus on 'improving' it, is only to continue to feed and clothe and house it."[18]

The process of self observation requires total honesty with yourself. It requires a willingness to look at everything that occurs inside and to recognize that it is there. At the same time, it means letting go of judgment and attempts to fix or justify. It means simply observing what arises with no attachment.

One thing that may help in impartially observing what arises is the idea that nothing about the personality self can be trusted; that which arises is simply what an ego at that stage of consciousness would put forth. As <u>A Course in Miracles</u> says, "The whole purpose of this course is to teach you that the ego is unbelievable and will forever be unbelievable" (T-7.VIII.7.1). By observing, you will see that "I" is never constant. How one behaves is a function of which role one is playing at the time. The real "I" is a witness to all of those roles.

There is no definition to what it means to be spiritual. It is not something you "do"; it is the awareness behind the doer. Letting go of any expectations of what it means to be spiritual, or any attempts to get there, is the most effective route. The small self is standing in the way of spiritual insight. Any personal agenda about the right way to handle a situation stands in the way of guidance from the Divine.

Although it is true that one tends to move up the emotional scale with growth in consciousness, feeling good is not the purpose of self observation either. Once allegiance fully moves to the Higher Self, the small self that is looking for happiness will no longer exist.

The following exercises are designed to aid in development of the skill of self observation:

1. Resolve to change allegiance to the inner world rather than the outer. As best you are able, make this resolution from the heart rather than stating it as an intellectual activity.
2. Begin watching the breath as you did previously. Be aware that you are the observer watching the breath come and go. Who or what is feeling this?
3. Go for a walk outdoors. As you walk, observe yourself observing the things around you. There is [your name] walking along the road. Now he/she is looking at that tree. Now [your name] is looking at that flower. In a bit, see if you can observe yourself without verbalizing. The observer is SILENT. As you walk, simultaneously see with your eyes what is in the external environment and at the same time see yourself walking and looking. Each time you latch on to something in the external environment or to a thought in your mind, return to observing the environment and yourself as soon as you remember that you meant to be observing.
4. Begin to use your name or he/she instead of the words I, me, and mine. At first, do this internally, only in your thoughts. When you are brave enough, begin doing it externally. For example:
   - This is Debby's side of the bed.
   - Debby went to the store to pick up milk.
   - She stopped for gas on the way home.
5. As you go about your daily tasks, begin practicing present moment awareness. As Ram Dass says, an example is that of making tea. To make tea consciously, one brings together everything needed, including the knowledge of how to make the tea. Then, one focuses solely on each step of the process as it is done. Things that are not present moment awareness include: worrying about how the tea will turn out, worrying about whether you're good enough to make the tea, planning whether you should serve the tea with milk or lemon, and reliving how you made the tea incorrectly in the past. Although worry, planning, and living in the past are humorous in this example, beginning to note them in daily life is the first step in letting them go.
6. When you are part of a group, begin to observe what is going on inside of you while listening to the conversation going on around you. Notice your inclination to attach to the comments being made - to agree or disagree with them and to claim them as of value.

7. Make a decision to say as little as possible for a given day. Instead, focus on your inner world as you go about your activities. Observe what is taking place inside as you go about your day.

8. Once you have become proficient with observing, see if you can move to the awareness behind it. Approach this with a relaxed receptive feeling, that whatever happens is acceptable, that there is no need to react to anything, and that you will just be with whatever is.

9. The next time you see someone you know well, change your focus. Instead of seeing the individual standing before you, see that person as embedded in a network of relationships.

10. As you say the following affirmation, note what occurs inside of you:
    "What I need is already here."

11. Return to your ideals worksheet. With the sheet in front of you, see your Higher Self as the source of the ideal you have set and the wisdom that will guide you in your actions. See your lower self as what obscures this guidance and envision it gradually fading away.

Uncovering the Personality

There are a number of assessment tools available in the marketplace that can help one to see the lens or filter that one is looking through. I am including a few of these tools here because I think they can:
- Create an awareness that everyone is looking through a filter
- Increase understanding of others so one can be of greater assistance to them
- Provide clues to what one personally needs to release

The risk in using these tools is that initially they can give you the impression that your personality type is who you are. In fact, you are the pure conscious awareness that sits behind the personality structure being described. The benefit is the increase in awareness that comes from recognizing the strengths and weaknesses of your "self."

Myers-Briggs

When I was in my 40s, I had the good fortune to take a three-day experiential Myers-Briggs course offered at my place of work. I count it as one of my life-changing experiences for two reasons: One is that I have an unusual personality type and for the first time in my life I felt understood. Two, it made it very clear to me that everyone is looking through a filter. Furthermore, by understanding another's filter, I can better communicate with that person.

The Myers-Briggs Type Indicator (MBTI) is based on the work of Swiss psychiatrist Carl Jung, who saw his theory as an aid to self understanding. Using a series of questions, it maps the answers to those questions on four scales and creates a four-letter code indicating personality type. There are thus a total of 16 personality types. A typical Myers-Briggs personality type description will include discussion of where one falls on these four scales, as well as the strengths and challenges of that personality type. Although there is a natural preference for a particular personality type, Jung also put forth the idea that, to achieve balance, the secondary process (opposite of each letter in the personality type) needs to be developed in support of the dominant process.

These days, the Myers-Briggs Indicator has somewhat fallen out of favor because different results sometimes appear over time, other more inclusive tools are available in the marketplace, and the results have sometimes been misused in the workplace. However, as a tool for self reflection and increasing self understanding, it is a quick and easy tool to use. Simple assessment tools can be found on-line or the official version can be obtained from the Myers & Briggs Foundation for a fee. There are multiple books available in the marketplace to help with understanding of each four-letter code.

Human Design

Human Design is described as a "blueprint of your personality."[19] The book <u>Human Design: Discover the Person You Were Born to Be</u>[20] describes it as being based on a natal astrological calculation using time and place of birth as well as three other ancient wisdoms: the chakra system, the <u>I Ching</u>, and the <u>Kabbalah</u>. My personal take on Human Design is that it outlines "natural tendencies" that are a reflection of the sign under which you entered this planet. That sign, in turn, reflects past sojourns as well as the conditions that were suited to the life purpose and the lessons you have come to learn in this lifetime.

Edgar Cayce saw astrology as a tool that could be used to increase self understanding but with the caveat that nothing supersedes the free will.

"...but let it be understood here, no action of any planet or phases of the Sun, the Moon or any heavenly bodies surpass the rule of man's will power, the power given by the Creator of man, in the beginning, when he became a living soul, with the power of choosing for himself." (Edgar Cayce Reading 3744-3)

My recommendation if you choose to use this tool, is to pair an online assessment with a good book to help with interpretation, as the chart itself can be very confusing without a good explanation. Again, this is about increasing self knowledge. What rings true with me as I read this material? How does it help me to understand self and others?

Energies of Love

My third recommendation for increasing self understanding is Donna Eden's work on <u>The Energies of Love</u>. Donna Eden has the gift of seeing energy. In collaboration with her clinical psychologist husband David Feinstein, they have written multiple books in the area of energy medicine and energy psychology. In this particular book, the authors talk about four fundamental ways of internally representing the world - "feeling (kinesthetic), sound (tonal), sight (visual), and logic (digital)."[21] While we all have access to all four aspects of these modes of processing information, what Eden has been able to see is that "the [energy] band that is closest to the body determines the sensory representational mode the person will viscerally trust and rely on during times of distress [stress]."[22] This book not only gives insight into how we perceive the world, but is very helpful in understanding relationships and how perception impacts those relationships. Again, there are strengths and weaknesses to each style that can provide tremendous insight to the self. While the book is good, this is an instance where I also recommend the DVD.

The use of these three tools makes the personality, tendencies, and one's natural inner response mechanism more visible. Self knowledge stemming from the three tools makes it easier to see one's own filter.

Summary

- Learning to direct attention, both internally and externally, is the base on which the skill of self observation is built.
- With self observation, we begin to observe the self or ego, rather than perceiving from it.
- The goal of self observation is to see the ego arise (in the form of thoughts and feelings) as a foundation for releasing attachment to it.
- Self observation is a skill that can be learned just like any other skill.
- Self knowledge enables conscious choice.
- Assessment tools that reveal aspects of the personality self can be of value in raising awareness if kept in the proper perspective.

Chapter 8 - Working with Thoughts

So far, we have looked at the topic of oneness and a few metaphysical models to develop a better understanding of our true nature and what it means to grow in consciousness. We have looked at some general spiritual principles, as well as aspects of the ego (beliefs, emotions, thoughts), the role of the will, and the self-perpetuating nature of the ego. In this chapter, we delve deeper into what can be done to break this egoic cycle.

Before developing this further, it may be helpful to understand what this means in terms of our inner world. If we look at our inner world, it is as if there are two streams within us - the true or Higher Self and egoic consciousness, as depicted in the diagram below. In every moment, we have a choice about which of these two streams we give our allegiance to. The true Self is always present and always calling us to it. In ordinary consciousness, we are unaware of the presence of the true Self and give our allegiance to the egoic self.

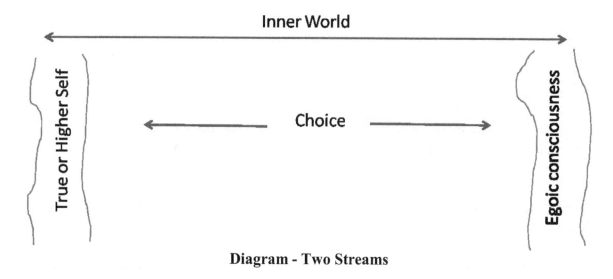

Diagram - Two Streams

When we choose to align with the Higher Self, we take guidance from our true nature. The logical mind is still able to function, but is now in service to the Higher Self, and the diagram changes to look as follows:

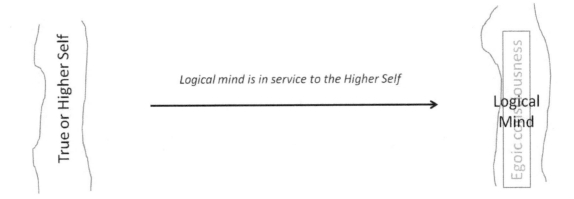

Diagram - Inner World with the Logical Mind in service to the Higher Self

We are still creative beings and continue to manifest - it is simply a matter of choice. As we begin to recognize and disassociate from the aspects of the ego, we come to rely more and more on the true or Higher Self. The diagram below again depicts these two aspects within us with the power of choice. Do we choose to give our allegiance to that which comes from oneness or that which fosters separation?

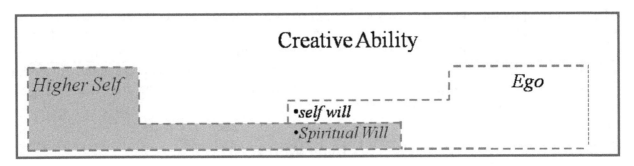

Work on Being

To grow in consciousness, we need both the knowledge of how to grow in consciousness and the slow, steady effort of "work on being." In other words, intellectual understanding alone is not enough. These days, we have ready access to spiritual knowledge in the form of books, videos, seminars, etc., but the point is that they are of little value if they are not accompanied by this inner work.

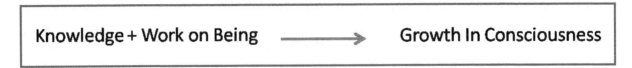

Learning to focus attention, self observation, recognizing and giving up identification, coming to know the self and one's own strengths and weaknesses, and developing and making decisions from the ideal are part of what it means to work on being. In this chapter, we begin a deeper exploration of what it means to work on being.

Energy Inputs and Energy Leaks

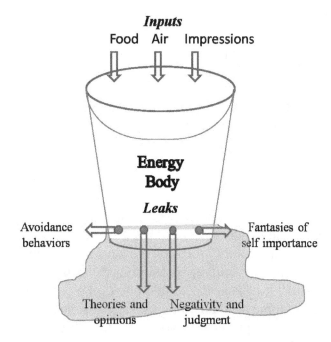

Bucket Diagram of the Energy Body

One way to think about raising human consciousness is to see it as raising the vibration of the body. If we think of the body as an energy system, we impact it by what we put into the body and by what we lose from the body. Eating healthy food and breathing clean air are examples of inputs that raise the vibration of the body. The impressions we take in from the world around us are also an input. We have already looked at how mind is the builder and the physical is the result. It makes sense then, that what we feed ourselves mentally is as important, or perhaps more important, than what we take in physically.

A heightened awareness of what you are taking in as you watch, read, or listen to the news, watch movies, listen to advertising, and interact with the people around you is a step toward controlling the impact of those impressions. For example, what we watch on the nightly news or read in the newspapers might leave one with the impression that we live in an unsafe world. Similarly, many of the movies we watch might leave one with the impression that violence is the answer to perceived threats. Advertising often implies that acquisition of material things is what is important in life. With awareness, we can learn to isolate ourselves from some impressions and open ourselves to others.

Leaks to the energy body might include the following:

Mechanical avoidance behaviors - Into this category we put intellectual meanderings, idle talk, and busyness. The idea here is that while all of these give some sense of pleasure and fill time, they are mechanical avoidance behaviors. In a sense, this is about taking back control of the mind and the objective is to break oneself of habitual distractions through the development of discipline. We might think of these as "doing" rather than "being."

Fantasies of imagination - In this category are uncontrolled daydreams and imagining non-existent powers within the self, where self is the center of focus and the imagination is embellishing one's own importance. By allowing the mind to wander down these paths of fantasy, we waste energy and also create illusions that we then build on. Fortunately, these flights of fantasy are easy to stop because as soon as you move awareness to them, you see how silly they are. It is worth mentioning that not all imagination is an energy leak. When imagination is attuned to the Higher Self, we call it visualization, creative thinking, inventive thinking, etc.

Intellectual theories and opinions - As discussed earlier, we do not perceive reality as it is, but rather as we perceive it to be based on the values, beliefs, and expectations we hold, current emotional state, and even the thought processes we employ. And yet, we continually form opinions about whether something is good or bad and attempt to assign meaning to situations, when in ordinary consciousness, we are incapable of having an accurate picture of the situation.

Negativity and judgment - Most would agree that the largest leak to the energy body is negativity and judgment. Negativity drains energy from the body and leads to suffering. One of the early steps in spiritual development is learning to recognize and let go of negativity and judgment.

Negativity and Judgment

The key point about negativity is that it comes from within. While it is common in our culture to say things like, "He said this, and made me angry," that anger is, in fact, self-generated. In choosing to play the role of victim, we abdicate responsibility for what we have created ourselves.

Negativity is very accepted in this culture, so learning to be negative could be thought of as both learned and sanctioned behavior. It is so accepted that one of the common ways for strangers to bond is to share in complaining about a topic of mutual interest. The first step in plugging the leak of negativity, then, is a heightened awareness of its presence in yourself and the culture around you.

Why does all of this matter? There are four basic reasons we want to eliminate negativity:

1) Negativity stands in the way of our ability to feel the higher emotions of peace, love, and joy. We cannot enter the state of oneness while we continue to foster separation.

2) Negative thoughts are strengthened when we allow them to continue, so the sense of separation becomes even greater.

3) To attain higher states of consciousness, we must take control of our own thoughts and emotions.

4) Negativity creates energy imbalances and is the major leak to the energy body. It lowers one's vibration.

To summarize, negativity matters because it prevents further development.

When negativity and judgment are present, we have moved into identification or attachment. That is, we have consciously or unconsciously taken a given situation and chosen to personalize it. We allow a victim mentality to enter the mind along with its distorted impressions of what occurred. Justification of our own position begins.

Inner peace comes with the ability to accept people and events as they are. We have to take everything as it is - we cannot change it or them, we can only change ourselves. A thing happens a certain way because it could *not* be any different. People's actions are based on their level of consciousness. If what occurred could be different, it would have happened differently.

This is not to say that we do not act to correct perceived injustices in the world, but rather that we remove the emotional attachment, judgment, and corresponding loss of energy from the situation. There will be times when you know you are right or when what occurs around you is totally unacceptable. Becoming identified in those situations simply lowers your own vibration. The point is that moving to a higher place of oneness where you can keep the situation in perspective results in less suffering, keeps your own vibration high, and increases the ability to be inner guided when action needs to be taken.

Each of us has certain patterns of negativity we have developed over time. Some examples include seeing others' faults but not your own, self-pity, self-doubt, fearfulness, blame, laziness, hopelessness, and anger. To let go of negativity, it is necessary to become aware of what those patterns are. Use of self observation as events occur, and reflection after the fact, are helpful in identifying those patterns. Clues include how easily and often we employ a pattern, how immersed we become while employing it, and how difficult it is to let go of once it is seen. It is helpful to spend some time reflecting on what colors your world view.

As we go about our day, we become immersed in - or attached to - one thing after another. We are so used to operating from a state of identification that we typically are not aware that we are identified, but, because identification is synonymous with separation, it is standing in the way of peace, love, and joy. To overcome that identification, it is necessary to move one's perspective to something larger than the small "self," and that means developing enough awareness to choose for the Higher Self.

We could think of this as a progression. First, we make a change in attitude with respect to negativity and judgment so we no longer see them as acceptable. In so doing, we are making a decision to give up victimhood and take responsibility for what we have created. Then, using self observation as we go about our day, we notice when negativity and judgment arise and use those moments as an opportunity to choose for oneness.

It is important to note that we cannot keep negativity and judgment from arising; that is what happens at a certain level of consciousness. There is no point in being shocked or embarrassed by what arises and there is no need to feel any guilt. The more effective, open, and honest path is simply to observe what arises without reacting to it and to see what arises as an opportunity to choose for oneness. Negativity includes all limiting thoughts, including those of failure, self-doubt, fear, thoughts of illness or harm to the body, thoughts of potential negative outcomes, self-condemnation, etc. Judgment includes things like jealousy, criticism of others, dwelling on previously perceived wrongs, etc.

The important thing is to turn out negativity and judgment immediately. The longer they are allowed to remain in the mind, the stronger they become and the more difficult it becomes to turn them out. In entertaining those thoughts, we give them power until they eventually become what creates our reality.

We might think of negativity and judgment as falling into three groups that are illustrated with a sand, gravel, rock analogy. The sand is easy to clear out, the gravel is a little more difficult, and the rocks require real effort.

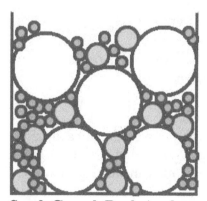

Sand, Gravel, Rock Analogy

With the little everyday irritations (sand), awareness via self observation and a simple choice to let them go will often be enough to release them.

The gravel represents irritations that appear less frequently, but are a little more intense. The creation of right attitude via the ideals process is often effective with these.

The rocks are the more intense, more difficult and fortunately rarer patterns of thinking that are more deeply rooted in limiting emotions and beliefs. I like to think of these as the ones that send us into the black hole for three days. For these, it is necessary to rely on a higher power, the Self, for assistance. This is a moment of will when you know you are doing something that will not be helpful and choose not to do it. I think of this as rising above the issue - taking a higher perspective to avoid becoming immersed and choosing differently.

While all of this can be thought of as what builds the will, it is in turning loose of the big issues that we make the greatest progress. Each time we make a choice for the Self over the self, we decrease identification with the body, mind, and emotions.

Learning to "Self remember" is a skill that can be acquired through practice. Prerequisites are a clear understanding of one's own aims or ideals, and a willingness to do this inner work. It might be said that the ability to see and take control of thoughts is necessary for Self remembering.

Summary

- There is within us two streams, that of the Higher Self and that of the ego self. In each moment, we have a choice of which stream we give allegiance to.
- Negativity is a choice.
- Psychological approaches to growth in consciousness involve not only knowledge, but also steady inner work.
- The impressions we take in matter from an energy standpoint.
- The *expression* of negativity and judgment is a major leak in the energy body and is an appropriate starting point for raising consciousness.
- We will need less energy if we gain control over our thoughts.

Reflections/Exercises/Practices

For Reflection:

1. Some of the methods that are *not* helpful but are frequently employed when negativity and identification arise include:
   - disassociation or withdrawal from a person or situation as an avoidance mechanism
   - acting out in some manner
   - repression
   - resentment/revenge

   Think through times when you have exhibited each. Is there one that you favor over the others? What might be a better thing to do when negativity arises?
2. Begin to look at your own attachments and identifications. Are there people and places you value more than others? How do you view your own race, religion, nationality, and ethnic group with respect to other races, religion, etc.? Do you consider your opinions to be of more value than the opinions of others?
3. Can you make a commitment to cleaning negativity out of your life - letting go of all discord, fear, doubt, suspicion, condemnation, criticism, judgment, and self-righteousness? What do you feel when you attempt to make this commitment from the heart? What would it take to make this commitment?
4. What resentments are you still holding? Can you let them go?

5. Think of a time you felt righteous indignation. Is there another way to perceive this situation?
6. Begin thinking about what your most deeply ingrained habit patterns might be.

Exercises:

1. Choose a person with whom you have trouble interacting and write out the ten best things about this person.
2. Begin to notice your energy level throughout the day. What happens to it when you interact with someone you do not care for? What happens to it as you interact with the media - (watch TV, listen to the radio, read the news, watch a movie, etc.)? What seems to raise your energy level?
3. For a few days, become aware of times when you speak just to speak. Are there times when you put forth theories on things you know nothing about? Are there times you try to come across as right or the expert when, in fact, you are not? How do the expectations of others impact you with respect to your need to speak?
4. If you see yourself begin to fantasize about your own self-worth, immediately turn it out. Notice how easy it is to stop fantasy if you catch it early.
5. Begin to notice how often you blame others for what occurs in your life. Become conscious of the phrase: "If only..."
6. Begin to notice how prevalent negativity is in this culture. When you speak, become conscious of whether what you are saying is negative.
7. Make a list of those events that cause you to become the most upset, the ones you have the most trouble releasing. Is there a common theme?

Meditative Practices:
1. In meditation, use the affirmation, "I am the cause of all that happens to me."

Working with Thoughts

With thoughts, emotions, and beliefs, the letting go process can be seen as a two step process: first seeing each aspect of the ego, and then letting go of each.

We now have an understanding of what it means to see our own thoughts - to become aware of them as we go about our daily activities. We have looked at various techniques to help with focusing attention and to develop the skill of self observation. Methods of looking at the personality self were discussed that might aid in making the personality more visible. All of this is preparation for letting go of attachment to thoughts. To let go of attachment, you have to be aware as it occurs.

As described in the previous section, it is not about stopping thoughts from happening; it is about letting go of identification with them. When we resist something, we give it energy by the very act of resistance. When we allow thoughts to enter and dissipate without picking them up and identifying with them, thinking gradually loses its power and begins to dissolve. In that sense, spiritual progress is a shedding of illusions so the true Self stands revealed.

Letting Go of Egoic Thoughts

Fortunately, those who have gone before us in making spiritual progress have left guidelines on what helps with this process of letting go.

Catch them early - The first guideline is to catch and release a thought when it first comes into your mind. If you dwell on it or give it any energy at all, it will become more difficult to release. (Note that constant self observation makes this possible.) With the sand, gravel, rock analogy, we talked about how there are many thoughts that will dissolve just by noting their presence. A good example of these is the tendency to make mental comments when a stranger passes by. There is no emotional investment or reason to attach to that thought, so simply seeing it is enough to let it go. With thoughts in which we *are* likely to become entangled, the earlier we can see them, the easier it will be to choose to let them go.

See them as worthless - We have already looked at the fact that each of us is looking through a filter. Our perceptions are colored by our personality, our past experiences, our expectations, our emotional mood, our beliefs, etc. We have already done an exercise where we looked at how we have misperceived things in the past. Why would we think that our thoughts are accurate?

The approach to take here is that the egoic mind doesn't really *know* anything. Opinions are worthless. They come from separation and they reinforce further separation. The undisciplined mind feels the need to comment on everything, but those comments are of no value and can actually be destructive. We have already discussed how thoughts can subliminally impact another and they are even more destructive if they are shared or acted upon.

The ego is inclined to take everything personally. A good way *not* to take things personally is to see your thoughts as of no value.

Giving egoic thoughts value implies that the ego is real and further strengthens it. By devaluing those thoughts, the basis of the thinking process is undermined and its dissolution has begun. As shown in previous diagrams, the proper use of the logical mind is to solve problems and that should be done in service to the Higher Mind, in other words, from a position of oneness.

It is this uncontrolled mind activity and the constant expression of negativity that drains the energy body and obscures the guidance available from the Higher Self. It is not possible to serve two masters. In each moment, we have a choice of which we give our allegiance to.

Withdraw attention from them - It is attention and interest that keeps egoic thoughts going. It is picking up thoughts, owning them, giving them value, and giving in to the urge to play with them that sustains them. When you are conscious of your thoughts, you are able to step back into the role of observer and let them run themselves out. Without interest and attention, thoughts cannot survive. Adopt the attitude that you do not care what the ego has to say.

I think multiple things come into play here. One is the momentum of habit. We are used to relying on our thoughts. Lacking understanding, we perceived them as who we are. Our culture values intellectual pursuit and rewards those who live in the world of thoughts. With attention and choice, it is possible to give up the seduction of experiencing thoughts.

The problem is that this thinking process uses up energy and diverts attention from the true mode of "knowing" that is present when allegiance is moved to the Higher Self. In that sense, there is a direct cost to continuing to indulge the ego.

See them as "not me" - That leads to the next guideline, which is to cease to identify with egoic thoughts as who you are. The ego is simply a mental image we hold of ourselves. Our true identity is the awareness behind all of this. As thoughts arise, simply say, "These are not me, I am not my thoughts, I am the awareness behind them." Begin to think of the ego as "it" instead of who you are. Since the ego is not who you are, perceived threats to "it" are meaningless. Once thoughts are depersonalized, they lose their attraction.

Get rid of the incentive - The ego is always out to get some internal gain or pleasure from a situation, however misguided that may be. For example, if you are prone to judging everything and everyone, see if that makes you feel better about yourself. If so, in becoming aware of and denying this satisfaction, the ego will have no reason to continue to judge. If you are prone to play the victim, ask what you are receiving from that role.

Give up judgment and interpretation - Giving up interpretation of situations as they arise is another way to make progress. The concept here is that you are not fit to judge any situation. There is no way the egoic self can know the circumstances and motivations present in any situation. By trying to make sense of it or apply your own interpretations, you will simply become further embroiled in a situation you cannot possibly properly perceive. This applies to personal experiences and to what goes on around you. Later we will see that the inclination to judge is a means of hiding one's own feelings and vulnerability.

One of the survival mechanisms of the ego is making value judgments about what takes place. The ego creates duality where things are perceived as either good or bad, positive or negative. In reality, both ends of the spectrum exist simultaneously, but one of them appears more desirable at any given moment because of the selective nature of the ego's perception. To recognize the wholeness of life, we need to integrate all aspects of the psyche (the two polarities) and give up the tendency to assign value to what occurs.

As an example, the following table contains "opposites." If you take any one of the rows and look at it, you realize that neither of the words is whole in itself; it is the balance between the two that creates wholeness. For example, consider the words "work" and "play". We might perceive work as a good thing (it allows us to earn a living and to create many things) but eventually we realize that all work with no play is unbalanced. Similarly, we might perceive play as a good thing. It allows us to enjoy life, but eventually we realize that all play with no work is also unbalanced. In giving up judgment, we open to the opposite and allow this balance to occur.

Childlike	Mature
Selfish	Unselfish
Work	Play
Assertive	Receptive
Victim	Perpetrator
Light	Darkness
Male	Female

Table Polar Opposites

We are looking to be fully present with what is in any given moment - in a state of being with what is, un-interpreted and un-judged.

Give up the past and the future - As you are watching your thoughts, let go of those that dwell in the past. Who you really are dwells in the present moment. By turning out memories, you allow the present moment to be what it is uncolored by the past. The past is what has brought you to where you are now. Thank it for that and let it go; it no longer serves you. Similarly, the ego colors all future events with the history of the past. Once you have mastered letting go of past thoughts, refuse any thoughts of worry about the future.

Give up negativity - As we saw earlier, negativity is the single largest drain to the energy body. A mental diet that eliminates negativity and judgment can be life changing.

Give up justification - Justification also fosters separation. It does not matter whether you are "right" or "wrong." It is the need to defend your position that creates the separation. When you feel resentment and attempt to justify your position, you are giving away your own power and happiness as well as creating distortion in the relationship.

Recognize the nature of the ego mind - Recognize that you created this filter through lack of understanding and that you are capable of transcending it. See it as a software program that is running and can be stopped at any point, or as a camera lens obstructing your true vision that can be removed at will. Understand the nature of the ego. Note that triggering events will drastically increase the noise level because that's how egos operate, and that the loud voice is rooted in unjustified fear. See it as an antiquated mechanism that you are disassembling through awareness.

Set clear priorities, goals, and intentions - Failure to make progress can occur simply because one does not have a clear idea of what one is trying to achieve. A process like the ideals identification process previously discussed needs to be in place so there are clear standards to measure progress against. In going through that process, one becomes familiar with internal triggers, raising awareness of their presence. One outlines and then practices preferred methods of acting. It is possible to transcend temptation in the heat of the moment by thinking about the long-term consequences with respect to the ideal. New attitudes are put in place that call into question habitual patterns of thinking and acting.

Invoke a higher power - We have previously discussed the concept that we are already our Higher Self or that the Buddha Nature or Christ Consciousness already resides within us. That is our true nature and it could be said that who we really are is always calling to us. In A Course in Miracles, we read: "The holy instant does not come from your little willingness alone. It is always the result of your small willingness combined with the unlimited power of God's Will." (T-18, IV.4.1-2) If we look at the Creative Ability diagram at the start of this chapter, we see that Spiritual Will or the Will of God is already within us. When we become immersed in our own drama (misperception) and are unable to let it go of our own accord, the Course is suggesting that all that is required is the "little willingness" to give it to the Higher Power that resides within us. In that little act of willingness, we are turning away from the ego, asking for help, and acknowledging that who we really are is this Higher Self. I think of this as rising above the issue - taking a higher perspective to avoid becoming immersed and allowing the Will of God to lead. This means being able to step back enough to take responsibility, to recognize that there is a misperception present, and to ask for help. Within the process, there is implied an openness to a different way of viewing the situation.

Foster gentle awareness - Another way to de-condition the constant thought process is to begin sitting in a state of relaxed or gentle awareness on a regular basis. Other words that might be used to describe this state would be to become centered or to be in a receptive state. The idea here is to sit with your eyes open and just "be" without attempting to control anything. Just let go and sit in the natural state of awareness that is always there. There are multiple advantages to sitting in this state on a regular basis: it allows suppressed energies to be released; it gives access to the state of inner "knowing;" it allows one to align with the silence, so it is possible to see thoughts arise and to refuse them; and it makes it easier to return to this state when crises do occur.

Experience sensory overload - There is also some evidence that sensory overload can help in altering the thought stream. Cultures across time have used chanting, drumming, and dance to lead to an altered state. The issue again is that - for this state to become permanent - a corresponding change in consciousness is also required.

Stopping the Obsession

There will be times when, despite our best efforts, the mind becomes obsessed with a thought stream that will not stop. There is evidence for heart-brain interaction that explains the physical basis for the continuation of this process.[23] If one can catch it early, things that redirect (focus attention away from the situation) can be helpful. Examples of this might be taking the circumstances of the situation and modifying them to make them humorous, moving awareness to the heart, listening to uplifting music, or taking a walk.

When all else fails, it may be necessary to become the observer, and sit with the issue in gentle awareness until it runs itself out. Later, when no longer embroiled in the issue, it might be worthwhile to examine what led to becoming identified with that thought stream.

What Doesn't Work

Denial, suppression, and projection - We have already looked at how what is denied, suppressed, or projected is still present within the self and will appear again in similar situations until it is addressed.

Resistance - Fighting against thoughts gives them energy and leads to the belief that they are real and who you are.

Burying the issue and holding resentment - Resentment leads to loss of power and happiness in addition to the physical impacts it creates in the body.

Attempts to silence the mind via willpower - Stepping outside and becoming the observer is more likely to break the process than attempting to use the little will. Attempts to stop thinking about something simply make it more attractive.

Attempts to fix your thoughts to make them more acceptable - We are not here to convince the ego mind of anything. It is a waste of time to fix the ego, as it is not who we are. True freedom comes from realizing that thoughts have no control over the real Self.

Over-focusing on the problem - It is possible to feed a problem by giving it more energy than it deserves. Sometimes, it is better to simply observe and let an issue run itself out; then later, work with the situation from a higher perspective in terms of how one can grow from it.

Ongoing Process

It might be said that in every moment of every day there is an opportunity to choose for oneness or for separation. When we are not mindful of our thoughts, that choice is made unconsciously. It is mindful awareness via self observation that allows us to choose consciously. Complacency means that we have allowed awareness to slip. It is this constant vigilance that allows us to be mindful of every thought we have and every word we utter.

When fully awake, the rational or logical mind will only speak when requested to help. Reality is that we are all creatures of habit and that the undoing of these patterns is a process. Rather than become frustrated with repeated failure, changing perspective can help. One technique is to step into awareness and recognize that this is just what egos do. That gives the perspective that the ego is not the real you and creates distance from the undesired thought processes and behaviors. It may also be helpful to recognize ahead of time that you are not perfect and will make mistakes. That gives the illusionary ego less need to be defensive. It might be said that compassion for the misguided nature of the small self is the better path forward.

Summary

- Dissolution of the ego begins with making thoughts visible and then choosing to let go of attachment to them.
- Thoughts are sustained through attention and interest, identification, and acceptance of the belief that they are who we are. Thoughts are thus dissolved by seeing them as worthless, withdrawing interest from them, and recognizing the true nature of the mind.
- Invoking a Higher Power invites assistance from the Higher Will, which is always available to us.
- Sitting in a state of gentle awareness or receptivity allows suppressed energies to be released, gives access to the state of inner "knowing," allows one to align with the silence so it is possible to see thoughts arise and refuse them, and makes it easier to return to this state when crises do occur.
- Releasing attachment to thoughts is an ongoing process. Self compassion for the misguided nature of the small self is the more effective path when awareness slips.

Reflections/Exercises/Practices

For Reflection/Discussion:

1. What would help you personally to see and let go of attachment to your own thoughts? Sit with this question and see what comes.
2. When do you tend to become most immersed in your own thoughts?
3. What patterns have you noticed in your own thoughts? Which defense mechanism do you favor - denial, suppression, or projection?
4. If thoughts are of no value, what is of value?
5. What would aid you in moving allegiance to the Higher Self instead of to the ego?
6. What is your typical incentive?
7. What are your biggest worries about the future? Are they rooted in the past? How might you release this tendency to worry? If you were to write an affirmation for yourself to release this worry, what would it be?
8. What are the risks in letting go of attachment to the ego?
9. We have looked at how others pick up thoughts subliminally. Choose an existing relationship and reflect on how your thoughts affect your interactions with that person.
10. What resentments are you currently holding? Can you let them go?

Exercises:

Once again, these exercises are meant to be done on a regular basis over a period of time, until you see that there is a difference in your thought processes.

1. Tie yarn around your wrist or set a timer. Each time you notice the yarn or hear the timer, note your current thought.
2. Sit for ten minutes by yourself. Every time a thought arises, tell yourself, "This thought is of no value." Notice what happens to the thought stream as you persist in doing this.
3. For five minutes, with your eyes closed, become aware of how new thoughts arise. Focus strictly on the movement of the thought stream. See if you can observe a thought as it begins to arise. Instead of latching on to it, choose not to attach to it.
4. See if you can observe the change in your own energy as you latch onto a negative thought. Observe your energy level throughout the day. Note how it wanes as you allow the events of the day to wear you down.
5. When you meet someone for the first time, observe your thoughts. There is generally a judgment that takes place. Observe yourself making this judgment. What satisfaction do you get from this judgment?
6. Sit in a crowded area. As your awareness rests on each person, note any judgmental thoughts that arise about that person.
7. Make it a habit to sit in gentle or receptive awareness for a few minutes throughout the day whenever you have the opportunity.
8. Over the course of a month, give up each of the following items for one week, and observe the results. During that week, resolve to give up that item completely. Monitor your thoughts closely, so you know when it occurs and immediately let go of any unwanted thoughts. For example, with justification, resolve that you will not justify any of your thoughts or actions. As soon as you see justification occurring, let it go.
    *   Give up justification
    *   Give up interpretation
    *   Give up the past
    *   Give up negativity
9. The following exercise is one suggested by Bob Larzalere in The Harmony of Love[24] and is designed to show how powerful our thoughts are.
    *   Two people sit facing each other and decide who will be the sender and who will be the receiver
    *   The receiver closes his or her eyes
    *   The sender says "Start" and begins thinking nasty thoughts about the receiver
    *   The receiver signals when the sender stops thinking the negative thoughts
    *   The receiver opens his or her eyes, and the sender and receiver discuss how close the receiver came to knowing when the negative thoughts stopped
    *   After three or four times, the sender and receiver change roles
10. Begin observing how often your assumptions about other people and the situations around you are not accurate. Instead of assuming negative intention on the part of the other, be open to the idea that this person was speaking and acting with kind intent. If the situation is one you feel safe in, ask questions to determine the other's motivation and compare it to your assumptions.

11. Work with the phrase "don't take it personally." When you are tempted to react, see the ego as separate from who you are and not worth defending.
12. Give up adjectives for a week, both externally in your speech and internally in your thoughts. Note the impact on your tendency to interpret, to assign value, and to judge.
13. Write a poem or a letter showing compassion for the misguided ego.
14. Have a conversation with the ego. What would you like to tell it?
15. For a week, every time you see yourself become immersed or feel the need to take control and do it your way, instead give the situation to a Higher Power. Use a statement like "[Your preferred name for this Higher Power] help me to see this differently" or "[Your preferred name for this Higher Power] please show me how to move forward with this situation."
16. Take a subject or situation that produces a reaction in you and think about it with no justification or accusation of other people.
17. Emotional blackmail (the use of fear, obligation, and guilt), threats, and projected doom are ways in which the ego will try to survive. As you see these thoughts arise, recognize them as a survival effort on the part of the ego, and turn them out.
18. The next time you begin to obsess about something and are unable to let it go, move your awareness to the heart and begin watching your breath as it raises and lowers your chest. Choose a pleasant situation to focus your attention on and observe the impacts on your body.
19. One of the principles in this work is that of inner honesty. Practice describing to yourself what is going on around you in all kinds of situations, including human interactions. As you observe, follow the guidelines in the table below.

Do	Don't
Report facts only	Attempt to solve or resolve
Acknowledge your own likes and dislikes	Minimize or exaggerate
Be honest with yourself	Create theories about why something is so

Meditative Practices:

1. Close your eyes and focus your awareness on your thoughts. Simply observe the thought stream without latching on or immersing yourself in any given thought. Do not attempt to control or judge your thoughts, simply observe their coming and going. If you grab on and forget to observe, begin observing again as soon as you realize that you became lost in your thoughts.
2. Visualize the ego as a cloud or mist that is obscuring the view of your Higher Self. Gradually see this mist dissipating until you are at peace with who you really are.

Chapter 9 - Working with Emotions

This chapter will look in depth at the topic of emotions. Like the previous chapter on thoughts, it will do that with the objective of seeing your emotions so you can let go of attachment to them in order to align more closely with who you really are.

What Are Emotions?

There is no consistent theory[25] on where emotions come from. Some theories are evolutionary; they provide an analysis of emotions from a historical perspective and attempt to explain why we have the emotions we have today. Social theories explain emotions as the end product of living in a particular culture and society. Another set of explanations considers emotions an inner process and there are differences of opinion about whether "thinking" is a part of the process, a predecessor, or quickly follows the emotional response. For the purpose of this discussion, we will continue with the theory that emotions are part of a cyclic process.

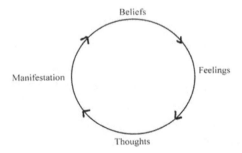

The Egoic Circle

Humanity's history and an individual's culture and society do impact underlying beliefs. although the cyclic nature of the process does leave open the possibility that preceding thoughts can impact one's feelings, we will continue with the theory that emotions lie between beliefs and thoughts,. I like to think of examining emotions as going one level deeper into the human psyche and the field of human consciousness, and therefore closer to where the original energy imbalance or distortion occurred, but also one step closer to who we really are.

9 - Working with Emotions

Value of Emotions

The value of emotions is that they point to parts of the self that are still in need of healing. Negative or painful feelings are a barometer, an indication that something needs to be looked at. The sign that you have come upon something that needs to be healed is that you overreact emotionally; you are too invested in the outcome. When negativity is present, there is an imbalance or distortion somewhere. By finding the feeling that preceded it, one can use the feeling to clear the imbalance or misperception. When you are connected to Spirit or who you really are, positive emotions are naturally present. When negativity is present, it is an indication that one is disconnected from the true Self.

Without this emotional guidance system, we would *not* be able to grow spiritually. Emotions, painful or not, are in that sense a gift. Emotions bring us information about the self that enables the ability to make changes and to continue to grow. It is not possible to align with who you really are until you become conscious of what is occurring emotionally within you. The cause of emotional pain is some aspect of the self that is not in alignment with the Higher Self and therefore not in harmony with oneness; it is an aspect that works against cooperation and a reverence for all of life.

Ideally, we would be fully aware of our emotions all of the time. If there was no negativity (distortions, imbalances) present, we would fully live without judgment with the awareness that nothing is good or bad, it just is. The following excerpts from the teaching "Resting from Mind Caused Suffering" by Jan Frazier explain what it is like to operate in this state:

When mind-caused suffering has stopped happening, you still feel. There is tenderness, openness, love. It's just that it isn't in the name of holding you together. It isn't about "you." ... But what doesn't happen is the story-making ... You aren't at a distance from life. You haven't become tough, or aloof. It's just that you no longer run everything through a filter. It's that you're no longer at the mercy of the mind, whose primary mission used to be to protect you ... How is it that you are really here and yet not attached to any of it? Reality doesn't bounce off of you anymore. It enters you, passes through you. You feel it, but it leaves you. It leaves you unchanged ... You want nothing. But life is here, happening. Sometimes it hurts. Sometimes there is a surge of joy. You're really here for it, all of it.

Barely Emotional

The issue for most of us is that we barely feel. Negative emotions are painful, and we have learned to avoid that pain in every way possible through denial/suppression or projection, using distractions like talking; watching TV; eating; smoking; working all the time; fleeing into thoughts, opinions, and compulsive activities; and the use of drugs, alcohol, or sex to numb the pain.

Social acceptance is a part of this process. Rather than make decisions from the truth of who we are, we sell out to what we are "expected" to do or be. The ensuing resentment and regret form the wall around the heart described earlier. The word "should" is an indication that one needs to look further at the motivation for a particular action or decision. Playing expected roles can provide a sense of self worth and even bring outside respect and admiration, but it can also lead one to be dishonest with one's self, to sell out to societal expectations. Roles and expectations can become a barrier to recognition of the true Self. This selling out begins so early in childhood, out of ignorance and fear, that by the time we are adults we do not even question it. The caution here is that "giving in" to expectations may relieve emotional discomfort but it does so at the expense of what is important to you. This is where having clear ideals for your life can make a difference.

If I were to draw our ability to feel emotions diagrammatically, it might look like this:

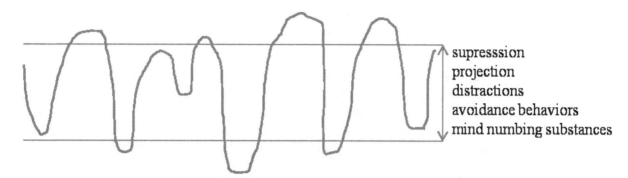

supresssion
projection
distractions
avoidance behaviors
mind numbing substances

Diagram - Blocking Emotional Awareness

For the most part, people are not aware of their feelings. Although emotions are occurring continuously as shown in the diagram, we are so used to hiding our feelings, even from ourselves, that it is only when they are very intense, in either a positive or negative direction, that we become consciously aware of them. It is not very pleasant to bring the light of awareness to the imbalances present in oneself. It is much easier just to distract oneself. There are two issues with this continual avoidance: the first is that we fail to grow spiritually and the second is that the intensity of the pain will eventually increase to the point that we will no longer be able to avoid it. Emotional awareness means becoming aware of feelings as they occur. Just as with thoughts, there is an opportunity in every moment.

When the same negative patterns occur in our life over and over, we want to blame a vengeful God or at least assume that a Divine Intelligence is sending us the same lesson over and over again. What we fail to see is that it is the distortion in our own perception that makes the issue seem to reappear over and over again. Pain and suffering come from the self and not from an outside source. The message of negative emotions is that something needs to be learned; a misperception needs to be corrected. Another way to visualize this is that the light of the Divine is always shining into us, but we block it by the misperceptions that we hold. From an energy standpoint, emotions tell us when and how we are losing energy and distorting that light.

When we permit these deeper, painful emotions to remain hidden, we act unconsciously and allow these unconscious patterns to drive habitual reactions. When we develop emotional awareness, we enable conscious choice and the ability to create new ways of acting and being. There are multiple routes to learning. We can take the shorter and less painful route of learning from our emotions, or we can take a longer and more painful route of experiencing suffering again and again until we choose to see and learn from it.

How Can I Feel Again?

Usually, the process of becoming more conscious and self-aware takes time and requires consistent effort. Thus, the use of self observation, letting go of identification (attachment), the implementation of right attitude, and moments of Self remembering lead to the growth in consciousness that begins to dissolve limiting emotions and enable the higher emotions. If by persistent right thinking we realize that we are the cause of all that happens to us, after some time right thinking becomes a permanent process and limiting emotions become less frequent. These moments of being emotional are in direct proportion to the efforts made to become more conscious. The process might be diagrammed as follows:

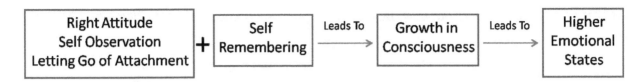

Diagram - Relationship of Consciousness to Emotional State

When we do see emotion arise, we need to use those moments as opportunities to let go of attachment, to remember who we really are, and to choose for oneness. When we are able to do this with emotions, we are working with a deeper level than thoughts and thus grow more from the experience. Some of the positive benefits of releasing the emotional charge include clearing cellular debris, clearing the auric field, lessening the misperception that you are the egoic self, and raising one's vibration and level of consciousness.

The remainder of this chapter will focus on how to put emotions in their proper context, how to recognize patterns in emotions to increase awareness, and how to work with emotions for spiritual growth.

Recognizing the Nature of Emotions

Negative (or limiting) emotions are of the ego. Higher knowledge comes from one's own intuition and is of the Self. These are separate processes and it is ultimately necessary to give conscious allegiance to one or the other. Negative or limiting emotions are part of the cloud of illusion that hides the true light. They arise from one's own misperceptions and are self created. Initially it may appear that external events "create" emotional responses, but, in fact, the emotions are an internal process. They may feel very real, but, in time, with emotional awareness and efforts to raise consciousness, it will become apparent that even the manifestation of certain emotions can be altered, since they are part of an internal process. Emotions themselves are not a good thing or a bad thing; they just are. There is no need to fear them or to be concerned about their power to overwhelm. They are a natural aspect of being human and are simply a reflection of one's state of consciousness.

Being self created, your emotions are unique to you and therefore the task of becoming emotionally aware and of taking ownership of how you respond is a task that only you can perform. The more meaning we give to a particular emotion, the stronger the emotion becomes. Conversely, the less meaning and significance we give to an emotion, the less strength it has. Thus, we need to see our own emotions impartially and with the view that they are here to inform us that we need to look at something.

While emotions are quicker than thought, the mind can be trained to "see" emotions after they arise, thus enabling a choice in how to respond. Feelings themselves are not a problem; it is how we choose to respond to them that can create problems. While we have no direct control over feelings that arise, we definitely can control how we interpret and respond to those feelings. Controlling our emotions means learning to process them and to respond to them in a healthy manner. Once we accept responsibility for how we respond, the emotions around a given situation tend to lose their hold over us.

Looking for Patterns

The suppression of emotions is a form of dishonesty to ones-self. The first step in working with emotions is thus to acknowledge or validate their presence. When we validate our emotions, we become more aware of and accepting of them, and we begin to understand what lies behind them. It is only by stepping back into this place of awareness that we can see what power we have given them. A part of dissolving the wall around the heart is this willingness to be vulnerable, and that can only occur when we are willing to be honest enough to look at what is really there.

Because these negative emotions have their source in unfounded fears, misperceptions, and misunderstandings, a given emotion can still be present within even if one is not currently reacting to it. In other words, each of us has habitual patterns of emotional response that we resort to when certain external circumstances arise, and we will continue to follow those habitual patterns until we recognize that they are there. Thus, a part of emotional awareness is spending time reflecting on what those patterns are for you. The more you become aware of your patterns, the more you are able to consciously choose how you will respond when similar experiences arise.

A key point in looking for these patterns is that the emphasis needs to be on what is occurring within and not on the details of the external circumstances. That is, the emphasis needs to be on your own emotions, and not on what "appears" to be causing them. For example, if someone repeats an instruction multiple times and you feel the person is talking down to you, the focus needs to be on your perception of being insulted or talked down to, and not on the triggering event (the words said, the tone of voice, previous interactions with this person, etc.).

Following are some methods that can be used to identify and reflect on these emotional patterns:

Look for connections between thoughts and self talk and your negative emotions - When you become aware that a negative emotion is present, look back at the thoughts and self talk that preceded it. Because of the cyclic nature of the ego, dwelling on certain thoughts can lead to an emotional response.

Look for connections between thoughts and physical discomfort - Begin to notice what occurs in your body with various types of thoughts. If you are feeling discomfort, look back at the thoughts and the frame of mind that preceded the discomfort. Look for patterns between a given physical discomfort and the associated thoughts that might share a common emotion. For example, a friend shared that she was about to change the cushion on the chair she sits in at the computer. Eventually, she recognized that it was not the chair itself that was giving her a backache, but rather that the backache would begin when she read emails that were upsetting to her. Part of emotional awareness is becoming aware of what you are physically feeling in your body. John Sarno, a medical doctor, wrote an interesting book called <u>Mind Over Back Pain</u>. In working with back patients, he became convinced (and cites strong evidence for the concept) that neck, shoulder, and back pain are rarely due to mechanical problems, but rather to tension. And by training people to correlate increases in pain with emotional rather than physical phenomena, that pain can often be relieved.

Notice what triggers a particular emotional reaction in you - Begin to notice what sets you off emotionally. Rather than focus on the externals of situations, look for commonalities in your own internal reactions.

Check your emotions throughout the day - Periodically, throughout the day, stop and ask what you are feeling. Go inside and feel what is going on with your body. Check in with your heart.

Watch your memories - Observe your memories as they arise throughout the day. Which ones recur on a regular basis? What patterns do you see between the memories? What emotion(s) lie behind those memories and patterns?

Identify other experiences of the same emotion - Once you identify an emotion, recall other times when you experienced the same emotion. Sit with this and see what memories come up.

Note the emotions in your dreams - The emotions in your dreams are likely the same ones you struggle with in everyday life. For example, when I feel like my life is not under my control (I am allowing outside expectations to control my life), I will have a dream where I am driving a car from the back seat and cannot properly control the car (I am not in control of my own vehicle).

Reflections/Exercises/Practices

For Reflection/Discussion:

1. What is your method for avoiding emotional honesty?
2. What role in your life do you most resent? Why did you create it? How would it feel to do things differently?
3. Can you accept emotional discomfort as a gift that will help you to grow spiritually?
4. How did your family handle emotions? Were there any emotions that were "off limits" in your family?

Exercises:

1. The next time you notice you are emotionally upset, take time to reflect on what you are feeling. Later that evening, sit with the feeling and ask to have memories of that same feeling come to mind.
2. In your own words, write out what Self remembering means to you.
3. Keep a journal of your emotional highs and lows for a period of several weeks. Briefly note the details of each event but place your emphasis on what occurred internally as a result of the event, both physically in the body and psychologically in the mind.
4. Reference the list of negative emotions at the end of this chapter. Which emotion on the list feels the most uncomfortable to you? Choose six that you feel most apply to you. (If an emotion you are aware of is not on the list, feel free to include that emotion.) Choose the three that you feel most strongly belong to you and write out how they feel in your body. For example, anger might feel like blood rushing to the head, heat in the upper body, tension in the neck, and throbbing at the temples.
5. Write your day from an emotional standpoint.
6. Make a list of the "little hurts" from your childhood and adult life that you can still remember. What commonalities do you see?
7. Each day for a week, take time to write out instances during the day when you "sold out." This may be times when you did something because you felt like you should; when you did not state your feelings on a subject because you told yourself, "It's not important enough to create a fuss about;" or where you agreed to something you don't really agree with, just to keep the peace.
8. Research one of your frequent emotions. Find out what the literature says is the root cause and how to work with that emotion. As you come across various theories and differences in what you find, listen within to see what rings true for you.

9. If you have a recurring pain in your body, begin to monitor what occurs prior to the onset of that pain. What thought processes precede the onset of the pain? Is there a common emotion that underlies these thoughts?

Note that at this point you should have a good idea of what your primary repertoire of limiting emotions is and what triggers them. You should also be positioned to choose differently when you see yourself start the familiar pattern of reaction. If you did the ideals work earlier, you may have already put in place some right attitudes to support your ideal.

Letting Go of Attachment

Once one has learned to be aware of limiting emotions, the process of releasing or letting go of attachment to them uses *some* of the same techniques as were used with thoughts.

Catch it early - As with thoughts, the sooner you can detect that a negative or limiting emotion has taken hold, the better. When you see that you are beginning to react to an event, move your focus from the outer world to the inner and recognize that a limiting emotion is present. Focus awareness on the emotion and not on the external circumstances. A technique such as watching the breath can help in interrupting the reaction process. Awareness that you are experiencing the discomfort of one of your ego's limiting emotions is the first step in releasing attachment to it.

Give up identification - The biggest challenge with a limiting emotion is the inclination to pick it up and believe that it is justified, that who you are has been offended in some way. Giving up identification thus has two aspects: 1) creating perspective about the emotion itself, and 2) recognizing that you are not your emotions.

To create perspective about an emotion, one or more of the following may be helpful:
- Observe the emotion as if it is within someone else. Note its characteristics, how it feels in the body, etc., as if you are doing so on behalf of another.
- Write about your feelings - in a journal, as a letter, as a poem, etc. Writing seems to create distance and give perspective.
- Look at the emotion and give it a name. Simply giving a name to or labeling a negative emotion calms the amygdala, the part of the brain where emotions are generated.[26]
- Remember that nothing is permanent, that this too shall pass.

It may be helpful to put identification or attachment in your own words. In doing so, recognize that identification occurs not just to things in the external environment, but also to "things" in your inner world. Detachment allows you to keep perspective and to navigate through, rather than becoming immersed in.

The following may help in remembering that you are not your emotions:
- Remember that within you there are two selves: the self and the Self. It is only the small self, the ego, that takes offense. The true Self is the real Self and the ego is not worth defending.
- Keep your aim or ideal ever before you, so it becomes more important than identification with any emotion.
- Recognize the nature of emotions, and that they too are part of the illusion of separateness.
- Recognize that it is lack of consciousness that leads to identification.

Reflections/Exercises/Practices

Exercises:

1. Write out what identification means to you.
2. Sit quietly and visualize what it means to be free of identification.
3. Choose a day you can devote to inner work. Throughout that entire day, notice how you move from identification (attachment) with one thing to identification with another. See if you can take notice of things (external events, the comments of others, thoughts, feelings, etc.) without identifying with them.
4. Notice what irritates you about other people. See if you can observe that same behavior and not be irritated by giving up identification with it.

Self Remembering

This ability to Self remember is developed through continual effort over a period of time and involves the ability to see and let go of attachment to thoughts, a willingness to go against habitual reaction patterns, giving up identification with limiting emotions, and dedication to a higher ideal. It is a moment of will.

In the last chapter, we saw that when we allow thoughts to enter and dissipate without picking them up and identifying with them, thinking gradually loses its power and begins to dissolve. We also looked at how resisting those same thoughts would simply give them more energy. And so it is with emotions. To dissipate a limiting emotion, it is first necessary to honor its presence - in other words, to fully feel or be with it, but at the same time to keep perspective on it so that one does not become immersed in it.

Sitting with an emotion is of value. It allows one to go deeper within, to understand what is drawing the emotion. As you fully experience an emotion, you realize that there is nothing to fear about the emotion itself. Whatever it is, you can survive it, because you are sitting with it and surviving it in the moment. As you observe yourself doing that, you realize that the emotion is not who you really are. Feeling or being with what is within simply means that you are owning it. Guidelines for feeling the emotion include staying with the feeling as opposed to moving into thought, staying with the feeling as opposed to dwelling on the circumstances that led to it, and going as deep as possible with the feeling while still maintaining perspective.

Once it is clear that you are not your emotion, it is possible to make a conscious choice to give up attachment to it. After a while, you realize that there is just no point in staying with something that no longer serves you. You can choose to wallow in it or you can choose to give it up. Once a negative emotion is given up, previous events associated with that emotion lose their charge, and become like threads in the fabric of your life, no more or less significant than anything else.

Pictorially, the process would look something like this:

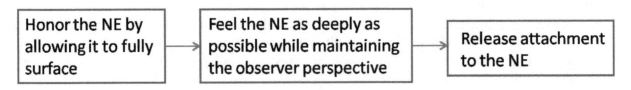

Diagram - Letting Go of Negative Emotions

There are a number of good books and processes available that describe methods of releasing this emotional attachment.

In <u>Transcending The Levels of Consciousness</u>, David R. Hawkins, M. D., Ph.D. gives the following steps for processing out negative feelings:[27]

- *Stay with the feeling and stay focused on it unswervingly. Realize that all pain is due to resistance. The suffering or loss stems from attachment and specialness.*
- *Be willing to become immersed in and surrender to the feelings without avoiding them. Notice that they come in waves and that surrendering to the most intense waves tends to decrease their emotional severity.*
- *Ask God's help and surrender the personal will to God.*
- *Be willing to endure and suffer out the process. If not resisted, it will process itself out and come to an end.*

When overwhelmed, he recommends temporarily and consciously setting aside major aspects of the situation, to begin letting go of smaller aspects.[28] The example he gives is job loss; one might surrender on the social aspects of no longer having lunch with colleagues, the familiarity of the workplace, etc., before attempting to surrender on the main event. He also says that if you are stuck with a particular feeling, simply surrender to the feeling of being stuck.[29] While fragments of an event may occur for a period of time afterward,[30] continual surrender will eventually release all attachment.

The concept of inviting assistance from a higher power is the method suggested in <u>A Course in Miracles</u>.

Everyone here has entered darkness, yet no one has entered it alone. Nor need he stay more than an instant. For he has come with Heaven's Help within him, ready to lead him out of darkness into light at any time. The time he chooses can be any time, for help is there, awaiting but his choice. And when he chooses to avail himself of what is given him, then will he see each situation that he thought before was means to justify his anger turned to an event which justifies his love. He will hear plainly that the calls to war he heard before are really calls to peace. (T-25, III.6.1-6)

<u>The Sedona Method</u> by Hale Dwoskin is another helpful book in understanding the release process. This book explains that welcoming a feeling opens consciousness, which begins the release process and allows the feeling to drop away. By diving into the core of an emotion, we come to realize that nothing is really there. In letting go of an unwanted feeling, we release attachment to what we - through misunderstanding - have held on to.[31]

The Sedona Method outlines a series of questions:[32]

- *Could I allow this feeling to be here?*
- *Could I welcome this feeling?*
- *Could I let this feeling go?*

If the answer is "no," then:

- *Would I rather have this feeling, or would I rather be free?*

If the answer is to have this feeling, then:

- *When could I release it?*

Another book I found very helpful in experiencing the release process is <u>Whatever Arises, Love That</u> by Matt Kahn. The underlying premise of this book is that each emotion is a cry for love from your own inner child. After owning and embracing the emotion, he recommends sending love to your own heart.[33] Since the subconscious mind does not care who is saying the words "I love you,"[34] the result is that you feel more loved and accepted regardless of what is occurring in the outside world. This process can be thought of as a surrender to love.

The Emotional Freedom Technique (EFT), also known as tapping, uses these same principles of acknowledging and staying with the feeling, accepting and loving the self, embracing the positive opposite, and willingness to release. In addition, there is evidence that tapping on the acupressure points helps to calm the amygdala, a part of the limbic system in the brain that plays a role in processing emotions.[35]

Note that it is not necessary to fully understand an emotion to release it. Even with aches and pains, one can place a hand on that spot, fully feel what is there, and choose to release it, give it to a higher power, or send it love. As one works with self observation of both thoughts and emotions, one becomes more adept at releasing attachment in the moment.

It is worth mentioning that fear of any kind is self created and the process for releasing it is basically the same. Once a fear is seen, owned, and fully felt, it is necessary to walk straight through it. That is, choose to give *no* validity to the fear and to act in opposition to it.

Also, note that venting does temporarily release the emotional charge associated with a particular situation, but does not address the underlying issue. When this venting is toward another person, it is likely to be harmful to the relationship. When emotional charge is let out in a safe way - screaming in an empty room, hitting a pillow, journaling, or talking with someone safe - it releases the charge. But until the underlying misperception is addressed, it will not be helpful long term.

There are also indications that other processes, such as breath work, emotional release work, deep body work, music and movement therapy, etc., can help in getting in touch with one's own emotions, although they are beyond the scope of this book.

After Effects

When this emotional baggage is released, one feels calmer and more centered, and there is a greater sense of freedom. Situations that previously were triggers will no longer be so, and there will be less inclination to take things personally. The energy spent keeping the emotions at bay will now be available for other uses. Once an underlying emotion is released, there is no longer a need for the thoughts it engendered and the mind becomes less noisy. As the wall around the heart begins to crumble, there is an opening to the presence of love. Once one realizes that all that is needed is within, the need for external approval diminishes.

Summary

- Emotions are a level deeper in the psyche and letting go of attachment to them allows one to grow more quickly than simply working with thoughts.
- Emotions bring information about the self that enables the ability to make changes and to continue to grow.
- For the most part, we have been conditioned not to acknowledge our emotions, but emotional awareness is something that can be developed.
- There is a relationship between growth in consciousness and higher emotional states.
- Self honesty and willingness are needed to identify one's own recurring patterns.
- The emotion itself is not the issue; it is identification with it and believing that one is that emotion that continues to support the ego.
- General consensus on how to release emotional charge involves these steps:

    ○ Honor the emotion by allowing it to fully surface
    ○ Feel the emotion as deeply as possible while maintaining the observer perspective
    ○ Release attachment to - or identification with - the emotion

Reflections/Exercises/Practices

Exercises:

1. Practice being honest with yourself. For example, if you are annoyed, recognize that you are annoyed. If you are angry, recognize that you are angry.

2. The next time you are upset, stop and ask yourself what is going on. Look at what you are feeling and how your body feels physically. Do *not* dwell on the circumstances of the situation, but rather look at what you are feeling.

3. The next time you become aware that you are judging someone or something, move your awareness to your body and feel what is going on in your body. Move your thoughts to how compassionate you feel toward someone (possibly a child or good friend) and notice the difference in how your body feels.

4. Practice taking ownership of your own feelings. For example, when you see judgmental thoughts arise, look within and see if you can define the feeling that is behind them and take ownership of it.

5. The next time you are saying good-bye to someone, observe what is going on within you. Are those feelings consistent with your view of the relationship?

6. The next time you are in a situation where you are talking to someone you would prefer not to be talking to, or are doing something you would prefer not to be doing, use the moment as an opportunity to feel within.

7. When you are struggling to keep a situation in perspective, envision yourself standing above the situation and looking down on it.

8. If you see a feeling arise at a time when you can work with it, sit with the feeling, talk to it, and ask what is driving it. Honor it and give it the space to talk to you.

9. Take the list of six emotions you selected from the list at the end of the chapter and define an opposite for each. When you see yourself move to one of these emotions, bring the opposite to mind.

10. When you recognize that you have responded to a person or situation with a habitual emotional reaction, spend a moment and decide how you would like to respond the next time you are in a similar situation. Let go of attachment to the situation and confirm "the next time I will respond differently."

11. Practice sending love to yourself. If you see that you are worried or anxious about something, move your awareness to your own heart and send yourself love. Recognize that you can give yourself the love you didn't get in the past. If you sense that your fears are based in something from the past, tell yourself, "That was then, and this is now."

12. Choose one of the "little hurts" you defined previously and work on releasing the emotional charge associated with it.

13. In the Self remembering section, multiple means of releasing attachment to a negative emotion were discussed. Although, in some sense, these are aspects of the same thing, it may be helpful to work with all three approaches and see which you personally find most effective.

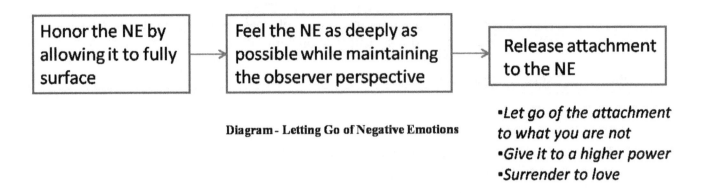

Diagram - Letting Go of Negative Emotions

Honor the NE by allowing it to fully surface → Feel the NE as deeply as possible while maintaining the observer perspective → Release attachment to the NE

- *Let go of the attachment to what you are not*
- *Give it to a higher power*
- *Surrender to love*

14. Pause for mini attitude adjustments throughout the day.
15. If there is a situation in which you feel overwhelmed, try Dr. Hawkins' technique of releasing on aspects of the situation.
16. Choose someone in the past who has hurt you. Say to your own inner child the words that you would like to hear from that person.

Meditative Practices:

1. Focus on your own heart and hold your focus there until you can feel the warmth/energy/light that is present within. Let go and feel your heart within the heart of God.
2. Choose a positive affirmation that reflects your willingness to own your own feelings. Repeat that affirmation within to focus the mind. When you are ready, release the words and stay with the feeling of those words. For example, "I created these emotions and it is within my power to release them."

List of Negative Emotions

Abandoned	Diminished	Indifferent	Perplexed	Uneasy
Abused	Disappointed	Indignant	Pessimistic	Unhappy
Accused	Disapproved of	Inferior	Powerless	Unheard
Afraid	Disbelieve	Inflamed	Preoccupied	Unimportant
Aggressive	Discouraged	Infuriated	Pressured	Uninformed
Agonized	Disgusted	Inhibited	Prideful	Unknown
Alarmed	Disgusting	Injured	Provoked	Unloved
Alienated	Disillusioned	Insecure	Punished	Unpleasant
Alone	Disinterested	Insensitive	Put down	Unsafe
Angry	Dismayed	Insignificant	Rejected	Unsupported
Annoyed	Disrespected	Insulted	Repugnant	Unsure
Anxious	Dissatisfied	Insulting	Resentful	Untrusted
Appalled	Distressed	Interrogated	Reserved	Untrusting
Ashamed	Distrustful	Intimidated	Restless	Unwanted
Attacked	Dominated	Invaded	Restricted	Unworthy
Bad	Doubtful	Invalidated	Ridiculed	Upset
Beaten down	Dull	Invisible	Robbed	Useless
Bitter	Embarrassed	Irritated	Sad	Vengeful
Blamed	Empty	Jealous	Scared	Victimized
Bored	Enraged	Judged	Shaky	Violated
Bossed around	Envious	Labeled	Shamed	Wary
Brushed off	Fatigued	Lectured to	Shocked	Weary
Cheated	Fearful	Left out	Shy	Withdrawn
Cold	Forced	Lied about	Skeptical	Woeful
Conflicted	Frightened	Lied to	Sorrowful	Worried
Confused	Frustrated	Lonely	Stereotyped	Worthless
Contemptuous	Grief-stricken	Lost	Stressful	Wronged
Controlled	Guarded	Manipulated	Stupefied	
Cowardly	Guilty	Misled	Suffocated	
Criticized	Hateful	Misunderstood	Sulky	
Cross	Heartbroken	Mocked	Suspicious	
Crushed	Helpless	Neglected	Tearful	
Cut down	Hesitant	Nervous	Teased	
Cynical	Hostile	Obligated	Tense	
Defensive	Humiliated	Offended	Terrible	
Dehumanized	Hurt	Offensive	Terrified	
Dejected	Ignored	Over-controlled	Threatened	
Depressed	Impatient	Over-protected	Timid	
Deprived	Imposed-upon	Over-ruled	Tormented	
Desolate	Imprisoned	Overwhelmed	Tortured	
Despairing	Inadequate	Pained	Trapped	
Desperate	Incapable	Panicky	Uncared about	
Despicable	Incensed	Paralyzed	Uncertain	
Detestable	Indecisive	Pathetic	Underestimated	

Chapter 10 - Working with Beliefs

In this chapter, we look more closely at underlying beliefs. As we saw earlier, core beliefs are the basis on which the rest of the structure stands. As a reminder, core beliefs are the views that we hold about ourselves, other people, the world, and the future. They serve as guides to making sense of the world. They can be thought of as a filter through which all of our experiences pass before coming into awareness.

Beliefs are, for the most part, not conscious. We want to break free of beliefs that no longer serve our development, so growth in consciousness can be seen as a process of making our beliefs visible, then letting go of attachment to them.

Beliefs are yet another level deeper than emotions. Our limiting beliefs and misperceptions are the major roadblocks to the perception of the true Self. In fact, one could view the purpose of a given lifetime as an opportunity to let go of attachment to a set of misperceptions - a little experiment in growth in consciousness. The life lessons one has come to work on are just this: "I think I will try this in this lifetime and see if that helps me to 'get it.'" The earth plane is an environment where there is enough contrast to facilitate the undoing of these beliefs. For each person, situations are in place to help him or her see what is not being seen.

Being willing to let go of limiting beliefs, including the belief that we could ever be separate from our Source, is what the earth experience is all about.

Ideally, we want to come to the point where we allow everything to just be. This is about letting go of past and future, of being in the present moment, and fully experiencing everything that happens with no filter. It is about coming to the realization that there is no good or bad, that everything is in balance, and that all is as it should be. The goal is to come to the point where one can truly say "I know nothing" and trust that what is needed will come at exactly the right time.

Beliefs are easier to undo once they are made conscious. As with the previous chapters on thoughts and emotions, this chapter will look at how to bring limiting beliefs to conscious awareness, and will then look at what helps in letting go of attachment to them. The intent is *not* to create a better personality; but rather to let go of all misperceptions about the true nature of the Self and reality.

Willingness to Question Everything

It is sometimes said that a prerequisite to growth in consciousness is an attitude of openness and a willingness to question everything. Let us look at a couple of examples of what this means. A simple but telling example is the simple puzzle that follows. When asked to form a square from the puzzle pieces at the left, most people will unconsciously choose one of the two right angled pieces in the middle as the starting point.

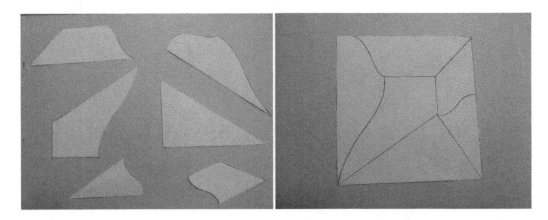

For most, there is prior conditioning to assume that a piece with a right angle is a corner piece. We are surrounded by right angles as corner pieces in the construction of our homes. One of the starting points with a jigsaw puzzle is to build the border first by locating all the flat-sided pieces first and, in particular, the corner pieces with a right angle. With this particular puzzle, that assumption makes it difficult to complete the puzzle. But what happens if we become conscious of that assumption - if we ask, "What if the right angle is not the corner piece? Are there two other pieces that together form a right angle?" At that point, the puzzle becomes easy. This is a simple example of a classic assumption, but it aptly demonstrates how unconscious assumptions dictate our path forward.

A common assumption in this culture is that resources are limited. That leads to the concept that competition is good. The result at the individual level is thoughts such as, "Well, at least I am better than so and so", or "I am justified in taking more than I need right now, because I have to ensure that I get enough to make my future secure." But what if resources are not limited? How do we know that they are? What would happen if we cooperate instead of compete? Is it possible that there would be no need to fear for the future if we understood that we are all one?

Yes, this does create confusion and a state of uncertainty. Like it or not, embracing this confusion and being willing to give up one's story and illusions in favor of a bigger picture is how we discover a deeper reality. The more open-minded one can be - the more willing one is to consider that there might be another way to look at things - the more one is positioned to let go of limiting beliefs.

When we unconsciously follow these limiting beliefs and allow them to influence our behavior, we abdicate responsibility and believe that we are the victim of circumstances. Limiting beliefs provide some payoff in the area of avoiding responsibility. These unconscious beliefs make certain choices seem more sensible.

As one continues this process of continuous questioning of everything, inconsistencies will become clearer. If honesty is maintained, as inner awareness increases and these inconsistencies become more obvious, there will be a need to resolve them. It then becomes an inner process of asking whether "this" serves me well or not. Can I be open to other ways of perceiving this situation? Can I be flexible and open to other possibilities?

When we develop awareness of the inner world and adopt an attitude of openness to questioning everything, we come to realize that these categorizations of people and things are irrelevant and arbitrary. If one spends enough time with the inner "self," it will become clear that there is nothing there. It is all made up, conditioned, put on. Another way of approaching this then is to be open to the possibility that no beliefs are necessary. Of what value are they? They are just conditioned judgments that have been picked up and allowed to become the basis for one's thought processes. Maybe it is better to come from a place of stillness? Truth comes in the stillness.

Even with this understanding, habit patterns are strong, and it is awareness and the willingness to keep the ideal ever present that is key when it comes to action. This is about acting from a different place. It is possible to choose to rise above these limitations each time one feels or sees something arise within the self, to mentally picture the egoic circle and ask, "Do I want to get caught up in this?" If not, then it is better to look for that place of silence within and let the rest go. After a while, this too can become a habit.

Characteristics of Beliefs

Core beliefs manifest as general and absolute statements. Unlike thoughts, which vary across time, core beliefs are fairly stable and act more as "fundamental truths" that apply in all circumstances. They are often formed in early childhood, but one's own karmic past and familial impacts are also significant factors. Limiting beliefs may well have been created in previous lifetimes and brought into this lifetime, as we have already discussed that consciousness goes with us when we leave this earth plane. In choosing a family situation for a particular lifetime, one is entering an environment suited to the life lessons to be worked on in that lifetime. As with thoughts and emotions, beliefs are self created and therefore not something that needs to be feared. The list at the end of this chapter contains some common limiting beliefs.

Information Processing Distortions

Once limiting core beliefs are activated, we process information in a biased way that maintains the core beliefs and discredits contradictory evidence. These are some common information processing distortions.

- All-or nothing thinking – no in-between
- Mind-reading – you believe you can discern the thoughts of others
- Labeling – instead of labeling just the behavior, you label yourself or another
- Jumping to conclusions
- Emotional reasoning – assuming that feelings are facts
- Blowing things out of proportion
- Assuming the worst
- Generalizing - drawing a conclusion based on limited evidence
- Ignoring the positive
- Magnifying or minimizing one's own characteristics or those of another

Without intervention, this is a self-fulfilling process. We continue to create the same limited reality based on the same limiting beliefs and conclude that what occurs is confirmation of those beliefs. We have already looked at deconstructing this process by working with thoughts and feelings, and by putting ideals and right attitudes in place.

Identifying Limiting Beliefs

There are a number of ways to begin the work of identifying limiting beliefs:

Become aware of your information processing distortions - Become aware of which of the information processing distortions above you employ. One way to do this is to allow yourself to state only the verifiable facts of any given situation. Any tendency to distort or embellish those facts is a processing distortion. When you see or feel yourself resort to one of these, ask: What is going on? "What am I avoiding facing?"

Monitor attitudes, self talk, thoughts, and behaviors - Ask: "What are my characteristic thoughts and behaviors across various situations?" What life situations tend to repeat themselves? What am I saying to myself that might be reinforcing limiting beliefs? What triggers me? What might be behind this? Ask, "Why did I do that?"

Follow the emotion - Extremes of emotion are a pretty good clue that underlying beliefs are in play. The most effective way to uncover those beliefs is to follow the emotional charge. Ask, "Why do I feel that way?" Following the charge with emotions will lead to the misperceptions, fears, and limiting and misguided beliefs that underlay them.

As stated in the last chapter, we are used to employing various mechanisms to avoid uncomfortable emotions. Avoidance behaviors (denial/suppression or projection, using distractions like talking, watching TV, eating, smoking, working all the time, etc.) also distract us from the underlying beliefs and fears in our own mind. By staying with an uncomfortable emotion, we allow underlying beliefs to come to the surface.

The issue is that once one sees the misperception, the tendency is to believe that this is who you really are because it is so deep and has driven so much behavior. Again, it is necessary to keep it in perspective, to realize that all of this is the ego and it is all just conditioned, made-up unreality. The whole structure is self-created nonsense.

Dig deeper - Once you isolate a belief, look at what other beliefs are linked to it. In other words, dig deeper. Some questions for introspection include:
- How does this limiting belief impact my life now?
- What will happen if I continue with this belief?
- How strongly do I identify with this belief?
- What keeps me from being willing to let go of attachment to it?
- What other beliefs are supporting this belief?
- Am I ready to let them go?

Review life circumstances - Ask what limiting beliefs your environment might have led you to. What theme(s) run through your childhood? Through your adult life? If you look across your life, are there any themes that recur that might be a clue to underlying beliefs?

Find the payoff - Look at the payoff you get from a particular mode of operation. For example, if you are a perfectionist, ask what that brings you. Is there a better way to get what you feel you need? Why do you think you need that anyway?

Research and experiment - This can take three forms:
The first is classical research. Once you have identified one of your issues, for example perfectionism, do a little digging on that topic and see what beliefs are typically behind it. You can then assess and do further experimentation with whether those beliefs apply to you.

The second is to become an observer of humanity. When an event occurs, look at the various ways people respond to the situation. Note similarities and differences in the way they have responded versus how you would respond. What might be behind the way you choose to respond?

The third is to take a belief you think you have identified and experiment with it. For example, if you think you have uncovered a limiting belief behind your perfectionism, test it out. Take action that directly confronts that limiting belief and observe the results. Part of this process is demonstrating to yourself that the limiting belief is unfounded and taking action that directly confronts it is one way to convince yourself that the belief is indeed unfounded.

Exercises

1. Think back to an instance when you have used each of the following information processing distortions. Which distortion(s) are you prone to resort to?
   - All-or-nothing thinking – no in-between
   - Mind-reading – you believe you can discern the thoughts of others
   - Labeling – instead of labeling just the behavior, you label yourself or another
   - Jumping to conclusions
   - Emotional reasoning – assuming that feelings are facts
   - Blowing things out of proportion
   - Assuming the worst
   - Generalizing - drawing a conclusion based on limited evidence
   - Ignoring the positive
   - Magnifying or minimizing one's own characteristics or those of another
2. Choose a situation that is troubling you. Write down the facts of the situation. What emotion are you feeling? Sit with that feeling and see if you can intuit what limiting belief might be behind that feeling.
3. Although it is better to work from emotional charge, those who have been doing self observation for a while may be aware of limiting beliefs. Choose something from the list at the end of this chapter that you think may be one of your limiting beliefs. Sit with it and inquire within: If this limitation is present, why did I choose it? How is it serving me? If I were to let it go, how would things be different? Am I willing to see things differently, to give up identification with this belief?
4. Choose an item from the list of limiting beliefs that you feel is one of your limiting beliefs. For a few days, watch your thoughts, feelings, actions, self talk, and tendencies to distort information to see if this belief could be driving your thoughts, feelings, and actions.
5. Take a recurring thought that you are having trouble letting go of. First write down the thought. Then ask, "Why do I care?" Write down your response. Again, ask, "Why do I care?" Continue doing this until you come to something that feels like a limiting belief. Go back through your responses and identify the processing distortions that were present in your responses. Next to each response, write out any facts that would contradict your distortions.

Thought:
Repeatedly ask "Why do I care"?

Response	Distortion	Facts

Limiting Belief:

For example:
Thought: She constantly criticizes what I do.
Ask: Why do I care?

Response	Distortion	Fact(s)
I hate being constantly criticized	Generalizing All-or-nothing thinking	She asked if I would do something in a different way
It makes me feel unimportant	Emotional reasoning	Being asked to do something in a different way is a reasonable request
She should care about me instead of criticizing me	Jumping to conclusions Mind-reading	She does show that she cares about me in other ways
I want her to see me as someone she respects		

Limiting Belief: I need to be perfect to be loved

6. Choose something that you have always wanted to do, but have not. Write out a statement like, "I have always wanted to travel to Europe, but..." Look at what comes after the "but" to see if these are limiting beliefs.

7. Write out a list of experiences that tend to recur in your life. Sit with the list and see if you can identify a limiting belief for each.

Recurring Experience	Limiting Belief
Example: I get overlooked in a group.	I'm unimportant

8. Pay attention to your own self talk. What limiting beliefs do you see present there?

9. As you go about your day, become conscious of the assumptions you continually make.

10. Choose a couple of people you know well and think about what their life lessons might be - what limiting beliefs they have come to let go of. Once you have done that, pretend you are an observer of your own life situation. What lessons have you come to learn?

Working with Core Beliefs

If all of this is a facade, how does one go about recognizing that fact? As stated with the childhood dance story earlier, simply seeing and acknowledging minor limiting beliefs may be enough to dissipate them. Even with more deeply rooted beliefs, the commitment to search for the truth begins to draw alternate ways of looking at things. One or more of the following may be helpful in letting go of attachment to limiting beliefs.

Experiment with the positive opposite - Since this is about convincing yourself that the limiting belief has no value, embrace the positive opposite and see what happens.

Challenge it - As mentioned above, another way to convince oneself that there is nothing to a limiting belief is to challenge it in some way and see what happens. That could be as simple as finding another way to interpret the events that led to the belief, especially if it was formed in childhood. For more deeply rooted beliefs, it may be necessary to try other ways of thinking and acting, and to perform actions that demonstrate to yourself that the belief is not true. Basically, this is about convincing yourself that the belief is not valid, and that it was made up at the time to serve a purpose, but is no longer of value. What if this is not true? What if I fly in the face of this supposed belief? What happens? Nothing. It was never real to start with. If necessary, find a recurring situation and write out how you will approach it differently the next time you encounter that situation.

Put processes in place that reinforce the new - Expose yourself to information, people, and environments that support the new way of being. One book suggested that the reason Jesus often told the people he healed to "tell no one" is that he knew they would return to an environment of unbelief and that unbelief had the potential to "undo" the healing benefits. We, similarly, return to environments where we are expected to behave as we always have, which makes it difficult to act out new ways of being. One way to counteract these influences is to associate with groups of people of "like" mind on a regular basis and to regularly read or listen to materials that support the new way of being. It might also be helpful to mentally rehearse how you will respond when you return to familiar situations. Part of what we are saying is that we live in a shared illusion with shared cultural beliefs. In becoming aware of the impact of the shared environment, one is better positioned to resist the influences of that environment.

Step out of the circle - Ultimately, this is about realizing that the whole ego process is illusion. There is nothing behind it; it is simply a mist that is blocking visibility of who we really are. So, how does one step outside the egoic circle and look at it from a different perspective? The following items are things that help us to step outside the circle:

- **Ask for help** - Give limiting beliefs to a Higher Power, ask for help in releasing them, and envision them being removed from your consciousness. In doing this, we align with our own Higher Self and step outside the circle.
- **Send love to the self** - Send love to the "child" who felt the need to create the limiting belief, whether in this lifetime or a previous one.
- **Affirm "I am not the ego"** - "My personality self is acting out the belief that it is not good enough, but I am *not* that personality self. I am a pure and holy child of God."
- **Pray and meditate** - Employ prayer and meditation which open one to the Higher Self and expose what is within.
- **Read materials that reinforce this understanding** - Read materials like A Course in Miracles that call into question assumptions about unworthiness and not being loved and put forth our true nature as that of a pure, holy, and flawless child of the Divine.
- **Use an affirmation** - Use an affirmation such as: "I release all limiting beliefs, known and unknown, from all levels of my being."

When letting go of limiting beliefs, it is important to remember that they were formed as a means of understanding and protecting the self from the surrounding world. In letting go of them, it is better to assure the child who created them that if this belief is released, everything will be OK. That is to say that when one detects a limiting belief, it is more compassionate to gently assure the self and feel one's way into releasing it, than to take a chisel to it. You can't just think your way into a new belief, you have to feel your way into it.

Summary

- Limiting beliefs and misperceptions are the major roadblocks to the perception of the true Self.
- Once limiting core beliefs are activated, we process information in a biased way that maintains the core beliefs and discredits contradictory evidence.
- An attitude of openness and a willingness to question everything facilitate the change in perception that is necessary to release attachment to limiting beliefs.
- Following the emotional charge is the best way to uncover a limiting belief.
- Ultimately, this is about realizing that these misperceptions are self created and are meaningless.
- This change in perception allows one to see the ego as illusion and the Higher Self as the true Self.

Reflections/Exercises/Practices

For Reflection/Discussion:

1. If the only way out of this illusion is a change in perception, what else could lead to that change in perception?
2. If every lifetime is both an opportunity to let go of attachment to limiting beliefs and an opportunity to create additional limiting beliefs, how will we ever get out of this illusion?
3. What if heaven and hell are states of consciousness?

Exercises:

1. Choose a limiting belief you would like to release. Feel the limiting belief in your body. Use one of the following to assist in releasing attachment to it:
   - See it as a cloud or a mist, and observe it dissipate
   - See it as a piece of worn off clothing that you take off and put in the trash
   - Write it on a piece of paper and burn it
2. Define a positive opposite for the following limiting beliefs and any others you feel drawn to:

Limiting Belief	Positive Opposite
I am not good enough	
I must be perfect to be loved	
My needs are never met	
I can't trust anyone	

3. Choose an event from your childhood that still bothers you and see if there is another way you can interpret that event.
4. Choose something you feel may be a limiting belief and experiment with it. For example, if you feel your needs are never met, approach the experiment in a positive manner, start expressing what you need, and see how people respond.

5. Write an affirmation for something you perceive as a limiting belief. Read it several times a day and post it in an obvious spot so it often comes to mind. Observe the impact on your perception.
6. Which of the items listed under "Step Out of the Circle" would you be willing to do?
- Ask for help
- Send love to the self
- Affirm "I am not the ego"
- Prayer and meditation
- Read materials that reinforce the understanding that you are not the ego
- Use the affirmation: "I release all limiting beliefs, known and unknown, from all levels of my being."
7. Declare an "opposite" day. For each action you are about to take, consider doing the opposite. How does this make you feel? What would be the consequence(s) of taking the opposite action? If appropriate, try out a few of these opposites.

Sample Limiting Beliefs

I am [not good enough/unwanted/different/uninteresting]
I am not lovable
I am not safe
I am [helpless/powerless/incapable/incompetent]
I am responsible for everyone and everything
I have to do everything myself
I must be perfect to be [loved/worthwhile]
If I don't excel, then I'm inferior and worthless
I must be approved of by everyone
When people treat me unfairly, that means they are bad people
If something is dangerous or fearful, it helps to worry about it
It is frustrating when things do not work out as I want them to
Misery comes from outside forces that I can't change
It is easier to avoid life's difficulties and responsibilities than to face them
The past controls my present and future
Happiness comes from doing as little as possible and doing only what I enjoy
I have to work hard to get what I want
Suffering is good for us
You don't get something for nothing
Things that are simple aren't worth much
I can't be my real self or I'll be found wanting
I can't fall in love or I'll get my heart broken
I can't ask for what I need or want because I will be disappointed
If I assert myself, people will not like me
I can't be happy if I am alone
I can't change
If I allow myself to feel, I will lose control
I need to control myself
I can't trust people because they will betray my trust
I can't pursue my dreams because I may fail
I don't need to be successful, so I'm not going to strive for success
I am not bound by the rules that apply to other people
It's too late to pursue my dreams
My needs don't matter

Chapter 11 - Aligning Aspects of the Self

What does it mean to be in alignment? That all that comes to you is perceived in its true state. That there is no impediment to the truth.
*****

At times it seems that regardless of how much one has worked with a particular issue, it seems to still be present within the self. One of the reasons this appears so is that different aspects of the self are still working against each other. For example, one may set a conscious desire for a particular result while an unconscious belief says that result is impossible. Likewise, if feelings are going one way and the head another, it is likely that the desired result will not be achieved. This chapter will be devoted to looking at what it means to align aspects of the self and recommendations for how to do that.

Inconsistency

Before we reach some sense of a united self internally, we tend to behave differently in the different roles we play throughout the day, based on the circumstances around us and what society expects of us. It is through the use of self observation that we position ourselves to see the inconsistencies between the different roles we play and the different personalities we adopt. In that sense, self observation enables the process of unification of the self.

Although what we really are is pure conscious awareness, the observer can be thought of as the foundation for that awareness - an aspect of the personality founded in the ideal. The role of the observer is to see the false personalities we have adopted and, being positioned in the ideal, to aid in letting go of attachment to them. Here, what is false is defined as that which fosters separation. At the point we start this process, we do not know our real identity, so we begin with self observation and study of these false personalities. The following Cayce reading describes the difference between what he calls individuality and personality.

"Personality is that ye wish others to think and see. Individuality is that your soul prays, your soul hopes for, desires." (Edgar Cayce reading 5246-1)

Little by little, who we really are becomes more apparent as we let go of these false personalities and continually choose for the Self over the self.

Conscious and Subconscious

Although what is in the subconscious lies below everyday awareness, the beliefs, values, and attitudes held there are very powerful in affecting our thoughts and behavior. These two quotes attributed to Carl Jung, the Swiss psychiatrist and psychotherapist who founded analytical psychology, testify to the power of what lies outside the conscious mind.

"Until you make the unconscious conscious, it will direct your life and you will call it fate."
"One does not become enlightened by imagining figures of light, but by making the darkness conscious."[36]

What then is the value of uncovering the shadow? We are no longer driven by what is automatic and/or suppressed. Uncovering the shadow is pure gold to self growth and allows us to integrate all that is inside us. It allows us to make choices from a place of full awareness instead of being driven by what resides in the unconscious.

For most of us, the unconscious has two parts: aspects of the lower or personality self that are no longer in conscious awareness (the subconscious) and that which we really are, the Higher Self.

One way to think of the subconscious is as a map for navigating one's world. Into it, one has placed all of the habit patterns that have "helped" navigate the world in the past (ways of interacting with the world that have become habitual) and all of the "rules" one created to represent what society, culture, familial group, etc., were saying. Just as moving skills like learning to ride a bike or drive a car eventually become automatic functions, our mental and emotional habit patterns have also become automatic functions. The rules we perceived and later reinforced have become our values and beliefs. Like any map, it is only a guide for navigation and not an actual representation of one's world.

The subconscious can be thought of as habit patterns from each of our aspects (physical, mental, emotional, spiritual) as well as the memories associated with each. Uncovering what is in the subconscious then becomes making what has become automatic, visible again. As has been described in the earlier chapters, we do that through increased awareness. As we will see later, there is evidence that mental and emotional habit patterns have also become ingrained in the body and that there is a physical component to undoing old patterns.

Also below conscious awareness are all of the repressed thoughts, feelings, and ideas that we have chosen not to look at. It takes a lot of energy to keep these things hidden. Earlier we discussed the concept of the heart wall and how suppressing emotions can inhibit the capacity to love. As the shadow is uncovered, that energy also becomes available for higher functions.

The conscious and subconscious can be thought of as much like an iceberg where the conscious is the small protrusion above the water, and the subconscious is the much larger portion below. The implications of this are that most of our perception and processing is done below the conscious level using our mental and emotional patterns and underlying beliefs as the filter for that processing. I once had an instructor who made the statement that change does not occur as a result of your thoughts; change occurs in direct proportion to the impact those thoughts have on your subconscious mind. While the conscious mind has gained a new understanding or chosen to approach something in a different way, until the subconscious is on board, the subconscious has the power to thwart.

The issue is that what has been understood at the conscious level is not passed directly to the subconscious mind. The literature describes what could be thought of as the "critical mind," which sits partially in the conscious and partially in the subconscious. It acts as a barrier between the two, which either allows or prevents information from passing between them.

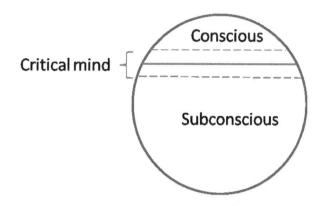

**Diagram – Critical mind sitting between
conscious and subconscious**

The critical mind can be thought of as a gatekeeper that contains our underlying beliefs and conditioning. Information that comes into the conscious mind is evaluated and compared, and that which is consistent is allowed to pass to the subconscious. When there is an inconsistency, status quo is generally maintained as the subconscious is more powerful than the conscious.

Creating new patterns then is a process that occurs over a period of time, which allows the subconscious to gradually recognize new habit patterns as the norm. By continuously thinking a new thought, consistently choosing a particular emotion, or acting your way into a new belief, the subconscious gradually accepts a new way of being. This happens as long as what is being put forth is consistent. That is why it is so important to watch what you say to yourself and to others. The subconscious has limited capacity to work with language and does not differentiate between right and wrong. It simply accepts and reacts to what it is told. When it receives conflicting inputs, it becomes confused. If you think you believe a certain way, but your inner self talk and/or the words you say aloud contradict that belief, how can you expect your being to be aligned?

The use of affirmations - repeating a verbal statement over and over - is one way to eventually get the subconscious on board with a desired thought pattern. Continuous affirmation of the new way of being makes it familiar and acceptable to the subconscious. Until the subconscious integrates the new way of looking at things, however, it may feel as if these two parts of the self are in conflict with each other. All of the work described thus far in this book is also designed to make this gradual change.

One of the exercises earlier in the book was to begin practicing relaxed or gentle awareness (also described as becoming centered or being in a receptive state). Getting into this state sets the stage for information to move from the subconscious to the conscious and vice versa. The subconscious is most effectively accessed through the lower brainwave states known as Alpha and Theta and eventually Delta, as opposed to normal consciousness or Beta. These states are available through meditation, which is the most consistent and readily available means to reach them.

There are two natural points in the day when these states are accessible: on first awakening and as falling asleep. I describe them to myself as halfway states because the conscious mind is still present but the altered state is either still available (waking up) or has already begun to take over (falling asleep). This is called the hypnagogic state. It is useful to become aware of this state on first awakening in the morning and one can learn to extend its length. Pre-sleep CDs take advantage of the period where one is falling asleep. The idea is that by playing desired suggestions during the pre-sleep state, one is able to get those suggestions into the subconscious more easily.

When we are asleep, the conscious mind is set aside and we are by definition in the other states. Symbolism is the natural language of the unconscious and that becomes apparent in dreams. One of the ways to get at what the subconscious is trying to tell you is to begin keeping a dream journal and to work with what the symbols in the dreams mean to you. A portion of what comes through comes from spirit and it is interesting to see what spirit deems important compared to what your personality self deems important.

Hypnosis or hypnotherapy is another way to reach the subconscious. In his book, The Law of Psychic Phenomena, Thomas Jay Hudson summarizes the bulk of knowledge about what he calls the subjective mind. A few statements from this book will serve to increase understanding of this topic:

- The subjective (subconscious) mind is constantly amenable to control by the power of suggestion. (p.91)
- The subjective mind has absolute control of the functions, conditions, and sensations of the body. (p.151)
- If the suggestion made to it is not counteracted by something from the objective mind, it will always be unhesitatingly accepted. If it is controverted, the strongest suggestion must prevail. This law is universal. (p.360)
- Experiments demonstrate the impossibility of controlling the hypnotic subject so far as to cause him to do that which he believes or knows to be wrong. (p.129)

Hudson makes a distinction between hypnotism where the client is in a relaxed state and the operator is not, and mesmerism where both the client and the operator are hypnotized. The advantage of mesmerism, according to Hudson, is the presence of telepathic communication, which is as much a suggestion to the subjective mind as oral speech (p.120). Hudson also says that the subjective mind of an individual is constantly controlled by the suggestion of his own objective mind (p.197-199) as previously discussed, and that not only is it possible to hypnotize oneself but that at times we unwittingly do so. It is possible to do intentional self hypnosis although that should not be taken lightly or undertaken until one has a good depth of understanding of the self.

It is worth noting that because symbolism is the natural language of the subconscious, the use of imagery and visualization are helpful in transmitting information to the subconscious.

It is also worth mentioning that kinesiology (muscle testing) is a means for accessing what is in the universal field, including what is in your own subconscious. It is therefore useful as a tool to self knowledge and a way to access truth.

At times, the conscious portion of the critical mind may also resist. This may be due to a number of factors - payoff, laziness, unwillingness, what is asked puts one outside the comfort zone, lack of understanding, one has not seen the need, etc. A way to bypass the conscious portion of the critical mind, that has been used a few times in the exercises in preceding chapters, is pretending or playing "what if." So, for example, to undo a limiting belief, one might envision what it would be like to live without this limitation. Pretend it is true, feel how it feels in the body, let the imagination play with the implications of the new way of being, and visualize actions that would stem from it.

Subliminal messages, designed to pass below the normal limits of perception, are also a way to bypass the conscious portion of the critical mind.

In Chapter 1, we used a spiral to represent growth in consciousness. This is not a linear process. As we work with each aspect of the self, we gradually make progress, returning many times with increased understanding in an ever-expanding spiral of awareness.

A Path to Self Remembering

Summary

- Work on growth in consciousness includes exposing what is currently unconscious so that choices can be made with full awareness.
- The world around us is a reflection of what we believe, so to become conscious creators, we need to make known what is currently unknown.
- Failure to make progress on an issue may be due to lack of alignment between different aspects of the self.
- The subconscious has the ability to thwart one's efforts if not understood.
- By consistently thinking a new thought, choosing a particular emotion, or acting one's way into a new belief, the subconscious gradually accepts a new way of being.
- Hypnotherapy, making use of the hypnagogic state, and pre-sleep CDs are also tools to transmit new ways of being to the subconscious.
- Dreams and meditation will bring forth information from the unconscious.
- Pretending and subliminal messages are ways to bypass the conscious portion of the critical mind.

Reflections/Exercises/Practices

For Reflection/Discussion:

1. Earlier in this book we talked about the heart wall. How does becoming more familiar with the contents of the subconscious begin to deconstruct this wall?

Exercises:

1. Close your eyes and visualize your conscious and subconscious. See yourself shining a light into all aspects of your subconscious.
2. Repeat the following affirmation on a regular basis:
   "I am a pure and holy child of God. I am wisdom. I am power. I am love. I am a child of the light."
3. Choose a relationship you are having difficulty with. Visualize what it would be like if that relationship was healed. Feel how it feels.
4. On waking, while still in the hypnagogic state, with deep intent, ask: "How can I serve you and your people today?" Close your eyes, be receptive, and listen. If you have the luxury of staying in bed, get close to the sleep state again. Be prepared and willing because you may get an answer.

Chapter 12 - Opening the Heart

"Rejoice that your heart is not deceived, for herein lies your path to true remembering."[37]
--A Course of Love (C:8.30)
*****

To this point, we have focused on the illusion: how to recognize the various aspects of it (thoughts, feelings, and beliefs) and how to let go of attachment to them. Once one has developed the skill of self observation and is relatively consistent with releasing attachment to these aspects of the ego mind, there is a transition that needs to occur that involves integrating the head and the heart. That transition and the explanation of its benefits are the focus of this chapter.

Two Belief Systems

There are within us two systems or streams: that of the ego self which is founded in separation, and that of the Higher Self, which is founded in oneness. One is illusion and the other is real. Although each system is consistent within itself, the two systems are diametrically opposed to each other. In any given moment, it is possible to operate from one or the other, but not from both simultaneously.

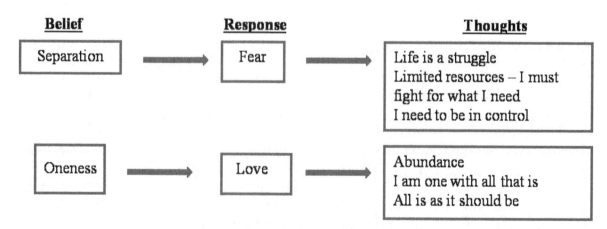

Diagram— Separation or Oneness

Thus far we have worked with how to let go of attachment to the limiting beliefs, the fear-filled emotions, and the limiting thoughts defined in the first stream. This is the stream associated with the personality self or the ego and is what is described here as coming from the head. This movement or change of allegiance from the head to the heart is the basis of operating from a position of oneness. Wisdom, power, and love reside within the heart. It is by turning to the heart that one is guided in the path of oneness. It could be said that the heart is the link between the lower and the upper aspects of one's self or, more poetically, the link between earth and heaven.

Nature of the Heart

Founded in oneness, the heart is aware of a bigger picture and can assess every situation from a higher perspective. It is the heart that allows us to move from thinking to a remembering of our original state of wholeness. Being aware of the bigger picture, the heart is in that sense a higher intelligence. The wisdom received from this position of oneness is sometimes described simply as "knowing." It is the heart that integrates all aspects of existence. Where the egoic mind is interested in maintaining status quo, the heart is open to all possibilities that serve the greater good. Driven by love, the heart knows the most life affirming path to take.

In Chapter One, we equated God with love or that which is life affirming. If love is the energy that powers all that is, and the heart is the perceiver of that love, then it is the heart that yearns for a return to oneness and it is the heart that will lead the way home. The love that is always present within is perpetually calling to us to return to our natural state. The heart is our access to wisdom, power, and love defined as follows:

Love - the life affirming energy that supports all that is
Wisdom - a greater knowing that takes the whole into consideration
Power - the strength that comes from knowing who we really are

Transition to Higher Emotional States

There is a saying attributed to Albert Einstein that "we cannot solve our problems with the same thinking we used when we created them." By the same token, we cannot escape the limitations of the mind via the mind. Yes, it is the starting point, as that is the only place we have to start. But spiritual literature says there will come a point beyond which the intellect can take us no further. In other words, we can't think our way to God.

While this transition does not have to be difficult, culturally we have learned to rely heavily on the intellect. There is much positive reinforcement for intellectual accomplishment and we are used to turning to the mind when decisions need to be made. Going within and turning toward this source of higher wisdom is a change of allegiance that becomes easier the more it is used.

Once we have done the preliminary work with thoughts and emotions, the higher emotional center can begin to function until eventually the higher emotional and higher intellectual centers begin to operate together. When the ego is fully gone, the heart leads, but the heart and brain are operating as one. The highest levels of consciousness involve both the heart and the head. It is in this way that the Divine becomes manifest. As Jesus says in A Course of Love (C:19.13), "It is only in combining mind and heart with a focus on letting heart lead that love can be combined with thought in such a way as to actually transcend thought as you know it."[38]

The basic premise here is that there is an emotional intelligence that must be developed before we can use the higher emotional center. In his book Emotional Intelligence, Daniel Goleman describes the aspects of emotional intelligence as: "self awareness in the sense of recognizing feelings and building a vocabulary for them, and seeing the links between thoughts, feelings and reactions; knowing if thoughts or feelings are ruling a decision; seeing the consequences of alternative choice; and applying these insights to decisions." He continues to describe it as: "recognizing strengths and weaknesses; and seeing yourself in a positive but realistic light."[39] He further defines managing emotions as: "realizing what is behind a feeling, and learning ways to handle anxieties, anger, and sadness" and "taking responsibility for decisions and actions; and following through on commitments."[40] These are the very things we have been working toward in the preceding chapters.

The term self regulation is often used to describe this ability to recognize and direct emotional energy. In learning to self regulate, we have positioned ourselves to turn to the wisdom and guidance of the heart. In learning to release limiting emotions, we open to the positive emotions of love, peace, and joy that are naturally present as part of who we really are. The heart is like a receiver. Love and acceptance are the frequency of the universe and are always available to us. We simply need to let go of the negativity that acts as static in the system and tune in to the frequency of love. When we remove blockages to that frequency and tune in to it, we naturally resonate with it.

The word discernment is often used to describe the ability to distinguish what comes from oneness versus what comes from the head - in other words, to recognize which of the two belief systems something is coming from. Perception of what comes from the heart is developed through practice and is strengthened by listening to and following (putting into action) what comes from this position of oneness.

Integrating Head and Heart

As we saw earlier, there is still a place for the rational or logical mind. It is simply that it now functions in service to the higher awareness of the heart.

Another quote sometimes attributed to Einstein is that "the intuitive mind is a sacred gift and the rational mind is a faithful servant." As we saw in the last chapter, a mind and heart in conflict (feelings going one way and thoughts another) results in conflicting desires and is a block to creation. It is when the head and heart work together, founded in the greater wisdom of the heart, that true creation happens. It is love that is the creative life affirming force and the heart that provides the direction and the power. As we will see later in this chapter, there is increasing evidence that "in order for the mind, emotions, and body to perform at their best, the heart and brain must be in harmony."[41] The mind and the heart of God are one and it is as we integrate these two that we move closer to recognition of our own divinity.

In <u>Esoteric Psychology II</u>, Alice Bailey describes this process:

"...the soul anchors itself in two streams of energy at two points of contact: the life stream in the heart and the consciousness stream in the head. This consciousness aspect is itself dual, and that which we call [S]self-consciousness is gradually unfolded and perfected until the ajna centre [third eye], or the centre between the eyebrows, is awakened. The latent group-consciousness, which brings realisation of the greater Whole, is quiescent for the greater part of the evolutionary cycle, until the integrative process has proceeded to such a point that the personality is functioning. Then the head centre begins to awaken and the man becomes conscious in the larger sense. Head and heart then link up, and the spiritual man appears in fuller expression."[42]

Feelings as the Gateway

Feelings are the gateway to higher states of consciousness. How one feels is intuitive guidance from the heart. We have previously looked at how emotions are a barometer that can be used to determine when changes need to be made. There is a lot of power in emotional energy, but - unfortunately - most people unwittingly let the mind take that power and squander it on judgment and other leaks to the energy body.

The good news is that we have control over our emotions. When an emotion comes in, with awareness, we can choose to make a shift. We do have a choice about what we want to feel next. In making a shift from the head to the heart and choosing to release any perceived limiting emotion, we open to the love that is always there *and* the power residing within the heart.

The challenge lies in getting the head (the intellectual center) to surrender to the heart (higher emotional center). We have looked at how "mind" is the builder and the physical is the result. Negative emotional habit patterns formed over the years are reflected in the neurology of the body. In turning to the heart, we call upon the power and strength residing within the heart to assist in releasing those ingrained patterns. By *consistently* turning to the heart and choosing a better feeling emotion, we reprogram not only the "mind" but also the body. As we act from the heart (in love and acceptance), we begin to re-pattern both the "mind" and the physical brain and nervous system.

Evidence for the Heart

Although modern society has assigned control of the body to the brain, many cultures in the past have seen the heart as the primary control unit of the body. Aristotle, for example, saw the brain as second to the heart in importance and the two functioning as "a unit that controlled the body."[43] The idea of the heart as the seat of intelligence and emotion was held in many earlier cultures, such as the Egyptian, Mesopotamian, Babylonian, and Indian cultures and by many indigenous groups.[44] For example, traditional Chinese medicine focuses on the spirit of the heart and sees this spirit as the primary force that animates the body.[45] The heart represents the fire element and although the Chinese didn't believe there were actual flames in the heart, others such as St. Germain see the fire of purification as resting there. Additionally, the Kabbalah (a Jewish school of thought) sees the heart as the "Central Sphere," which touches all other spheres.[46]

Interestingly enough, current findings - such as the work of the HeartMath Institute - are providing physical evidence for the primary control function of the heart within the body. A detailed description of this work is not within the scope of this book, but one or more of the HeartMath® books are helpful to get a better understanding of physiological evidence and for practical exercises on how to work with the heart. A few of the more salient concepts are listed below:

- "There is more information going from the heart to the brain than the other way around and this information influences regions in the brain that affect decision-making, creativity, and especially emotions."[47]
- The heart communicates with the brain and other bodily organs and systems in four ways:
    - "Neurologically - through the transmission of nerve impulses
    - Biochemically - through hormones and neurotransmitters
    - Biophysically - through pressure waves
    - Energetically - through electromagnetic field interactions"[48]

- There are neural cells located in the heart and the heart "can process information and make decisions about cardiac control independent of the central nervous system."[49] It turns out "that 60 to 65% of the cells of the heart are actually neural cells," "the same connecting links called ganglia, with the same axonal and dendritic connections that take place in the brain, as well as... the same kind of neurotransmitters found in the brain."[50] About half of those cells are involved in processing information from other parts of the body and about half are in communication with the brain.[51]
- The heart has both long- and short-term memory.[52]

The work of the HeartMath Institute shows that it is heart rate variability (HRV), the "measurement of beat to beat changes," that is most closely tied to inner emotional state.[53] There is a strong correlation between the heart's magnetic field, heart rhythm (HRV), and emotional state[54] which are independent of heart rate.[55] In a sense, HRV patterns reflect how well we are balancing our lives emotionally.

Coherence

Also coming out of the HeartMath® work is a concept being labeled as coherence." When a system is coherent, all of its component parts are working in harmony, and minimal energy is expended. Coherence is used "as a general term that encompasses entrainment, resonance, and synchronization."[56] Coherence is defined as "an optimal state in which the heart, mind and emotions are operating in-sync and balanced. Physiologically, the immune, hormonal and nervous systems function in a state of energetic coordination."[57]

This work is showing that feelings affect the electromagnetic signal of the heart. Positive emotions are associated with coherence and produce fluent sine-wave-like HRV patterns. Negative emotions are associated with lack of coherence and produce erratic HRV patterns. These in turn create corresponding changes "in the electromagnetic field radiated by the heart."[58]

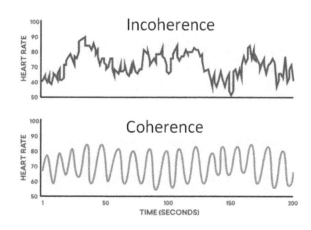

Diagram - Coherence vs. Incoherence[59]

The good news in all of this work is that by going to the heart and choosing to feel a positive emotion (such as love, compassion, non-judgment, patience, sincerity, forgiveness, appreciation, gratitude, courage, etc.), we can move from incoherence to coherence, generate these fluent sine waves, and in turn impact the physical functioning of the body in a positive way. In coherence, the heart and brain synchronize. As discussed above, the heart has the power and strength to overcome ingrained emotional patterns. Through consistently choosing to feel coherence-producing emotions, we create new neural pathways in the body and these patterns then become increasingly familiar to the brain.

This work underscores the importance of moving to the heart, as it has an ability beyond that of the personality/thinking self/brain to perceive things from a different perspective and to restore coherence, even under the most difficult circumstances.

Relaxation versus Coherence/ Breath

Research is also showing that "coherence is a higher order function than relaxation"[60] and is "physiologically distinct from relaxation because the system is oscillating at its resonant frequency."[61] This suggests that there may be benefit in adding focus on the heart to relaxation and meditation techniques.

There also appears to be a correlation between emotional state and breathing rate. "Agitated states... increase the breathing rate" and "positive emotional states slow the breathing rate."[62] Slow rhythmic breathing stimulates the vagus nerve, which ultimately impacts the heart's rhythmic patterns to help generate coherence. The HeartMath® techniques make use of all of these aspects - heart focus, breath work to begin the entrainment process, and feeling positive emotion - to generate coherence.

Gifts of the Heart

The gifts of the heart are many. From a physiological perspective, it is increasingly clear that what we think, the attitudes we adopt, and our emotional state all impact the physical body (mind is the builder, the physical is the result). In the paper <u>The Coherent Heart</u>, the authors put forth the premise "that the physiological, cognitive, and emotional systems are intimately interrelated through ongoing reciprocal communication."[63] In moving to the heart and invoking positive emotional states, we have the ability to impact our own health and - with sustained practice to improve our health and emotional stability - gradually replacing destructive habit patterns embedded in the body and the psyche with those of coherence. As outlined above, coherence is a highly efficient mode that confers a number of health benefits. In his book <u>Resilience from the Heart</u>, Gregg Braden says that "stress from negative emotions increases the levels of cortisol and adrenaline" while "rejuvenating emotions... support stronger immune response and greater amounts of DHEA,"[64] sometimes described as the youth hormone because of the many benefits and the sense of well being it provides.

Similarly, there is increasing evidence that "global coherence must be present for the brain and nervous system to function efficiently and effectively."[65] In his paper, Dr. Rollin McCraty states: "Learning to maintain our coherence has a lot of benefits - increased ability to self-regulate, 40% improvement in long-term memory, 24% improvement in short-term memory, increased ability to focus, increased ability to process information, increased reaction times, higher test scores."[66] It appears that mental clarity is also a positive outcome of the coherent state.

Earlier we looked at negative emotions as leaks to the energy body. In turning to the heart and consciously choosing life affirming emotions, we are able to sustain higher energy levels.

Coherence also produces a sense of psychological well being. As described in <u>The Coherent Heart</u>, "the subjective experience of this mode is a state in which the intrusion of mental and emotional 'chatter' is reduced to a point of internal quietness, to be replaced by a profound feeling of peace and serenity and a deep sense of being centered in the heart."[67] In the coherent state, the body and mind are balanced and in the present, the state sometimes referred to as "present moment awareness" or "being in the now."

A Path to Self Remembering

The expression "with grace and ease" is sometimes used to describe what comes to us without effort when we are in tune with the universe. Once we move past the concept that life is a struggle, we recognize that we can draw what we desire through intent, and that love is the power that provides. It is interesting that those who bring new creations into existence often describe the new ideas as coming from beyond them in a moment of quiet reflection. Creativity might be described as an experience where the heart, the mind, and intention are all aligned.

Operating from the heart provides a certain resilience that is not present when operating strictly from the mind. There is a strength that comes from knowing who you really are (the Self). Viewing things from the larger context of oneness allows one to accept whatever occurs as what is needed at the moment, and positions us to see human suffering as a necessary aspect of the growth process. It is possible to view all events with hope and meaning when viewed through the heart.

Purification

The heart has the ability to purify what is brought to it. In historical drawings of the Sacred Heart, it is depicted as a three-fold flame of wisdom, power, and love. As the spark of the Divine within us, it is our access to the true love that comes from the heart of God. In taking life experiences to the heart, we have access to a power greater than the self that will perfect and purify what is brought to it. Within the heart lies a power greater than that of the mind, a power that has the ability to change even the most ingrained emotional patterns.

Intuition

Intuition is a natural ability given to all to perceive in a manner beyond that of reason. Intuition is founded in the larger picture of oneness (union) and the greater good. Properly used, it moves us toward our highest potential. The basic premise here is that there are ways of knowing that cannot be reached by intellect alone, but rather can only be reached by going within. Intuition is knowing more than what comes from the five external senses. Truth, which transcends culture and time, is arrived at intuitively.

While everyone has what might be termed "gut" instincts, these are largely unconscious survival instincts. One of the benefits of self regulation is the ability to *consciously* choose to listen to one's intuition. Once we begin to operate from a non-dual state of mind, we have conscious access to the intuitive guidance that is always present. Perception of this inner knowing is hidden by the habitual thoughts and emotions coming from the ego - those rooted in social conditioning and ignorance and reflected as opinions, desires, fears, negativity, and bad habits. It might be said that as the noise level (both inner and outer) goes down, the ability to perceive intuitive guidance goes up. Self regulation and learning to rely on what comes from within - rather than without - position one to remain centered regardless of what happens in the outside world.

Early in this book, we looked at multiple models for understanding human consciousness to try to wrap our minds around what can only be understood by experiencing it. Intuition is also one of those topics where there are many ways to look at it, but real understanding comes from experiencing it, as the manner in which intuition is perceived varies from person to person. We will approach the topic from a few different viewpoints to establish some basic understanding.

General consensus says that there are three points within the body that are the access points for intuitive information: those typically described as the abdomen or gut, the heart, and the third eye. These are sometimes called the organs of subtle perception. This led me to question whether there is a relationship between the three parts of the brain and the three organs of subtle perception, although there appear to be no studies that confirm or deny that.

Author, educator, and psychologist Frances Vaughan says that the three centers are interconnected and that spiritual practices clear an opening for spiritual energies to manifest through all three organs of inner perception. Although these are the connection or access points, many, including Vaughan, have described how to perceive intuitive information.

In her essay, Mental, Emotional, and Body-Based Intuition, Vaughan describes "four distinct levels of intuitive awareness: physical, emotional, mental, and spiritual:[68]

Physical - Paying attention to physical or body-based intuition means paying attention to subtle body responses, as they "are a source of information about the self and the surrounding environment."[69]

Emotional - "On this level, intuition comes into consciousness through feelings."[70] Intuition at this level might appear as a sensitivity to the energy of others, or a feeling of like or dislike for someone or something.

Mental - At this level, intuition may come related to thinking, such as what occurs as insights in problem solving and creativity. Patterns may be perceived or inferences drawn based on limited information. Mental intuition is associated with images and ideas.

Spiritual - Spiritual intuition is described as being "associated with mystical experiences."[71] There is another way of knowing called "direct knowing" that is beyond the previous three levels. It is a direct transpersonal (beyond the self) experience of the oneness of life. Because mystical experiences are beyond the self, the signals coming from body, mind, and emotions would only serve as distractions. While what comes from the realm beyond time and space cannot be scientifically proven (known by means of reason), what is reported by those who have mystical experiences is consistent (universal).

Another way to work with intuition is to work with the four energy bands described in Donna Eden's work.[72] The four basic styles of perception might be used as follows:

Kinesthetic - Kinesthetic focuses on body awareness. It is turning inward and feeling what is taking place in the body in response to a given question, person, or situation. For example, in response to the question, "How will this relationship be perceived going forward?" I received a let-down reaction as if getting ready to nurse a baby. Once I became aware of that reaction, I received through claircognizance the word nourishing. That body reaction and awareness of it are the use of kinesthetic intuition.

Visual - Intuitive responses received visually will appear on an inner screen in the area of the third eye in the form of pictures, much like during the dreaming state.

Digital - Intuitive responses received digitally will come as metaphors or phrases. For example, I will sometimes receive a phrase from a song and realize that it is a response to something I have been internally working with.

Auditory/Tonal - Auditory or tonal responses come as words but are more subtle than the voice of the ego. The challenge with responses received tonally is to learn to distinguish what comes from the ego versus what comes through intuition.

Some say that we have internal senses, just as we have external senses. That implies that internal taste and smell can also provide intuitive responses. For example, I have smelled cigar smoke while internally speaking to my deceased grandfather. On another occasion, I had just attended a meeting where the exercise we were assigned was to try something different in preparation for meditation. While driving down the road, I wondered if I had ever used incense in preparation for meditation in a past life. At that point, I clearly smelled incense, which I took to be intuitive confirmation via the sense of internal smell.

Some points to understand in working with intuition are these:

- Although we all have access to all of the ways of receiving intuitive guidance, some may be more developed than others. For example, I rarely perceive guidance visually. Since we live in a very visual culture, even inner work is often visually based. I have often been asked, "What are you seeing (internally)?" For me, the answer is usually "nothing." It is important to recognize that inner vision is only one of many ways of receiving guidance.

- For a given individual, there is generally a primary and secondary means of intuitive perception.[73] Learning to recognize and use those styles first will make the process of discernment easier. Donna Eden's DVD on The Energies of Love is helpful for identifying and understanding intuitive styles.
- Intuition is subtle. Once you move into questioning, the connection is lost and you are back in ego mind. Part of learning to trust intuition is thus learning to go with that first impression.
- Intuition will *never* guide you to anything that violates oneness and the good of all.

Being one of the subtle centers, the heart is a connection point to intuitive guidance. In shifting from the mind to the heart, we open to this guidance. Most authors describe the language of the heart as feelings, although there is a distinction that needs to be made between feelings coming from identification (of the ego) and feelings coming from a connection with Spirit. It is possible to be highly emotional and yet be out of touch with your own heart. Heart-based connection thus requires learning to perceive from true connection rather than emotional identification or moral obligation. The inner awareness work and the practice of releasing attachment to limiting emotions have all been preparation for discriminating between emotional identification and the more subtle perceptions that come into awareness when the baser emotions are stilled. Again, although the language of the heart may be feelings, how that information is most easily perceived varies from person to person.

In sleep, the conscious mind is totally out of the way. Thus, dreams have access to pure intuition. Honoring what comes in the dream state (believing that dreams are there to provide guidance, working to understand them, and acting on that understanding) is also a way of using intuition. The more we work with our dreams, the clearer they become. Tips for remembering dreams include the following:

1. Make a conscious decision to remember your dreams
2. Get enough sleep
3. Drink water before going to bed so you will wake during the night
4. Maintain sleeping position after waking
5. Focus on recalling your dream as soon as you wake up
6. Write every time you wake up during the night and in the morning
7. Act upon the dreams – record, tell, put the insights into action, and try out truths by experimenting with them

Other Gifts

Another gift of the heart is the ability to connect to universal consciousness. Studies[74] are showing that the body receives and processes information about future events before they happen. Intuition appears to have access to information that is not limited by time and space. The heart is, in that sense, one of the connection points to universal intelligence or all that is.

Getting in touch with the heart allows us to become more aware of our interconnection with each other. We are each, in a sense, broadcasting our own emotional state and receiving the emotional state of those around us all of the time. A positive aspect of moving into coherence is that, in the coherent state, we broadcast a signal that can be of benefit to those around us. "The more love and care you send out toward a person (or issue), the more you come into alignment both with your spirit and with that person, and the more your intuition comes on-line."[75] On a practical level, turning to the heart allows us to see behind the surface behavior of other people to the pure and holy spirit that is present within each individual.

An interesting aspect of our ability to influence each other is the small number of people required to effect a positive change. The idea that it takes the square root of 1% of a population to effect change has been around for a while, and studies are indeed showing that groups of meditators have significant impact in furthering non-violence in target populations.[76] The Global Consciousness Project originating out of Princeton University is showing that human consciousness influences the behavior of physical systems.

Cayce described each of us as a corpuscle residing in the heart of God. When one awakens, it is as if a corpuscle of God lights up and provides light to the entire circle. A little bit of light makes it easier for all to see. The more we awaken, the more we can be a light to our solar system, to our universe, to the cosmos, etc., in an ever-expanding circle of love.

The most significant aspect of the heart is its ability to connect us with the Divine within. By turning within to the depths of being, and with sincere desire to know the God within, it is possible to experience the Divine directly. The following Cayce reading confirms this access to the Divine:

(Q) What is the highest possible psychic realization - etc? (A) That God, the Father, speaks directly to the sons of men - even as He has promised. (Edgar Cayce Reading 440-4)

This experience may come as that of a personal God or as that of an impersonal God (a response from the universe that is known in every cell of the body).

Expression of Individuality

Each of us is a unique gift to the universe by the very nature of our being. Learning to live from the heart gives access to that true Self; it allows us to be connected to the essence of who we are, which is far more than the individual personality. Listening to the heart, rather than conditioning and social expectations, positions us to present those unique gifts to the world.

Summary

- In each moment, we have a choice whether to operate from separation or oneness.
- Once the lower centers are in balance and we have learned to self regulate, we are positioned to move allegiance from the head to the heart.
- The heart operates from a higher perspective and an all-encompassing state of wholeness.
- In coherence, the heart and mind work together at their resonant frequency.
- We can choose to move into the positive emotional states that generate coherence.
- Benefits of operating in a coherent state are physical and psychological well being, improved cognitive function, increased energy levels, drawing what we desire with grace and ease, resilience, greater access to universal consciousness via intuition, and access to the Divine within.

Reflections/Exercises/Practices

For Reflection/Discussion:

1. What are your personal energy drains (judgment, self-inflicted stress, pretending things are fine when they are not, lingering resentments, unresolved feelings of guilt, taking things personally, falling into fear, etc.)?
2. What energy drains do you see in the world around you? How can you work with those drains to minimize their impact?

Exercises:

1. Watch the documentary <u>Heart vs Mind: What Makes Us Human?</u> which at the time of publishing is available on YouTube.com.
2. Read a HeartMath® book, or download the e-book <u>The Energetic Heart</u> - which at the time of publishing -is available for free on the HeartMath® website.
3. Determine your intuitive style(s). You can do this through self observation, research and reflection, using muscle testing as recommended by Donna Eden in <u>The Energies of Love</u>, etc.
4. Experiment with controlled breathing. Try conscious, slow, relaxed breathing with your awareness focused on different points in the body (third eye, heart, solar plexus, lower abdomen, etc.). Determine which you find to be most beneficial. What impact do you feel to your overall well being?
5. The next time you are struggling with letting go of attachment to a thought or feeling, take it to the heart for purification.
6. Explore the Heartfulness Meditation website.
7. Keep a dream journal and pen by your bedside. Each time you awake from sleep, record any dreams that occurred. Refer to the previously outlined tips for remembering your dreams.

Chapter 13 - Turning Towards God

As the deer pants for streams of water, so my soul pants for you, my God. My soul thirsts for God, for the living God. When can I go and meet with God?
--- Psalm 42
*****

I like to think of coming to know God as having two parts: letting go of attachment to what stands in the way (misperceptions, limiting beliefs, fear-filled emotions, and limiting thoughts) *and* turning towards the light within. In the last chapter, we began to look at what it means to turn toward by exploring what it means to move to the heart and how to recognize one's own intuition. This chapter will continue to explore what it means to turn towards God.

Change of Allegiance

In the end, this is about a change of allegiance. We tend to define ourselves as the body and the intelligent mind. In fact, we are the pure conscious awareness that lies behind both; we are the Spirit within. Moving from identification with the self to identification with the Self is what leads to lasting peace. At heart, all enlightenment "methods and techniques" (and honestly all life experiences) center around either letting go of what you are not or turning toward what you truly are. Enlightenment is a shift from association with what is happening to association with the field in which it is happening.

There are some fundamental shifts in perception that underlie this change of allegiance. One of them is that there is nothing you need to do to get to God, because you are already there residing in the Heart and Mind of God at peace with all that is. When we first start on this spiritual path, we think it is the self in search of the Higher Self. In time, we come to recognize that there is no self. There is only the Higher Self and all we need do is remember who we really are and move our allegiance there. The next chapter will be devoted to an exploration of the will, but - as creative beings - we get to choose what we wish to experience, and it is in choosing to align with the universal Christ consciousness within that we find lasting peace. Seeking ends when we recognize that we are already one with our Source, that Love is all there is, and that our sole purpose is to be a vehicle for expression of that Love.

The awakened mind realizes that things come through us and not from us. Some of the characteristics of the awakened mind include:

- Mind chatter ceases
- A feeling of interconnection with all of Life
- Absence of judgment and acceptance of what is

- The free flow of all that arises within - thoughts, feelings, perceptions, and experiences - and recognition that whatever arises is alright, because one can choose for love
- Increased capacity for discernment
- Knowing as the mode of operation
- Acting from the truth within, rather than externally imposed values
- Forgiveness (seeing the other as pure and holy) as a standard practice

Where ordinary consciousness sees separateness, the enlightened person sees the presence of the Divine in everything. Peace is the result of this change of allegiance.

A fundamental part of this shift is the recognition that truth lies within. The implications of this statement are profound. It means that we should never look to anyone or anything in the outside world as our authority. It means that the definition of "good" as defined by society is irrelevant. In fact, the definition of what is good and moral has changed and will continue to change over time, but truth and the best way to respond to any situation can only be found within. By turning within, you will always have access to the most appropriate and loving response to any circumstance - that which serves the greater good. At the personal level, the implication of truth being within is that one must give up the need for external approval.

Feelings as the Gateway

We have previously discussed the importance of emotions in the Self remembering process. In The Way of Mastery[77], Jesus confirms the importance of feelings to the awakening process with the following statements:

"...[L]earn more and more to lead with the body, to lead with your feeling nature, not your intellect."(p.10)
"Feeling - unbridled, unblocked, unobstructed feeling - is the doorway to that Love that sets you free!"(p.78)
"Even that which arises as fear or anger should never be judged or obstructed."(p.373)

It is by placing focus on the inner world and fully feeling whatever arises, whether it be light or dark, that we are best positioned to move forward spiritually. As we saw in the last chapter, the power to transcend negative emotions comes from the wisdom, power, and love that reside within our own heart. In bringing what arises to the heart, we are best positioned to release limiting emotions and beliefs. Simply by choosing to take negative emotions to the heart, we have already begun the process of releasing them. The heart has the ability to alter the perception of any situation.

In the HeartMath Solution, it is recommended to spend five to fifteen minutes a day focusing awareness on the energies of the heart.[78] An exercise recommended in The Way of Mastery is to sit for the same amount of time and experience yourself as Christ.[79] Both exercises allow one to experience the feeling qualities of the heart and to begin to operate from a higher perspective.

The Power of Sincere Desire

However you would like to phrase it, a powerful criteria on the path to enlightenment is the sincere desire to know God above all else. The power of that desire begins to draw exactly what is needed to fulfill that desire, including drawing circumstances and situations to you that lead to growth *and* bringing up that which is buried in the unconscious for healing. It is important to feel that desire with all of your being, rather than treating it as an intellectual statement. Where you focus your energy is what you get, so why choose anything less than coming to know the God within you? It is things of the spirit that give life meaning and the only relationship of true value is the one with your Creator. When that is in alignment, all else flows effortlessly.

Pure Intentions

There are many books written on the power of intention and its ability to draw things to you. We are creative beings and - conscious or unconscious - the thoughts that run through our minds create our reality. By default, they become our intention. In the earlier section on ideals, we looked at how to spiritualize intentions. If you set your intention on spiritual things, spirit grows. A sincere desire for spiritual qualities begins to draw those patterns to you.

One of the aspects of turning toward the Divine is to become aware of the intention(s) behind our own feelings and actions. A story anecdotally attributed to Edgar Cayce describes twin brothers where one of the twins was born blind. When the parents inquired about the blindness, they were told that, as brothers in a previous lifetime, the brothers had been charged with putting out the eyes of captured enemies. One brother grew to enjoy the act, while the other did it as his duty. The brother who enjoyed inflicting suffering was born blind as an opportunity for soul growth. The point of this story is that the same act can have very different energy based on intention.

Evidence for the power of our intentions can be found in the work of Masaru Emoto, the Japanese author, researcher, and photographer, who took pictures of water crystals after exposure to various words, pictures, and music. Positive intention created more aesthetic crystals when the water was frozen, while negative intentions produced "ugly" formations. With our intentions, we mold the unlimited supply of energy emanating from our Source. Non-harmonious thoughts and feelings create a resistance that blocks the free flow of that energy.

When setting an intention, there are a number of things that will help bring it to fruition:

- Let go of any thoughts about the past and any limitations you may be holding about why the intention cannot come to fruition.
- State your intention in detail, being specific about the desired outcome, but letting go of any expectations about how it will be achieved.
- Get centered and connect with the field of energy that is your true nature.
- Visualize the intention as having already occurred. Use all of your senses (hear it, see it, feel it, etc.) to know it as completed. Don't just think it, feel it.
- Surrender the process to the universe for completion. Let go of any doubt or need to control the process or the outcome.
- Trust that you have called to you exactly what you need.

The combination of conscious intention and confidence in a positive outcome is a powerful force. It is the difference between force and drawing things to you. Force requires much effort, while intention comes with grace and ease. Obstacles to intention include dwelling on what you see yourself as lacking, engaging in activities that lower your own vibration, and trying to control the outcome.

Commitment

Accompanying the sincere desire to know God above all else is a commitment to "keep the eye single." That is, to let that desire become the motivation for all that you do. Aspects of that commitment include:

- A commitment to retraining the mind until it desires only Love
- A commitment to being fully aware of what you are choosing in each moment, and a commitment to choose for oneness over separation
- A commitment to listening to - above all other voices and expectations - the inner voice of the Divine within
- A commitment to being the presence of Love in the world and to the extension of your own gifts for the benefit of all

In taking responsibility for what you think, feel, see, and experience, you are reclaiming your own power as a creative being. You are the only one who can change your present reality. This is less about changing the circumstances of your life and more about the commitment to abide differently, right where you are. Inner spiritual evolution is of more value than anything you can do and dedication to these processes is a surrender to the Divine.

Trust

Life is as we believe it is. What we believe and the expectations we have shape our reality. Trusting that:
- There is meaning to life
- The Creator has defined a pathway that leads to freedom and increased consciousness
- All of creation is interconnected
- Life is abundant
- There is a win-win solution to every problem
- What we need will be provided in the most appropriate manner exactly when we need it

...makes this path easier to follow. Confidence in the wisdom of the Divine provides a sense of certainty and security that allows us to overcome doubt.

Focusing on the Positive

If the thoughts we hold in our conscious and subconscious mind are generating our reality, then there is benefit in keeping those thoughts focused on the good, the holy, and the beautiful. A part of this process then is being vigilant about what you allow into your mind. It is almost as if the mind is a two-year-old child who needs to be constantly redirected toward the positive. Turning out negative thoughts is a big part of what it means to focus on the positive, but there are many other aspects.

One is to become very aware of the negative thoughts that abound in the world around you, with the objective of disengaging from those energies. The violence on the evening news, war movies, political bickering, etc., all foster the perception that this is a dog-eat-dog world, and that we need to live in fear of it. In fact, there is much good that occurs in the world each day that does not get publicized. In the chapter on negativity, we looked at the three energy inputs and saw that the impressions we take in are more important than food and water with respect to the energy body. Becoming extremely aware of discord and refusing to buy into it in its many forms are means of fostering the positive.

A corollary of this concept is the idea that we cannot stamp out anything by fighting against it. Wars of any type - be they political or social (such as the war on drugs) - cannot be "stamped out" by fighting against them. It is better to be *for* something positive than to fight against something negative. Energy is immediately withdrawn from a situation the moment you choose to disengage from it. Energy is first patterned at the level of mind and it is at the level of mind that true and lasting change can be made. The expression "be peace" means that you have chosen to disengage from conflict in favor of peace and that, in doing so, you are affecting the overall consciousness of humanity in favor of peace.

Another means of fostering the positive is to look for the best in each person or situation and to minimize the faults. Looking for the positive automatically activates beneficial vibrations and keeps one connected to the heart. A corollary is to look for commonalities and minimize differences. Expectations are a part of this equation also. Look at what you expect from yourself, from others, and from situations and focus on making those expectations more positive - that is, expecting the best instead of the worst. One way to re-contextualize people who irritate you is to see them as your best teachers.

Another way of fostering the positive is an acceptance that the present moment is just as it should be and is beautiful and holy just as it is. We do not need to focus on future happiness or goodness, because it can be present right here and now if we simply choose to perceive it. It is in fully engaging with life by openly and honestly experiencing and acknowledging what is, and by seeing it as a gift from God regardless of how the outside world perceives it, that we become aware of the one spirit that permeates everything.

Another form of the positive is unconditional compassion and kindness to everyone and everything. Simple kindness is a powerful transformational force. That kindness includes giving others the benefit of the doubt, giving up assumptions about motives, and total acceptance of self and others just as they are.

The benefits of gratitude and appreciation are many and include the following:

- Drawing to you more things to be grateful for
- Strengthening and amplifying coherence
- Aligning one with the Higher Self
- Strengthening positive emotions
- Allowing us to connect with and open our own heart
- Boosting serotonin and dopamine levels and reducing stress
- Changing the focus from fault-finding to finding the good in situations and people
- Changing the focus from lack to abundance

Some of the ways to enhance the feeling of gratitude include thinking about someone or something for which you are grateful, meditating on gratitude, journaling about things for which you are grateful, and thanking another in either a verbal or written manner. Being grateful is a choice that, over time, can become a habit.

Union With All That Is

The Self is one - that is, in union or relationship with all that is. Does it make sense then that part of moving allegiance to the Self is being in union with what is around you, whether that be the people in your life or the environment in which you live? Who we really are (the Higher Self) only exists in relationship and that implies that recognizing our true identity means being in union or oneness with everything.

One way to begin to recognize union with "all that is" is to take oneself out of the center of the picture. The ego mind tends to see itself as the center of the world with everything that happens being done to and for it. Simply changing perspective to see the self as part of a larger picture begins to move awareness from the self to the field in which it resides. Taking focus off the self and feeling union instead eventually leads to the understanding that there is no self and that we are one with everything.

It is the heart that is capable of perceiving this union. It is in dedicating thoughts to union and perceiving with the heart that we begin to see the true essence of what is around us. In A Course of

Love, Jesus says: "For every joining, every union you enter into, your real world is increased and what is left to terrify you decreased."[80] (C:5.28)

An aspect of being in union is the willingness to be open. When we are willing to share our deepest thoughts and fears, we create a safe space for others to do the same. When I first started this work, I was told that, in the end, all will be made known. I initially found that openness to be a scary thought. But eventually, I came to understand that there is no self to defend. As Jesus says in A Course of Love, "What you withhold from the world, you withhold from yourself." [81] (C:7.16)

Asking for Help

We are not in this alone and one of the most powerful things we can do is to ask for help. Asking for help may mean asking to see your own core issues or deepest emotions, asking for assistance to change an attitude or perception, asking for guidance, asking for information and direction, etc. Because we are beings with free will, it is necessary to ask, as nothing and no one can intervene with our free will.

There are many to turn to: God or Source itself; enlightened beings who have gone before us; saints and angels; the Holy Spirit; your own Higher Self; guides; turning to the wisdom, power, and love within your own heart; etc. Does it make sense that if all is One, that these are all aspects of the same thing?

If we remember that the Higher Self (our true nature) is always calling to us, in asking for help we are invoking that Self and our own higher Will to assist us. The basic premise of A Course in Miracles is that when we see the self struggling, all we have to do is give it to the Holy Spirit and ask for help in seeing things differently. It is the Divine in its many aspects that has the power to transform.

When working with something specific, it may be helpful to invite the assistance of experts in that particular field, dead or alive, to provide insight. For instance, when writing a paper on holistic education, I invited holistic educators (Montessori, Steiner, and Krishnamurti) to provide insight. One of the most powerful uses of this energy I have seen was in a meditation space. Pictures of enlightened and high vibration people, again dead or alive, were placed on the shelves in the room and the energy of those people was invited to assist in creating the meditation space.

Being with Like Minded People

Meeting with like-minded people in small groups has multiple benefits. One is that it provides a sense of validation. When choosing to follow a path that is outside the norm of the predominant culture, there is a tendency to question how valid the path is, to struggle with how open one can be and still be socially accepted, to feel alone, and to slip back into conventional thinking. Joining with others of like mind helps alleviate all these tendencies. Being part of a small group is thus a source of motivation to stay on the path.

There is a synergistic (that is, the whole is more than the sum of the parts) energy that comes from group work. When small groups align with sincere intention and a common ideal, they invoke an energy beyond that of the individual members.

What is typical in these groups is to read and discuss inspirational literature. Deeper insights into the material can be obtained by hearing the perspective of others in the group. The literature creates a setting to discuss everyday issues and how others have overcome issues one may be struggling with. Being with those who are at a higher level of consciousness can have an uplifting effect and inspirational works, such as poetry, stories, scriptures, reading about the mystics, etc., can be a source of motivation whether done individually or in a group.

A healthy group encourages individuality even as it seeks for commonality. A small group should be a safe space to talk about concerns and to be known and accepted as you are. In that sense, it encourages the openness described earlier. Being part of a group and monitoring your own response to others in the group is also a way to work with your own issues, but in the safety of a group that values the individual.

Nurturing Your Own Spirit

Another important aspect of this process is to do that which brings you joy, and that which touches your own spirit. Some typical activities known to raise the vibration are art, music, being in nature, and being with young children and/or animals.

The state of flow is one where a person becomes so absorbed in an activity that time ceases to exist. There is a selfless immersion in the present moment. The early childhood educator Maria Montessori realized that, by the time they come to preschool at the age of three, most children have already lost touch with their own spirit due to conditioning. What she found is that when the child was allowed to concentrate fully on freely chosen work, it put the child back in touch with his or her own spirit. That concentration calmed the child to a point that was so notable that she coined a term for the process, "normalization." While we as adults have far more conditioning than young children, doing what we love still has the ability to put us in touch with the present moment and the deeper part of ourselves.

Using What Is Given

Service helps take the focus off the self and put it on the other. It is a form of demonstrating love and is thus a deterrent to fear. One way to think of this is as a spiral of continuous growth. As we come to increased understanding, we put that understanding into practice in the outside world. This is a process of continuous understanding and application. Service needs to be given freely - that is, with no attachment to the outcome.

Honoring intuition means acting on what is given. Empathy is a form of attunement and love is the highest form of attunement. The process of using one's intuition then becomes a process of recognizing a need, attuning to one's Higher Self, and application or using what is given.

Teaching, which forces one to clarify one's own understanding and commitment, is also a means of service to others.

Entering the Silence

The Self can only be known when mind chatter ceases - that is, in the stillness. If the objective is to move allegiance from the self to the Self, then spending time in moments of silence is what allows us to experience the Self and to create a deeper identification with it. Throughout the book, we have discussed how to create these moments of silence. Some of the ways to take advantage of this silence are as follows:

Learn to recognize and extend the hypnagogic state - There is a space of silence on first awakening in the morning and again just before falling asleep at night. In the morning, the mind is fully awake, but the mind chatter has not started yet. It is easy to turn out thoughts at this point and extend this state of silent awareness.

Create moments of silence - As you go about your day, periodically pause for a moment of silence. If the mind is still racing, look to the horizon. Sometimes, just a change of perspective to the broader picture can create enough of a shift to allow the silence. Another tool to silence the racing mind is to focus on the sound "mmmmmmmmm" to block out thoughts and stimulate the pineal gland.

Feel the stream - Beneath the constant mind chatter, there is a stream of awareness. Periodically feel for that stream throughout the day.

Feel the energy around you - Feel the energy in the empty spaces - between your own thoughts, emanating from objects, in the heart-to-heart connection with others, in your relationship to God, etc. Moving the emphasis to feeling will lead to an inward focus and reduce mind chatter.

Pose a question and sit in silence - Whether an answer comes or not does not matter; it is learning to sit in silent listening that is the point of the exercise.

Focus awareness on the heart, the solar plexus, or the third eye - As connection points to the Divine, there is a calming that occurs as a result of moving awareness to them.

Lighten up - By taking life experiences more lightly, we allow the deeper reality to surface.

Meditation

Meditation allows us to directly experience the Self as pure conscious awareness. It is only through attunement to our true nature (the Spirit within) that we come to know who we really are. If there is an objective to meditation, it is to reach that silent stillness within, that place of being that is beyond the limited mind and its activities. Meditation is *being* the field of awareness, rather than the thoughts that arise from that field. In deep meditation, there is total peace. It might be thought of as the ultimate "letting go" of the conscious mind.

Because meditation requires a focusing of awareness and the ability to direct attention, it is helpful to have worked with awareness exercises and to be using the process of self observation.

The process of meditation itself is one of watching the thought stream and seeing thoughts come and go. Rather than latching onto them, it is important to detach and let them go. Eventually, it is possible to feel a thought begin and choose to refuse to allow it to arise. Initially, this process of watching what arises begins as an observer function. But it is possible to associate more and more with the field from which things (thoughts, emotions, and sensations) arise. For me, meditation feels like it has two parts: non-attachment to what arises and giving up the control function.

There are many benefits attributed to meditation, including:
- More coherent brain waves and increased integration between emotional and cognitive processes (head and heart)
- Increased cognitive processing and mental clarity
- Increased access to intuitive information and conscious awareness of it
- Increased access to the subconscious and Higher Self
- A calming effect (more activity in the prefrontal cortex and less in the amygdala)
- Increased sense of well-being
- Higher vibration of the energy body
- A spiritual centeredness

In addition to the personal benefits, there are now a number of studies demonstrating the benefits of meditation to the surrounding environment, particularly in terms of crime rate.[82]

There are many meditation processes and practices available, and which to follow is personal preference. There is an equally diverse number of preparations for meditation. The value of these preparations is that they encourage turning toward the Divine within, and they begin calming the body in preparation for meditation. If a given aid is used regularly before meditation, eventually, simply beginning use of that preparation will signal the body that it is time for meditation. A few of the more common preparations for meditation are:

Prayer - Prayer is a good centering practice in preparation for meditation. It is less about the specific words used and more about turning towards God. Prayer can be in your own words, but equally effective is a prayer someone else has written that touches your own heart. One of the Cayce recommendations is a prayer of protection before entering meditation: "As I open myself to the unseen forces surrounding the throne of grace, beauty, and might, I throw about myself the protection found in the thought of the Christ." (Based on Edgar Cayce Reading 262-2) A nice accompaniment to this prayer is visualization of a bubble of white light surrounding and protecting you.

Relaxation - Many meditation practices begin with a relaxation process. This can be as simple as systematically relaxing the muscles in the body. This process not only begins relaxation of the nervous system, but also brings the focus inward and starts directing attention where desired.

Opening the Energy Channels - Yoga and body work that open the energy channels allow energy to move more freely. The Cayce meditation process uses "head and neck" exercises to loosen the area along the spine, so energy can move more freely.

Rituals and Aids - Some like to use incense, a cleansing process, oils to clear the aura, crystals to clear the chakras, etc. If you find that they help, then use them.

Breath Work and Chanting - These work with the vagus nerve, which impacts the heart's rhythm and helps generate coherence. Slow, rhythmic breathing is a common practice, because it is easy to follow and easy to return to if the mind gets caught in a thought.

Mantra - Use of a mantra is also a common meditation practice. The mantra is a short phrase such as "Be still, and know that I am God" that is said slowly over and over to focus the mind. Eventually, one should move from the mental saying of the phrase to the silent feeling of the phrase, and then into total stillness. Again, if the mind gets caught up in thinking, one can return to the mantra and begin again.

Some tips for meditation include:
- One should approach meditation with an attitude of surrender and openness, free of any expectations.
- First thing in the morning - before the mind fully awakens - is usually most effective, but not always possible.
- It is better to practice regularly, preferably at the same time of day and in the same space.
- Accept whatever arises without judgment and let it pass without picking it up or responding to it in any way.

- If concentration wanes and you get caught up in thinking, return to the breath or mantra to refocus the mind.
- Some days will be more difficult than others. Continue anyway. The discipline of continually refocusing the mind carries over to everyday consciousness.

As we meditate, not only does the conscious mind relax, but the subconscious mind does also. It is discernment that enables us to make a distinction between what comes from the Divine versus what comes from our own subconscious memories and conditioning, the voice of any outside authorities that have been internalized, or other non-divine entities.

The voice to honor is that of the Divine. The others are distractions and one should see them and let them go. Some report visual effects, rocking motions, etc., during meditation. When these things occur, allow them to arise without resistance, but do not pick them up or attach to them in any way. As with the subconscious, just observe without getting involved. The same is true for any insights that come during meditation. Note their presence, trust that they will be available when you need them, and return to the silence.

Summary

- Enlightenment is a fundamental shift of allegiance from the self to the Self.
- The Self is always calling to us.
- Truth is within and it is by turning within that we find it.
- It is by placing focus on the inner world and fully feeling whatever arises that we are positioned to move forward spiritually.
- A powerful anchor on the path to enlightenment is the sincere desire to know God above all else.
- The combination of conscious intention and confidence in a positive outcome has the power to draw to us what we desire.
- A commitment to placing the relationship with God above all else means that desire becomes the motivation for all that one does.
- What we believe and the expectations we have shape our reality.
- Trust in the wisdom of the Divine provides a sense of well-being that allows us to overcome self-doubt.
- Vigilance about what one allows into the mind means turning out negativity; becoming extremely aware of negativity and discord in the environment, and refusing to buy into it; and intentionally focusing on the good, the holy, and the beautiful.
- Gratitude and appreciation are powerful ways to reconnect to the heart and raise one's own vibration.
- We only exist in relationship. There is no separate self.
- Help is available if we ask.
- Using what is given to be of service to self and others draws more of the same (internal guidance) to you.
- Working in small groups combines the benefits of being with like-minded people with the study of uplifting materials.
- Moments of silence allow us to hear the voice of the Self.
- Meditation allows us to directly experience the Self as pure conscious awareness.
- Meditation involves non-attachment to what arises and surrender or letting go of control.

- There are many preparations and aids to meditation. Use those that you personally find helpful in creating a deeper state.

Reflections/Exercises/Practices

For Reflection/Discussion:

1. How do you personally know when someone or something (written material) is speaking the Truth?
2. What are a few of the externally imposed values (cultural, familial, societal) that you would most like to give up?
3. If things come through us and not from us, what is the nature of our being?
4. How would you personally go about deciding what is right for you, as opposed to what society dictates as right?
5. How would you demonstrate to yourself that you are not the body or the mind?
6. What filled you with joy as a child? Are those things part of your life now?
7. How would you go about achieving a balanced mood? What helps you avoid extremes of emotion?
8. What is your most sincere desire?
9. How do you sabotage your own desires?
10. What in your present life is self-created? What would you choose to create differently?
11. In what areas of your life do you lack trust?
12. Reflect on the thought that you only exist in relationship.
13. Can things occur that are outside the realm of possibility?
14. Reflect on individuals who you feel have contributed greatly to the spiritual consciousness of humanity. What does this say about your own role in the world?
15. What does the statement "All will be made known" mean?
16. What puts you in touch with your own spirit?
17. In what way(s) can you be of service in the world and use the gifts that are uniquely yours?

Exercises:

1. Throughout the day, as you sense that you are defining yourself as the body, the mind, or your feelings and emotions, use the following affirmation:
   I am pure conscious awareness. I release all attachment to the body, to the mind, to the emotions that arise, and to any limiting beliefs I may be holding.
2. Once in bed, give each troubling person or situation to your Higher Self to handle.
3. When you see that you are getting upset because another does not appreciate something you have done, re-contextualize the situation as being between you and God, as opposed to between you and the other. Take a deeper look at the motivation for your actions.
4. Define a plan for how you will respond to troubling emotions when they arise. Include those things that you know will calm you when you are troubled.
5. Choose one of these exercises to practice fifteen minutes each day for the next week:
   - Sit with your own heart and focus awareness there
   - Sit and experience what it feels like to be Christ in the world

6. Define the phrase you would use to express your desire to know God. Go within and feel the strength of that desire. Speak to God and express that desire with all your heart. Keep that desire before you as you go about your daily life.

7. When you start to get frustrated that something you want has not happened, give up the frustration and instead feel what it would be like to have that occur.

8. Become very conscious of the words "I am." What intentions have you been unconsciously creating when you use these words?

9. Create an "I am" affirmation for yourself. As an example, one might say "I am love incarnate."

10. Work with the belief that this is a safe and nurturing world - that exactly what you need is being provided to you. If thoughts that contradict that belief arise, visualize them as stones that you take and fling away from yourself.

11. Make a commitment to release all that stands in the way of happiness and coming to know the God within you.

12. Take a statement you use regularly and restate it as a more positive "I am" statement. For example, the statement "I am getting old" might be restated as, "I am thankful that I am in good health and am able to do all that I do."

13. Observe your reaction when you interact with someone who is a stranger. Instead of focusing on differences, focus on what you have in common.

14. Bring to mind a situation that you do not like, such as spending time with someone you do not enjoy, family obligations, or work encounters. Look at your expectations for this situation. Approach this scene from two different angles: how can you release your expectations about the situation to make it more positive, and what can you learn about yourself from this interaction?

15. Choose to see everything that happens as a gift.

16. Every time you see yourself start to worry about a future event, breathe deeply and bring your attention to the present moment. See the perfection in this moment.

17. For a few days, when you see yourself move into negativity with a person or situation, choose to re-contextualize it instead. What are possible reasons this person is behaving this way, or this situation is happening this way? Since you do not know the motivations of the person or, the full circumstances of this situation, is it better to assume the best or to make no assumptions at all? Ask your heart to show you things to appreciate about this situation.

18. Choose a time when your attitude is not good and use one or more of the following techniques:
    - Find something positive to think about: read something inspirational, see an inspirational movie, or move your thoughts to something you enjoy doing or someone you enjoy being with
    - Go for a walk or do some exercise
    - Smile
    - Look out to the horizon
    - Bring to mind your ideal and your commitment to make it your guiding force
    - Act as though you feel good

19. Before you fall asleep at night, mentally list all the things you are thankful for. Become aware of the impact on how you feel upon waking in the morning.

20. Practice taking yourself out of the center of the picture. Wherever you are - sitting in a room, sitting in the car, etc. - mentally move your position to be at the periphery of the picture. How does this change your sense of importance, and your sense of relationship?

21. With each person or thing that you interact with throughout the day, see yourself as only existing in relationship to that. Erase any thoughts of a separate self.

22. Experiment with sharing a few of your innermost thoughts and feelings with someone you trust. Observe the impact to the relationship.
23. Rather than looking at the external appearance of things, begin to feel for their essence. Move past the name you have given to each object and look at it anew. Feel for the common Source that underlies it.
24. Ask for help from whatever source you feel most comfortable invoking.
25. When you are struggling with an issue, invite enlightened beings who are experts in that area to assist you.
26. Explore the possibility of joining or starting a small group in your area.
27. Explore various activities to see if they help you to get in touch with your own spirit:
    - Listen to soothing music
    - Spend time doing an artistic activity
    - Go for a quiet walk in nature
    - Take a hot bath
    - Spend time with an animal
    - Do something calm and repetitive - rocking in a chair, sewing, etc.
    - Sit and repeat a mantra
    - Act on what is received via intuition
    - Experiment with some of the suggestions for finding silence
    - Learn to recognize and extend the hypnagogic state
    - Look for the spaces between your thoughts
    - Create moments of silence
    - Feel the stream
    - Feel the energy around you
    - Pose a question and sit in silence
    - Focus awareness on the heart, the solar plexus, or the third eye
    - Lighten up
28. For one minute of each hour that you are awake, close your eyes, watch your breath, and just be. Set a timer or tie a yarn around your wrist to remember.
29. Practice walking mindfully. Be attentive to each step and be mindful of your breathing.
30. Begin a meditation practice. If you are already meditating, experiment with the various preparations for meditation to determine which are most effective for you.
31. Explore prayers that touch your own heart. Write your own prayer using what you have learned through looking at the prayers of others.

Meditative Practices:

1. Imagine the circle of humanity with each soul representing a point of light in the circle. Imagine the light that Jesus and other enlightened masters brought to the circle. See your own point of light within the circle and how it also provides light to those who will follow.

Chapter 14 - The Will

The will is likely the most misunderstood aspect of our humanity and yet proper use of the will is essential to spiritual growth. The key is effective use of the will, which requires:

- An understanding of the creative process and our power to choose
- Internal consistency and some sense of a permanent self founded in the ideal, so one aspect of the self does not undo the work of another
- Self-awareness and recognition of habitual patterns of the mind, so one can make conscious choices

This chapter will explore these various aspects of what is required to use the will and what choices and behaviors foster continued growth.

Our Nature as Creative Beings

At a fundamental level, the energy comprising all relationships and all events is neutral. Earlier in this book, we looked at the concept that we are not perceiving anything directly and that what we perceive is filtered by our own beliefs. That concept is confirmed in The Way of Mastery: "...All webs of relationship, all energy fields, are absolutely neutral. What creates experience is how you decide you will view that web of relationship, that field of energy" (p.107).

Jesus uses the analogy of pebbles selected and thrown into a pool. Each pebble creates a ripple that then comes back just as it was sent out. That analogy reflects the concept that we are creative beings: We have the power to create the world we choose to see, because every thought we think sends out a vibration that is then returned to us as the events of our life. Essentially, we have the perfect learning environment. We each have the power to choose what we put out. That, in turn, attracts to us certain vibrational frequencies. Based on the experiences returned, we then have the freedom to choose differently.

The implications of this process are key:

- In putting out low vibration thoughts and holding low vibration beliefs, we draw to ourselves low vibration events such as war, death, disease, unhappiness, and the sense of being separate. Conversely, in putting out higher vibration thoughts and holding higher vibration beliefs, we draw to ourselves higher vibration people and events.
- The choice to perceive oneself as a victim is abdication of one's own power.
- If you are not creating the life you want (including being enlightened), you need to look at something in your own consciousness.

Another key point in this process is understanding that each time a ripple returns, there is an opportunity to choose how you will perceive the effect of that ripple. The Way of Mastery says, "And if you experience it with unconditional freedom, with unconditional acceptance and Love, forgiveness, neutrality and innocence, you literally defuse the effects of that ripple ..."[83]

Patterns of Energy

Archetypes - which are a concept introduced by Carl Jung that helps us perceive the patterns in humanity's consciousness - are related to this process. An archetype is a collectively inherited idea or pattern of thought, universally available in its abstract form. How the archetypal ideal or energy pattern is visualized varies across cultures and societies, but the core archetype or pattern at the level of the universal mind is the same. For example, the archetype of Victim has specific characteristics that are common to all victims, while the mental image of a victim varies according to the culture and society of the individual visualizing a victim.

Archetypes are universal psychic patterns, waves, or disruptions in the field of consciousness. And because we are all one, the wave comes from beyond the individual; it comes from universal human consciousness itself. Archetypes help us to see patterns in the unconscious, so they can be brought back into balance. Awareness of the effects of archetypes on our way of thinking – and resolving to free ourselves of those archetypes - can lead us to oneness instead of duality. Myths serve a similar role in that they explain the world around us and are a way of inspiring people to behave in certain ways. Through awareness and choice, we can free ourselves from being at the affect of archetypes, this collection of beliefs and feelings in the collective unconscious. Our role is to choose which ideas or patterns we hold within our own mind. Those choices determine what creates our reality.

Eva Pierrakos who brought through information in a trance state, says something similar in Pathwork® Guide Lecture No. 75:

"Ever since the world of matter began, all these feelings — good or bad, positive or negative, joyful or painful — have existed and people have experienced them. That you seem to produce a feeling does not mean that you have actually done so. What you do produce is the condition of tuning into the particular force or principle of an already existing emotion...

According to your personal frame of mind, state of emotion, general development, character tendencies, as well as passing moods or outer happenings, you tune into one of these currents...

As long as you harbor the illusion that you are producing the respective emotion or life-experience, you are still unique, alone, and separate. When you begin to feel that you are tuning into what already exists, you automatically become a part of the whole and can no longer be the separate individual you have felt yourself to be."[84]

By making these patterns more visible, and recognizing them as what we tap into at a certain vibrational level, we realize that they are not who we are and that we do have the power to choose differently.

Importance of the Will

If we return to one of the early diagrams, we see the importance of the will as a crucial aspect of the soul.

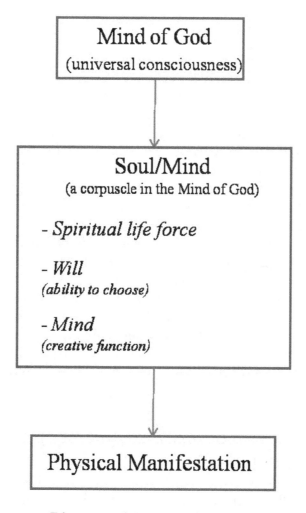

Diagram of Aspects of the Soul

As previously discussed, the Earth is the perfect learning environment for growth in consciousness and it is through making choices and experiencing the results of those choices that we move closer to, or further from, universal consciousness. We initially came into being to be co-creators with the Divine, and that means strengthening the will so we can realize our full potential. Spiritual teachers across time have attested to the importance of the will:

Edgar Cayce - *"Know that the birthright of every soul is choice, or will".* (Edgar Cayce Reading 2329-1)

The Way of Mastery - *"Consciousness - the power to be aware, the power to choose - is what you truly are."* (p.93)

Ouspensky - *"Two things can be developed in man - consciousness and will. Both are forces. If man overcomes unconsciousness, he will possess consciousness; if he overcomes mechanicalness he will possess will. If he understands the nature of the powers he can attain, it will be clear to him that they cannot be given; these powers must be developed by effort."*[85]

What is Free Will?

If we think of life (or our many lifetimes) as a journey to remember who we really are, then in some sense, the end of that journey is already determined. Jesus addresses this: "Having free will does not mean that you can elect not to take the only curriculum that life is offering to you in every moment. It means only that you do have the right to put it off yet another day."[86]

I have a friend who says free will does not exist for that very reason. Each time she chooses not to listen to the quiet voice within, she finds that she has simply taken a longer path to eventually choosing to listen to that voice. The implications of this are comforting in that we have not lost our true identity as offspring of Divinity, or as some say, "none can be lost." But it still implies that we need to remember who we are, and we do that through experiencing the results of the choices we make. Free will, then, is the freedom to make these ongoing choices.

Saint Germain says, "...when your emotions become disturbed over outer conditions, feelings, or concepts, there is a moment when you are yet able to wrest control of your energies from your own emotional body,"[87] and that is the moment of choice. Thus, will is a deliberate choice of that which is in opposition to habit. It is important to remember that we are constantly choosing, either consciously or unconsciously. Consciously choosing means that when we interpret an event received via the senses, we have enough awareness to observe what is occurring internally, to recognize that there are many patterns of response we can choose, and to choose for that which is consistent with the ideal. To break the cycle of limiting emotions, it is necessary to choose love over fear, oneness over separation.

Choosing Love Over Fear

What does it mean to choose love over fear? It means choosing God, or that which is life affirming. Being our very nature, there is nothing we must do to earn this state of love. By being open to receive it, it is available. There is however, a choice that must be made in each moment. Do I choose to perceive from my true nature of love (the Self), or from the self? Being an extension of love requires nothing but the choice for love.

Love and fear are mutually exclusive. In choosing for one, it is necessary to let go of the other. It is possible to choose for love in any situation, regardless of what is going on inside of you or what you perceive as occurring in the outside world. One of the ways to view things in the temporal world is to see them as a "call for love," or the longing to remember our true nature.

Fear is dissolved by awareness and choice. As with all emotions, resistance is *not* the answer. It is honoring the fear (in its many forms) and allowing it to fully surface, feeling the fear while maintaining the observer perspective, and releasing attachment to it that allow one to choose for love.

Choosing for the Self then is moving to that place that is beyond all that is temporal and returning to the quiet of the heart. Self remembering is these small moments of the will - the continuous choice for what is real. The goal is to consistently be in that space where every thought and every action comes from love. In the end, it is simply a quiet choice to be the presence of love in each moment.

Self-Discipline and Development of the Will

Self-discipline is something we learn for ourselves, not something innate or something that can be imposed effectively by someone else. It must be developed from within by use. The only way to improve self-discipline is through intentional and dedicated practice, by repeatedly going against what is habitual. Once again, we see that the environment of the earth plane is the perfect environment for growing in self-discipline. We are experiential beings, and it is through making choices and experiencing the results of those choices that we grow and become happy.

These small moments of letting go of self will, of going against ingrained habits, are what leads to growth in consciousness or Self Will. It is in our darkest moments that the opportunity for growth in consciousness is the greatest. The idea of dying to the self could be interpreted as these continual moments of giving up self will in favor of the Self.

In Every Moment

The choice for what is real is not limited to decision-making; it is about every thought we have and every emotion that arises. Life is about choices; every situation, every interaction, every thought, and every emotion is a choice. It comes down to a question of: "What am I choosing in this moment?" That is the value of present-moment awareness. It is only in bringing full awareness to the present moment and what is going on inside that we *can* choose consciously. There are countless opportunities to choose for peace in each day.

A negative emotion arises. Do I choose to move to the quiet of the heart and let it dissolve? Someone does something I do not like. Can I see this event as neutral or do I choose to personalize it? Would I prefer to be right or to be happy? Can I see the other as his/her Higher Self? Do I prefer conflict or peace? This ability to be fully aware and to make a conscious choice in each moment is the basis of lasting freedom and happiness. It is - by making all visible, integrating the will with the Will of God, and choosing for oneness rather than separation - that we find lasting peace. This is about relinquishing what no longer serves, and a conscious decision to be only the presence of love.

When people start down the spiritual path, there is often a feeling that there is something they need to be doing, such as a career change. Rest assured that there are plenty of opportunities to know God in your life just as it is. The bigger question is: How do I choose to be a Christ in this moment?

Shaping the Will

In the previous chapter, we looked at the power of intention and its ability to draw things to you. The power of intention is far greater than that of the individual will. It begins to draw to you what is needed to fulfill what you have envisioned, and does so with grace and ease. Earlier in the book, we looked at ideals and how the ideals process aligns body, mind, and spirit in a spiritual direction. The value of setting these conscious intentions is that, rather than struggling to overcome old limiting patterns, the focus is on moving to a new mode of perception. By envisioning the ideal, we begin to shape the will in the desired direction. Intention energizes willingness and begins to align thoughts and feelings; the conscious and the subconscious; and body, mind, and spirit.

Because this is the creation of something new, the path will feel unfamiliar. It is important to recognize this so one does not give up because of discomfort arising from the unfamiliar. This is a new way of being and it is important to allow what one is envisioning to be true. The difference between what you have and what you want creates a tension that is to be cultivated.

We have previously discussed how there resides within each of us the ultimate pattern of perfection that goes by many names: Higher Self, Christ Consciousness, the Buddha Nature, etc. In setting ideals or clear spiritual intentions, we begin to pattern our choices toward our true nature. Edgar Cayce expresses this:

14 - The Will

"As to whether circumstance or environ is to rule an entity's being or experience, or WILL, depends then - the most - upon what the entity or soul sets as its standard of qualifications to meet or measure up to, within its OWN self; or as to how well self may be guided by its standard in making decisions in those directions." (Edgar Cayce Reading 590-1)

The ideals process allows the visualization of desired results in specific situations and the act of writing them out sets a clear intention. The exercise in the previous chapter of sitting and seeing yourself as a Christ also sets this clear intention. Giving up self will means remembering the ideal and going against the self to act according to that ideal. In that way, the will is "developed" and thus disciplines the mind to keep attention focused on the desired mental patterns. It is by making constant small efforts to let go of limiting thoughts and limiting emotions, that we "develop" the will.

Awareness is power in that it enables conscious choice. To have self-control, we must first be self-aware - that is, practicing self observation. Thus, it might be said that learning to control attention is the beginning of will. Once we are able to control attention, it is then possible to choose what to use our awareness to focus on and thereby influence what we call into our life.

Fostering Development of the Will

There are specific tools and actions that can help foster development of the will

Dissolve limiting ideas of who you are - We are powerful beings. In essence, we are pure conscious awareness with full power of choice and the ability to be co-creators with the Divine. Fully accepting that as our true nature, and letting go of any misperceptions about who we are, positions us to step into that identity. Live as though you are a master and not an ego, and that will become your reality because what you believe is what you perceive and what in turn creates your reality. Again, it is a matter of choice. Do I choose to live as a Christ or something less than that?

Choose for what is real regardless of what others think - It is necessary to move to the point where what others think no longer matters; where what someone else chooses does not influence your choice. What is life affirming can only be found by going within and ignoring what conditioning, society, and culture expect. It is necessary to bypass the external senses and what the minds around you are convinced is true.

Present moment awareness - It is only in the present moment that we have the power of conscious choice. If we are not aware of what we are thinking and feeling, those moments of opportunity pass us by. It is the inner life that matters. What is going on in the outside environment is simply what you have created based on previous thoughts and feelings. The power lies in the present moment with the ability to choose once again.

Give up emotional attachment to the past - By projecting past incomplete feelings on the present, we color present moment awareness. The past is what has brought us to where we are now. It was neither good nor bad, it was just as it needed to be to bring us to where we are now. There is no need to repaint any of the events of the past in a better light or to dwell on how things could have been better. Staying in the present moment means that the focus is there and no longer on the events of the past or the future. A corollary is to view the people and events now in our lives as exactly what we need to continue to grow.

Become aware of the moment when you are yet able to wrest control - Become aware of the moment of opportunity described by Saint Germain when you are yet able to wrest control from your own emotional body. We have a tendency to add emotional significance to events and it is necessary to catch that tendency as it starts to happen. By catching the emotional response at that point, it is still possible to choose for peace. But once a limiting emotion is allowed to take control and the body picks up the lower vibration, it becomes increasing difficult to turn that around. When awareness returns, it is still possible to choose once again and the Heartmath® techniques are helpful in returning to a higher vibration. The more we detach and observe through self-observation, the less likely we are to become lost when an emotional reaction occurs.

Be honest with yourself - What remains hidden continues to unconsciously control us. To let go of what no longer serves, we have to be willing to acknowledge that it is there. In allowing limiting thoughts, emotions, and beliefs to surface, and in acknowledging limiting behavior patterns, we create a space for them to be healed. That is the value of choice. It is not what arises that is the issue, it is identification with what arises. In allowing fears, expectations, and limitations to be brought to conscious awareness, we realize that they no longer have power over us, because we can consciously choose not to accept them as who we are. That which we fear and have hidden is dissolved by awareness and choice.

Stay with it - It is important to see uncomfortable or painful situations as an opportunity and to stay with them until they are resolved. Limiting patterns will repeat until you decide to heal them. Making the decision to face painful feelings and to heal will attract what is needed to do so. Become good at tolerating emotional discomfort. Allow yourself to feel what you do not want to feel and be open to the possibility that you can see things differently. If you realize that you have slipped back into an old habit, when you become aware of it, simply choose once again.

Because habits are ingrained, there will be resistance to new ways of being. As we saw in the chapter on aligning aspects of the self, creating new patterns is a process that occurs over time, which allows the subconscious to gradually recognize new habit patterns as the norm. By continuously thinking a new thought, consistently choosing a particular emotion, or consistently acting your way into a new belief, the subconscious gradually accepts a new way of being.

Ask to have what needs to be healed put before you - Purifying your own mind is what allows the love that is your natural state to shine forth. Asking to have what still needs healing to be put before you implies a commitment and a readiness to heal it.

Invoke Higher Will - God's Will is always there; that guidance is always available. It is a matter of being open to it. As we discussed earlier, there is a difference between self will and Will, which is an aspect of the Higher Self. To silence the mind via self will is difficult and a constant struggle. By using the power of choice to invoke or turn toward the Will, we invite the assistance of a much stronger force. As A Course in Miracles says, "The holy instant does not come from your little willingness alone. It is always the result of your small willingness combined with the unlimited power of God's Will." (T-18.IV.4.1-2) There is a myth about Hercules cleaning the Augean stables that speaks to this ability to invoke a higher power. Hercules was able to perform the "undoable" task of cleaning out the stables in a day by diverting a river to wash through the stables. Likewise, by inviting the Higher Will, we have access to a power that can clean out our psyche in a manner we could never accomplish alone. Invoking this Higher Will is as simple as saying, "My will is Thine, O Lord."

Earlier in the chapter on Working With Thoughts, we discussed that Knowledge and "Work on Being" are both required to grow in consciousness.

If we create a table for developing the will, it might look like this:

Knowledge	Work on Being
Our true nature as creative beings	Setting clear ideals and intentions
The power of intention to draw what is needed	Being Self- or inner-directed
Law of attraction - what you put out is what you get back	Staying in the present moment
	Developing awareness of the moment of choice and choosing for what is life affirming
	Deep self honesty
	Persistence
	Surrender

Surrender

Surrender is the constant process of handing over whatever occurs to a Higher Power. To do that, it is necessary to let go of any limiting emotions and of any inclination to personalize or give significance to an event, and to instead act as a channel for love. Through this willingness, space is created for a Higher Power to work through us. Surrender is the willingness to set the intention to be loving, whatever the circumstances.

What are the advantages of surrender? The decision to release each moment to that Higher Power is what allows healing from the idea that we could ever be separate from our Source. It is, in that sense, the key to growth in consciousness and allows us to know who we really are. It opens us to a power that is capable of raising perception to a new level of understanding, and draws to us exactly what is needed with grace and ease, rather than effort. If pain and suffering are the results of fighting against, it is acceptance and surrender that allay that suffering. The root causes of stress are blocked feelings and limiting beliefs/expectations. In choosing to act from a deeper place and releasing results to a Higher Power, we give up attachment to those limitations and remove stress from our lives.

If surrender is so key to the development of higher consciousness, what helps foster surrender?

Cultivate humility - Humility is more a state of openness to what is larger than the self, than a state of meekness. Humility stems from the knowledge that there is something out there larger than ourselves and that our very existence depends on that Source. It comes from understanding that we cannot get there on our own - that growth depends on opening to that Higher Power. It is a recognition that the mind does not have the big picture, that its interpretations cannot be trusted, that it cannot tell the difference between truth and untruth, that thoughts and opinions are worth nothing, and that there is something present that is beyond intellectual understanding. In realizing that, "Of myself, I do not know," we are able to release the need to think and interpret, and to release the tendency to place emotional value on what occurs. This idea that there is a bigger picture than we are capable of understanding, and a greater force at work, is what positions us to give up struggle, to accept what occurs as what needs to be, and to rest in peace with what is. It is the beginning of the realization that what abides in time is temporary and will pass, and that its only value is in how we choose to use it to grow in consciousness. It is recognition that all of the events of our life are growth events and that in that sense, we can be grateful for the opportunity to experience them.

Humility is recognition that we are simply the vehicle for the larger Life Force that is flowing through us. In accepting that position, we allow the Mind of God to be expressed through us. One who is enlightened simply waits for guidance from and otherwise rests in a state of peaceful awareness. The symbol of an empty vessel reflects this state of consciousness. Insights come from beyond the self. In aligning with this Higher Will, one opens to the universal knowledge that is available via spiritual transmission. If intuition comes by getting self out of the way, then cultivation of humility is the path to wisdom.

Let go of expectations and desires - Perceived needs, comparison, likes and dislikes, projections and expectations all get in the way of inner peace. They are simply forms of attachment and the tendency to add emotional significance. We have previously looked at motivations as there is often some form of expected payoff behind them. To find lasting peace, it is necessary to let go of patterns of false desire, whether they be aversions or attractions, to give up projecting outcomes, and to give up all desire for control and gain. A subtle example of the difference in need to control is to contrast the two expressions "gaining enlightenment" and "being a Christ in the world." The first is phrased in terms of acquisition and still demonstrates the need to do and acquire; the second is a state of being where things simply flow through and the will is surrendered to a Higher Power. Even the longing for mystical experiences must be surrendered in favor of giving every moment to the Divine.

Just as with thoughts, desire will arise and just as with thoughts, it is what you do with it after it arises that is the concern. This statement from The Way of Mastery describes the intent of the process:

"Mastery of desire comes when you recognize that you are safe to feel whatever wave of desire might come up through your consciousness, because you decide whether or not you will act on it, whether you will bring it into the field of manifestation." (p.45)

Once again, this is a learning process and it is through choosing false desires that we realize that they have no ability to fulfill the soul. Conversely, by choosing for what is real, we find moments of peace.

Give up control - Control is the ego's attempt to assert self will on outside circumstances and people through force. To the ego, loss of control is synonymous with the end of its existence.

There are many control mechanisms - some passive and some aggressive. Aggressive forms of control include being loud, and using insults, blame, and sarcasm. Passive forms of control include procrastinating, forgetting, pouting, manipulative crying, and use of the silent treatment. As Deepak Chopra points out in How to Know God, even being overly caring can be a control mechanism: "Being a perfectionist, taking care of other people's needs even when not asked, taking charge of situations on the assumption that others cannot look out for themselves, and implicitly wanting to be thanked for one's trouble"[88] are all attempts to ensure acceptance and appreciation from others. While caring for others without expectation is a gift, caring for others as a means of winning approval is a control mechanism. Attempting to control the outside world to fill what is missing and avoid emotional pain is an error in thinking, as true fulfillment cannot come from without.

It is again in that instant when emotion arises - but before significance is added - that one can choose to forego habitual patterns of control.

Allow - Allowance is the process of letting things flow through you. It is the "letting go" that allows wisdom to come in. What happens when you give up the need to control anything, including your own mind, and let go to a Higher Power and a Higher Will? What happens when you are willing to let go of all perceptions and the need to interpret, and are willing to assume that there is wisdom in everything that happens even if you do not understand why? That openness allows a connection with Life itself. Pure intention and relaxation into the state of allowing are what opens one to Life's intelligence.

The Higher Self is always working in the direction of growth in consciousness, of well-being, and of bringing solutions that are for the greatest good. In opening to that Higher Power and allowing it to work through you, the events of your life no longer appear as obstacles, but rather as stepping stones to further growth. There is no need to control anything, no need to "try," no need to strive for perfection, and no need to seek. In fact, those actions get in the way of the flow. Allowance is more an attitude than a doing and incorporates openness and trust.

When fears arise, it is necessary to make a conscious decision, a choice, to let go of the fear and rest in the allowing. That choice includes a willingness to accept uncertainty and wait if necessary.

The Way of Mastery summarizes the essence of what it means to allow:

"To actively learn and master the art of 'you need to do nothing' to find that spaciousness within you in which you are willing to allow that voice within you that is eternally connected to your Source to be the vehicle through which you receive your guidance" (p.318).

Give all decisions to that Mind - It is the Higher Self or the Holy Spirit that knows exactly what is needed in any given situation. In moving allegiance from the ego to the Higher Self, one opens to that Higher Mind and Will that are always available. The part of the mind that is free from the ego, the Higher Self, is always present and can be accessed at any time by anyone. In any situation, the guidance needed to choose for Love is available. The more one works with this process of devaluing fear and turning to the Love within for guidance, the more the mind is refined and purified. It is through the human heart that Love is made manifest. That statement reflects both the understanding that the heart is the connection to the deeper Self and that the human heart is where God's Love is translated to a vibration appropriate for the earth. In choosing to act out of Love, we then become the hands and feet of the Divine.

The process of opening to this guidance incorporates concepts from the last two chapters:

- *Enter the stillness* - Go within and get centered. Focus attention at the heart or wherever you feel a connection to the Divine.
- *Express a sincere desire to know the Will of God* - Express a sincere desire to know the Will of God in this situation and intend that all will work out for the greater good.
- *Ask for guidance* - Open to the voice of love and ask for guidance, giving up all attachment to the outcome.
- *Trust* - Wait expectantly, trusting that the answer will come in its own time. Being at ease with not knowing is part of what allows the answer to come. Patience can be thought of as doing things in God's time.
- *Allow the solution to come from within* - Guidance comes spontaneously from within and cannot be forced. At times, it may be necessary to pose the question before entering the stillness of meditation or to "sleep on it." The guidance often comes with a peace and feeling of harmony that are confirmation that what was received is from the Higher Self.

Listening for guidance within and giving all decisions to a Higher Power are processes that are cultivated. If an answer is not forthcoming before it is necessary to act, simply make the best decision possible and put that decision up for guidance.

Take action on what is given - The "upward spiral" is one of coming to know and then acting on what is given. Cayce emphasizes this point:

"Then take the same considerations, with the answer, into the deep meditation and let there still be the answer from the deeper within - but abide by that given thee! Do not become one that asks and does not abide by the answers! For they would soon become as naught to thee!" (Edgar Cayce Reading 1246-4)

When I first came across these statements, I couldn't help but think, "But what if I do the wrong thing?" Eventually, I came to realize that the answer is simple: 'Just choose once again." We are on a journey, and this is about learning from our experiences. If you are not happy with a choice, simply acknowledge that the choice was less than ideal and resolve to choose differently at the next opportunity.

The aspects of surrender could be diagrammed as follows:

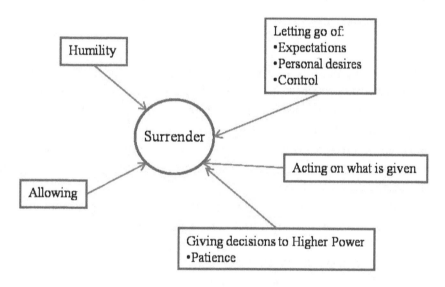

Diagram – Aspects of Surrender

In Chapter 2, we looked at three scales that showed the parallel between emotional state and level of consciousness. How we progress on these charts is a direct function of the willingness to surrender negativity and judgment. In a sense, development of the will could be thought of as this practice of letting go and surrendering to the Higher Power within, of choosing for love over separation. The more consistently we practice, the higher the rate of emotional growth and the higher the level of consciousness.

In "letting go," the focus should be on the function of surrender and not on what is being surrendered. For example, if a fear is seen to arise, it is not necessary to analyze the fear, to attempt to understand where it came from, etc. Rather, the emphasis is on the process of letting go of the fear, and any attachments to the fear or attempts to give it value. Ultimately, this is about moving from allegiance with the self to allegiance with the Self. In letting go of identification with content (our thoughts, emotion, beliefs, fears, etc.), we realize that we are the context (the background or pure conscious awareness that is behind all that is). We start first with surrender of our own personal perceptions and emotions, and eventually we move to surrender of those archetypal issues arising from the deeper level of humanity's consciousness. While the realization of higher states of consciousness is not under our direct control, it proceeds from setting clear ideals, commitment, and a consistent practice of surrender. Ultimately, the only motive for acting will be love and the desire to do the Will of God.

The following stands in the way of realizing our true nature, and is ultimately what must be surrendered:

- All limiting beliefs, opinions, attitudes, judgments, thoughts, and emotional responses
- All payoffs that come from the use of self will
- All self identities and the sense of a personal self
- All fears, including the fear of death or ceasing to exist
- Inclinations to let decisions be influenced by the expectations and desires of others
- Worry, control, efforts to over-manage, and lack of faith
- Struggle and negativity
- Any inclination to assign motives
- Self-judgment

Summary

- We are by our very nature creative beings. Creating unconsciously allows conditioning and habit patterns to dictate our choices. Conscious creating means setting clear ideals, developing self-awareness, and using that awareness to make conscious choices.
- What we put out is returned to us at the same vibration.
- We create our own reality by how we choose to interpret the events of our life.
- It is through making choices and experiencing the results of those choices that we gain or lose consciousness.
- Free will is the freedom to make these ongoing, moment-to-moment choices for fear or love.
- Self-discipline is an acquired skill that comes through practice.
- Setting clear ideals and intentions draws to us what we need to grow.
- The following foster development of the will:
    - Dissolving limiting ideas of who we are
    - Choosing from within for what is real, regardless of what others think
    - Present moment awareness
    - Giving up emotional attachment to the past
    - Becoming aware of the moment when one is able to wrest control from the emotional body
    - Deep self honesty
    - Persistence
    - Asking the Higher Self to put before us what we need to heal
    - Invoking Higher Will
- Surrender is the constant process of handing over whatever occurs to a Higher Power
- Surrender is fostered by:
    - The cultivation of humility - the recognition that there is something larger operating through us

- o Letting go of expectations and personal desires
- o Giving up the desire to control
- o Getting out of the way and allowing higher knowledge to flow through (allowing)
- o Giving all decisions to that Higher Mind
- o Patience
- o Acting on what is given
- o Gratitude

Reflections/Exercises/Practices

For Reflection/Discussion:

1. In The Fourth Way, Ouspensky says, "The worst kind of imagination is the belief that one can do anything by oneself."[89] Dr. David R. Hawkins says, "There is no inner 'thinker' behind thoughts, no 'doer' behind actions, no 'seeker' of enlightenment"[90]. What do these statements imply?

2. Earlier, we discussed the will and its relationship to obedience. What is your reaction to the word "obedience?" How has your understanding of this word changed or remained the same with respect to God?

3. In The Way of Mastery, Jesus says, "I learned... to drop only *unlimited* pebbles, that send out vibrations of unconditional acceptance and Love, forgiveness, unconditional and unbridled vision and revelation,..."[91] What are some of the pebbles you are currently dropping into your pool of awareness? What are some pebbles you would like to drop? (One way to approach this is by topic - politics, religion, personal relationships, etc.)

4. In what ways have you accepted the archetype of Victim? How might you go about releasing that perception?

5. If the will is so important, how might we raise our children differently to foster use and understanding of the will?

6. In reflecting on your own life, were there situations that you initially resisted that you ultimately came to see as what you needed to do? How might you have avoided that resistance in the first place?

7. How much of what you do is influenced by those around you? Why do you wear the clothes you wear, choose the foods you eat? Are your thoughts and beliefs influenced in the same way? How much of an impact do the thought patterns of those around us have on each of us?

8. What is standing in the way of you believing that you are a Christ?

9. How do you feel about the statement that "the ego" cannot reach enlightenment on its own?

10. What method of control do you employ? Do you prefer a passive or aggressive style? Under what circumstances do you normally resort to controlling behavior? What impact does the use of control have on those around you?

11. Reflect on the difference between making and creating.

12. What are some of the ways fear is fostered in our society? How can one live in this environment and not resort to fear?

13. What is the difference between "being a doormat" and surrender?

Exercises:

1. Give up defining yourself by any roles that you play. Turn out any thoughts that begin "I am this" or "I am that." Instead, feel for the deeper reality of who you are - that is pure conscious awareness.
2. Ouspensky speaks of overcoming "mechanicalness." One of the ways to do this is to design exercises for yourself that work against your tendencies and foster self-discipline. Choose something that you will do or not do this week as a form of self-discipline. Examples might be:
    *   Washing the dishes immediately after dinner, if this is a task you would normally put off
    *   Drinking your coffee without sugar if you would normally drink it with sugar
    *   Giving up gossip
    *   Walking instead of driving to a nearby location
    *   Dusting a particular piece of furniture each day, whether it needs it or not
    *   Taking a fifteen-minute walk at the same time each day
    *   Delaying decisions, if you are prone to quick decisions
3. What negative habits would you like to give up? Do not limit yourself to physical habits. Are there habit patterns of the mind that are limiting you, such as the need to be right, a perception of the world as a difficult place, etc.? Set an intention for eliminating each. Be specific.
4. Become very conscious of the moment of choice as you go about your day. Become aware of the habitual manner of responding. Recognize that there are multiple responses possible.
5. What are your own worst fears? In what ways do they rule your life? How might you go about letting each one go? Be specific.
6. Think back on three of the actions you performed today. Look at your motivation for each. Were they done from fear or love?
7. The next time you find someone or something as lacking, make a conscious choice to "choose for love" instead. Invite a change of perception.
8. Make a conscious decision to let the heart, rather than the head, take the lead. As you go through your day, constantly choose from a place of love.
9. The next time you are in a situation you do not like, become aware of how your attitude is shaping the situation. Ask what might lead to peace.
10. Review the ideals you set earlier. Have those ideals influenced your awareness and behavior? Modify those ideals to reflect current understanding.
11. If "what you believe is what you perceive and what in turn creates your reality," what limiting beliefs are standing in your way? Go within and release them using the head and the heart. Feel how it feels to be free of that belief. Envision yourself acting free of that belief.
12. Persistence in the face of discomfort is one of the factors in self-discipline. Define a plan for working through this discomfort when it arises.
13. Do something to raise awareness of the words "ought," "should," "must," and "have to." Some possibilities:
    *   Write them on an index card and carry it with you through the day. Each time you mentally use one of these words, question the validity of the need to "do."
    *   Write these words on a piece of paper and burn it.
    *   Envision these words on a white board. Erase them. Each time one of these words reappears, erase it again.

14. When you are ready, ask to have your own imperfections revealed to you. As you begin to see them, simply observe without judgment and be thankful for the additional self knowledge. Express a willingness to be open to new ways of being.

15. Become aware of the stress in your life. Recognize that it is self-induced. What pressures are you placing on yourself? Is there a limiting belief or attitude behind that pressure? Surrender and feel the difference within.

16. Instead of reacting to circumstances around you, begin to practice discernment by being still and waiting for guidance. (Observe any desire on your part to force a response rather than wait for it to arrive.)

17. Become aware of your desires. Does satisfying these desires provide fulfillment?

18. Sit with the phrase, "Of myself, I am nothing." How does that statement make you feel? Does any resistance arise? How can you overcome that resistance?

19. Take each of the following affirmations and repeat it constantly throughout a day. Write it on an index card to carry with you if necessary.
    - *The Lord is my shepherd, all of my needs are provided.*
    - *There is nothing I have to do to rest in the Love of God.*
    - *I am safe in God, there is no need for fear.*

    How does use of the affirmation make you feel?

20. Give all decisions, big and small, to Higher Power. Practice discernment by being still and awaiting wisdom. Trust in the process.

21. Choose something to surrender each day. (An indication that something has truly been surrendered is that it disappears - there is no longer an attachment to it.)

22. When you receive guidance, become aware of whether that decision is for the good of all. Examine your own commitment to the guidance; can you buy into it with both the head and the heart? If you are satisfied with its value and your commitment, make the decision to act on it, even if it is socially uncomfortable to do so.

23. Familiarize yourself with archetypes. Become aware of various archetypal energies. For example, take a few days and look for Victim energy as you go about your day, to raise your awareness of how prevalent that energy is and how the pool of Victim energy that surrounds us impacts you. What are your primary archetypes? What are the up-side and the down-side of those archetypes? Have a quiet session where you speak with each of those archetypes to understand why it is in your life.

Meditative Practices:

1. Choose a meditation session in which you feel God working through you, where you are the hands and feet of God in this world.

Chapter 15 - Forgiveness

This chapter will explore the topic of forgiveness. It will look at the difference between the ego's definition of forgiveness and the Self's definition of forgiveness. It will explore the relationship between forgiveness and karma, the benefits of true forgiveness, and the impact of not forgiving. Lastly, it will look at how to foster the forgiveness process.

Self Remembering

True forgiveness stems from Self remembering. True forgiveness, then, is Self to Self - that is from a position of oneness. It means remembering who we really are and, in so doing, recognizing other people as one and the same (a pure and holy child of God). We will later look at how to approach forgiveness, but tools and techniques are based on getting in touch with who we really are. As you use them, you come to realize that others are simply an extension of yourself. Until we can look at another and see him or her as a part of the Self, we are not able to forgive and blockages within ourselves are limiting the ability to forgive.

Firmly entrenched in its position of separation, the ego is incapable of forgiveness. Small self to small self (self to self) is by definition separation. Forgiveness, then, from the ego's perspective always involves victim mentality and some form of judgment, however keenly it may be disguised. In <u>A Course in Miracles (ACIM)</u>, Jesus makes a distinction between love and a call for love. In the same paragraph, he says:

"You cannot safely make this division, for you are much too confused either to recognize love, or to believe that everything else is nothing but a call for love.... For you do not respond to what a brother really offers you, but only to the particular perception of his offering by which the ego judges it. "(T-14. X.7.2-6)

At the point we are able to move past that judgment into Self remembering, there will be no separation.

Self Forgiveness

There is nothing that is unforgivable. Lesson 46 of <u>ACIM</u> says, "God does not forgive because He has never condemned. And there must be condemnation before forgiveness is necessary" (W-pI.46.1.1-2). This condemnation and the choice to see something as unforgivable occur only within one's own mind. It is part of the ego's delusional nature to continue to hold onto one's own past mistakes and to see them as unforgivable. We are on a path to total self-acceptance, and letting go of the illusion that we have done something unforgivable is the basis of that self-acceptance. If we return to the charts of consciousness, we see that guilt and shame are very low vibrations that stand in the way of spiritual growth. Feeling bad about the past simply impedes further progress.

Thus, the difference between what occurs when guilt and self-judgment are present, versus when they are not, might look as follows:

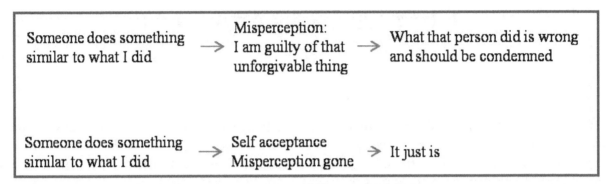

Diagram – Impact of Misperception

We have to accept that these "unforgivable" acts were done out of ignorance - that we were at an earlier stage of consciousness. If we look back at childhood, we understand that there is a growth process; what we are capable of at one age is very different from what we are capable of as we grow up. It is no different here. What we did was simply a reflection of where we were in consciousness at that time. We did not know what we know now. Those actions were driven by the ego and not the Self, which is our true identity. There is no point in continuing to feel bad about what simply needed to be at that level of development.

This process can be quite literal. Two stories of highly spiritual people demonstrate this point. One is of a psychic and healer who was sexually abused as a child by a male babysitter. She eventually "saw" a lifetime as a monk where she had sexually abused that same soul who was now incarnate as her former babysitter in this lifetime. The other is of a psychologist who was carrying his elderly mother because she could no longer walk. He had a flashback to a memory of carrying her as a newborn infant to leave her on the rocks to die because female infants were not valued in that culture. We have to realize that there were many things that occurred in the history of humanity and that, because we are "those people," we still carry those memories within us. Each of us would not need to be here now if we were pure as a lily. While this process can be quite literal, there is no point in struggling with the source of the imbalance. Not only do we have our own past lives to consider, but when we incarnate, we inherit through the DNA any number of misperceptions that come with the lineage. In addition, there may be contracts (things we have come to work on together) and we are always subject to influence from the archetypes that reside in human consciousness. Sometimes, when we release an issue, we are doing so on behalf of our extended family or humanity at large.

With every misperception released, the mist hiding your true Reality is further dissipated. There is a lot of conditioning behind the idea that "good" people don't do certain things and therefore it is easy to suppress or block memories of times when you did do those things, whether in this lifetime or in previous lifetimes. As events in the past come up from your own subconscious, it is important to acknowledge them, to own them, to accept that you were in a different place of ignorance when they occurred, and to forgive yourself. It is not possible to fully awaken unless you are willing to forgive the "unforgivable" within yourself.

A Path to Self Remembering

The Mirror

It is forgiveness of the self that releases the need to project onto another. <u>The Way of Mastery</u> reflects this understanding: "Each time you react to another, you are being given a sign that there is some kind of energy that has been presented to your awareness that you have not forgiven within yourself. "(p.35)

If we look at forgiveness from the perspective that this is all about forgiving the self, other people are then a mirror for the imbalances within the self. What we have suppressed in self is what we judge in others. When anger arises and we move into judgment, it is a sure sign that we are projecting onto another that which is within the self.

This is the Law of Attraction as described by Abraham Hicks: "That which is like unto itself, is drawn."[92] Abraham also says, "There is never injustice, because nothing can ever happen to anyone that is different from the vibration they are offering."[93] It is important to recognize that if you had not drawn a given person into your life, you would have drawn someone else, as it is the unresolved issue within the self that is putting out the attracting vibration.

Previously in this book, we looked at the difficult people in our lives and what annoys us about them. This information, along with broader life patterns of what keeps recurring, are opportunities to uncover limiting beliefs and unforgiven blockages. It is worth noting that it is not always the specific form of behavior in another with which we identify, but rather its underlying meaning. For example, one who perceives something that has been said as "criticism" does not necessarily imply that one is critical. It may be the deeper issue of feeling "not good enough" that is leading one to perceive the comments of another as "criticism."

When the same thing keeps reappearing, it is an opportunity to relive the event in a different form and to choose to see it differently. Once again, it is our choice. We can choose to continue to be a "victim" for the rest of this lifetime and many more, *or not*. The one thing we can be sure of is that the underlying issue will be with us until it is resolved and we will continue to perceive more of the same until the misperception is released.

Taking personal responsibility and releasing the victim archetype is humanity's major challenge at this time. Moving beyond victimhood means giving up judgment and the tendency to rationalize and justify our own behavior. As we choose to accept personal responsibility for what occurs, we reframe "negative" events as opportunities for personal growth and self-responsibility. It is personal responsibility that allows us to see the most difficult people in our lives as our greatest teachers. The more deeply repressed an issue is, the stronger the ego reaction.

It is the willingness to take personal responsibility that allows the change of perception from the self to the Self. The willingness to see things differently instead of blaming the other is what creates the space for healing to occur. Each perceived offence is actually an opportunity to look within and to choose for projection or forgiveness, for separation or for oneness. In responding to another with love and acceptance, we transform that same energy pattern within our own self. Anyone can be forgiven at any time, whether that person be dead or alive, simply by making a different choice.

Karma

So, where does karma come in? If we have truly forgiven the self, is it necessary to endure the same treatment we inflicted? I don't think so. Forgiveness can occur in a positive way. For example, one who raped in the past might choose to come here as a woman. There is within the psyche a need to forgive that action. Through awareness (observing dreams and what arises from the subconscious, what emotional reactions are present to external events), one can recognize this need to forgive the self of that action and choose to do so. And thus, rather than working toward self forgiveness by experiencing the treatment inflicted, one might, through introspection, reach self forgiveness by realizing that an energy imbalance was created in humanity's consciousness by those past actions. As a woman, that person would be positioned to help restore feminine energy to its rightful place.

Alternatively, through lack of awareness or choosing not to forgive, one can continue to project unto others. Unfortunately, that projection draws to us exactly what we do not want, because it still needs to be forgiven. By acknowledging what arises, and forgiving the self, there is no need for harsh outer circumstances to make the lesson more obvious. There is, however, still a need to help balance the energies that were put out of alignment through previous actions, even while there is no longer a need to endure the same treatment.

These statements reflect these understandings:

The Way of Mastery - "*In unconditional loving, karma does not exist. Unconditional love means that the mind has awakened and seen that nothing that occurs in life can cause it to contain or withdraw its love.*" (p.336)

Edgar Cayce - "*Karma is the natural law, yes. But there is the law of grace, and this is just as applicable as the law of karma.*" (Edgar Cayce Reading 2727-1)

St. Germain - "*However, forgiveness does not absolve the soul of the requirement to balance the energies misused.*"[94]

Keys to forgiveness thus are an openness and a willingness to work with everything that arises within, an awareness of how the forgiveness process works, and a willingness to forgive the self no matter what arises.

Definition of Forgiveness

Forgiveness is a process that occurs within your own mind. It means looking at a perceived injustice, reflecting on it, acknowledging your own feelings and inner hurt, and deciding to change your perception of that injustice. It is a willingness to let go of attachment to your view of what occurred. It is a willingness to view everything that occurs as "what is" and to accept that you are not in a position to judge anything. In the end, it is about forgiving yourself for the misperception that the other could ever be separate from you. It is an act of Self liberation. In choosing to perceive differently, you release the negative energy surrounding a person or event, and choose instead to have peace and to see the oneness that is always there.

Forgiveness is *not* justifying or condoning another's behavior. There is no need to minimize or excuse any wrong that was done or even to continue a relationship if you choose not to. This is an inner change of perception that releases your attachment to the situation and a recognition that it was simply what needed to be at that point in time.

Forgiveness is also not justice. It is possible to forgive and still pursue justice and/or retribution. That is simply done without the need to pass judgment or to place blame.

The following chart is an attempt to portray the difference in how the ego views events as opposed to how the Higher Self views events.

Ego	Higher Self
We are separate	We are one
Something wrong happened	There is a larger context where I drew this event to me so I could learn from it All energy is neutral - it is my perception that defines it as good or bad
Problem is "out there"	The problem is within me - I have a misperception
When someone does something wrong, I have the right to judge	The Higher Self recognizes that we are all engaged in a Self remembering process and that actions stemming from the ego are a part of this process The Higher Self knows our true nature as pure and holy children of the Divine
The ego is in control and will do whatever it takes to protect itself	The Higher Self uses every situation as a learning opportunity to foster oneness

When we truly forgive, we act from the Higher Self. In doing so, we not only release negative attachments but we reestablish the presence of the love that is always there.

Benefits

The benefits of forgiving are many. Forgiveness releases energy blockages within the body, so choosing to forgive is a way to better physical and mental health and to greater happiness.

Forgiveness helps us to live in the present moment by setting us free from the past. It restores a sense of personal power in that one is no longer repeatedly playing the role of victim. Forgiveness is release from the self-made prison of attachment. It releases attachment to painful memories so that what did not work in the past is no longer driving present behavior.

Forgiveness allows one to be aware of the peace that already exists within. The choice to perceive from oneness dissipates the mist that blocks true perception. Forgiveness changes the relationship with another. It allows the energy to flow freely in a relationship. Earlier, we discussed how others pick up changes in our own energy field and how that change of perception will be felt by the other. Forgiveness is a way to help others. When the relationship changes to one of acceptance, it creates a space for the other to choose differently and to heal. By perceiving Self to Self, we are open to guidance from beyond on how to be of help to another. It is in union, by joining with another, that separation (the ego) is undone. Every act of forgiveness is then a step toward dissolution of the ego.

Conversely, choosing not to forgive is a block to one's own ability to grow in consciousness. It is a choice to strengthen the misperception and energy blockages within the self. Former Catholic priest and speaker Ron Roth likened it to garbage, where the longer it is buried, the more it rots and stinks up your insides. What is not forgiven continues to be an energy drain within the self. Suppression of low vibration emotions, such as hate and anger, consume the energy that could be better spent on strengthening the will and working with the ideal.

The Forgiveness Process

True forgiveness can be felt. There is a feeling of freedom or liberation from the situation and a letting go of attachment to it. While *trying* to forgive is akin to the use of self will and feels like effort, with true forgiveness, the imbalance is released within a larger picture. It feels more like the use of spiritual Will, in that it comes from beyond the self. When attachment is fully released, the details of the situation become irrelevant. The ability to forget seems to be related to the degree to which one is able to let go of attachment and not take a situation personally.

Forgiveness can be thought of as a process and there are things one can do to facilitate the readiness to forgive. The following actions facilitate the forgiveness process.

Develop self-awareness - To even begin the forgiveness process, one needs to have the self-awareness to observe what is occurring internally and to openly acknowledge it. That implies that one can recognize anger, guilt, fear, and shame when they arise, and one is familiar enough with information processing distortions to know when one is engaged in them. Self-awareness also enables one to make a distinction between true and false forgiveness. It positions one to ask the hard questions:

- What am I putting out that is drawing this to me?
- Is it possible that I did this at some point in the past?
- If I had done this, would I want to be forgiven?
- What limiting belief could be leading to this?

Self-awareness positions one to own his or her role in the story and to recognize any reluctance to undertake the process. In a sense, the previous contents of this book have all been preparation for the process of forgiveness.

Give up victim consciousness - Give up the idea that you were and are a victim, and open to the possibility that you drew this situation to yourself and that you can grow - or have grown - from experiencing it. What do you have to learn from the situation? In what way(s) did it help you to grow? What disharmony resides within yourself that leads you to believe you are a victim?

Own what is yours - Honestly own your part in the situation. In what ways have you magnified in your own mind what actually occurred? Why have you chosen to perceive this in the other? What misperception(s) reside within yourself that you feel it necessary to project onto the other? Even when inappropriate treatment was inflicted, this self-examination and ownership of your continuing need to relive the situation is possible. Stick to the facts of the story versus your interpretation of those facts when reviewing what occurred, and focus more on the feelings within to uncover where your misperceptions are.

Release limiting beliefs - You must *believe* that you are already forgiven - that the you that is your Higher Self, your true identity, is as pure and holy as the day you were created. Let go of any limiting beliefs of unworthiness. The more we are able to believe that we are pure, perfect, and innocent, the more we are able to see the other as the same. It is that which enables true forgiveness. God or Source is always transmitting unconditional love. As we release our own blockages, we are able to perceive the love that is always present and to use that love to transform the events of our lives. It is total self-acceptance and forgiveness of the self that lead to total freedom.

Acknowledge and work with painful feelings - This is again where we turn to the role of emotions in the healing process. Not only are feelings the barometer for what needs to be healed, but it is only by fully feeling a suppressed emotion while choosing to move to a higher perspective that we position ourselves to choose forgiveness. Suppressed emotions are like time bombs just waiting for the right opportunity to go off. When they do arise and we are aware enough to perceive them, we have before us an opportunity for growth in consciousness. That is the opportunity for Self remembering. Pretending the emotion is not present when it arises is a form of Self *in*validation. It is giving up victimhood and owning that our feelings are self-generated (or what we choose to tap into at a certain vibration) that positions us to acknowledge and fully feel them. It is choosing to embrace our own feelings and sending love where it has been lacking within the self that allows us to release attachment to those feelings and sets the stage for the change of perception to occur. The more we are able to accept, love, bless, and release the charge associated with our own emotions, the more the wall around the heart is reduced so we can fully feel our true nature as beings of love.

Open to the idea that there is another way to look at any situation - Be open to the idea that there is a bigger picture at work. The world of spirit looks through a different lens. The more we can believe that things are as they should be, the more we are at peace with what is and the more we allow energy to move where it needs to be.

Weigh the cost of continuing to carry this burden - With all of the benefits that forgiveness has and all of the suffering that comes with not forgiving, is it worth it to continue to carry this? Your story is what has brought you to this point, but it is not necessary to continue that story. Yes, another may have hurt you, but is it also necessary to give to that person your ongoing happiness and peace of mind? Become aware of how continuing to carry this burden is a choice and how it might be more compassionate to yourself to choose to let it go.

Make a commitment to forgive - We have already looked at how the power of intention calls what is needed to make that intention a reality. The use of the phrase "a little willingness" reflects the same meaning as commitment and intention in that they all reflect a conscious decision to make the choice for forgiveness. That can be as simple as saying, "(Lord/God/Higher Self/Holy Spirit), help me to see this differently." Making that decision begins to draw what is needed for the change of perception to occur.

Turning the process over to a higher power, whatever you may choose to call it, reflects the understanding that true forgiveness comes from the Self and not the self. The little willingness creates the space for the change of perception. In that sense, true forgiveness is a combination of intention and surrender. It is recognition that the self is incapable of true forgiveness and that surrender to the Self (God, Higher Power, Holy Spirit) invites that healing to occur. Forgiveness comes not from effort, but from the willingness to surrender and be open to its presence. Trust that whatever is needed - insights, access to old memories, the release of emotional blockages, etc. - will occur.

The following quotes reflect this understanding:

"Your work... is not to seek and find love. It is merely to turn within to discover every obstacle that you have created to its presence, and to offer that obstacle to the great dissolver of dreams, the grace of the Holy Spirit. "(The Way of Mastery, p.72)

"Then thy attitude should be: 'Lord, they are thine, as I am thine. I am willing. I forgive. I present the problems to thee. Use me, use them, in whatever may be thy will in the matter. This then puts thee in that

position that there is no stumbling block, and that becomes then loving indifference. For ye have left it in the hands of the Creator, who alone can give life and withdraw it.'" (Edgar Cayce Reading 1152-2)

A part of this process might be feeling and visualizing what forgiveness would feel like without getting into how it will occur.

Be willing to re-contextualize - Being open to other ways of viewing the situation is key to the forgiveness process. That re-contextualization has many aspects:

- Be willing to recognize the past as something self-created so one could grow in consciousness. Questions one might ask are: How might I have drawn this? What was my attitude preceding the interaction?
- Be open to the idea that there is love in everyone and everything. That does not mean excusing an offense, but rather looking for the good and minimizing the faults. The more one can relate to the other as a fellow human being, the more one is open to forgiveness. Be willing to look at things from the other's point of view. What else might be going on in that person's life that explains that behavior? Remember that everyone is doing the best he/she can from his/her own level of consciousness.
- Recognize that we all make mistakes. When have I behaved this way in the past? Reflect on your own shortcomings and think of instances in which you needed forgiveness from another. Recognizing that we've all made mistakes will help you relate to someone who needs your forgiveness.
- Give up judgment. Loving acceptance of yourself and the other is reflected in your willingness to let go of the past and - in particular - your interpretation of the past. As thoughts of past painful events arise, refuse to honor them or to follow previous thought patterns. The techniques outlined in the chapter on "Working with Thoughts" can be used to work with this rumination.
- Give up any expectations you placed on the perceived perpetrator. In what ways were you looking for love outside yourself rather than within from your own Source?
- Depersonalize the situation. If you were listening to someone else tell this story, how would you see it differently? Be open to seeing your own story differently.
- Remember that we are all just passing through this world. Nothing is permanent. What is important is how we grow from the experience.

Keep Mistakes in Perspective - Recognize that we all make mistakes, that they come from lack of understanding, that there is nothing unforgivable, and that no one can be lost. Self-recrimination, guilt, shame, and blame are useless. They are also a decision and it is far better to choose to release them and move on.

Recognize incomplete forgiveness - In spite of the best intentions, sometimes forgiveness is not complete. It is better to openly acknowledge mixed feelings and to reaffirm the commitment to forgive. Sometimes it is possible to forgive some aspects of a situation while maintaining an attitude of openness to forgive on other aspects.

Readiness to Forgive

There is a change of allegiance from the self to the Higher Self that occurs with true forgiveness. This shift *is* the work of forgiveness. There is within each of us a capacity for love that is untouched by outer circumstances. Psychologically, it is difficult to forgive while we believe something was done to cause us harm. There are two forgiveness "prayers" that help in creating this little willingness to see things differently. In that sense, they help move the soul to the place where forgiveness is possible.

40 Day Forgiveness Prayer

The 40 day forgiveness prayer comes from Everett Irion, a longtime Association for Research and Enlightenment dream counselor, lecturer, and author. It goes like this[95]:

To the other:
[Name of the other], I am praying to you. Thank you, [Name of the other], for doing to me all that you have done. Forgive me, [Name of the other], for doing all that I have done to you.

To your own unconscious:
[Your name], I am praying to you. Thank you, [Your name], for doing to me all that you have done. Forgive me, [Your name], for doing all that I have done to you.

Guidance for the prayer:
- After doing the prayer each day, put it out of your mind so it can do its work undisturbed by your own thoughts, wishes, and expectations. (If you need to divert your attention from the prayer, say "Thank you, Lord" as often as necessary.)
- Don't tell the person to whom you are praying.
- Keep track of the 40 days on a calendar. If you forget a day, start the 40 days over again.

Ho'oponopono

Ho'oponopono is a Hawaiian practice of reconciliation and forgiveness. Recent attention was drawn to it by the Hawaiian therapist Dr. Ihaleakala Hew Len, who reviewed his patient's files and then looked within himself for anything that could be forgiven using a cleaning process called Self-I-Dentity-Through-Hooponopono. Ihaleakala knew that everything that exists also exists within his own soul, and thus he could assume one-hundred-percent responsibility by using the cleaning process. As he forgave within himself, the patients under his care also improved.

The phrases are simple but need to be said with feeling from the heart. When an opportunity for healing presents itself, with as much feeling as possible, say:

- I love you.
- I'm sorry.
- Please forgive me.
- Thank you.

Both of these prayers reflect the deep understandings that healing occurs within the self, that we create our own reality, that what we see in the other is within the self, that sending love is what heals, and that we are all one. They each reflect a willingness to see things differently and to forgive. Interestingly, the Psychotherapy: Purpose, Process and Practice supplement to ACIM reflects these same understandings.

Summary

- True forgiveness is Self to Self and is only possible when we move to Self remembering.
- The ego is by definition separation and is incapable of forgiveness.
- The need for forgiveness is self-created; God has never condemned.
- Forgiveness of self releases the need to project onto another.
- Grace is available, although it may still be necessary to help restore the energies misused.
- What we judge in another is what still needs healing within the self.
- Taking personal responsibility and releasing victimhood is humanity's major challenge at this time.
- The willingness to see things differently instead of blaming the other is what creates the space for healing to occur.
- There are many benefits to forgiveness, including: better physical and mental health, increased present moment awareness through letting go of attachment to the past, more peace, better relationships, and a means to be helpful to others.
- Forgiveness is a process and the following are aids to this change of perception:
    o Developing increased self-awareness
    o Giving up victim consciousness
    o Owning what is yours
    o Releasing limiting beliefs
    o Acknowledging and working with painful feelings
    o Opening to the idea that there is another way to look at any situation
    o Weighing the cost of choosing not to forgive
    o Making a commitment (setting an intention) to forgive
    o Being willing to re-contextualize
- The 40 day forgiveness prayer and the Ho'oponopono process may help in fostering the little willingness to see things differently.

Reflections/Exercises/Practices

For Reflection/Discussion:

1. Reflect on the statement, "Evil is the consciousness of humanity and not something external." Is it possible that evil is necessary? What purpose might it serve?
2. In his book Radical Forgiveness, Colin Tipping proposes a new set of questions for therapy:
    o "What is perfect about what is occurring for this person?
    o How is the perfection being revealed?
    o How can this person shift his or her viewpoint in order to accept that there might be a certain perfection in the situation?"[96]
   What benefits do you see to this approach to therapy?
3. Anger is a strong emotion. Is it helpful or harmful to get anger out? How would you propose working with anger?

4. If the need for forgiveness is all in one's own mind, how does that relate to karma and grace? What impact do your own beliefs about forgiveness have on what it takes for you to feel you are forgiven?

5. Reflect on Abraham's statement, "There is never injustice, because nothing can ever happen to anyone that is different from the vibration they are offering." What are the implications of that statement in your own life?

6. In what ways have you chosen to be a victim? In what ways do you continue to make that choice?

7. What are the implications of the statement that "minds can join, but bodies cannot?"

8. Is doing something bad the same as being a bad person? Are there places where you are hanging onto the idea that you are a bad person?

Exercises:

1. Bring to mind someone you are angry with. Work with re-contextualizing. Try to put yourself in their position. What would you have done differently? Is there a lesson that came from your interaction with that person? Can you forgive that person?

2. As you interact with the media (read the paper, watch the news, listen to political or climate change discussions, etc.) and see yourself move into judgment, choose instead to look for the perfection in the situation. Resist the inclination to go to fear or anger and open to the possibility that what is occurring is what needs to be; be open to the idea that there is something greater at work.

3. Choose an affirmation that reflects your true nature as an innocent child of the Divine and use it on a regular basis. It might be something like one of these:
   o I am as pure and holy as I was the day I was created.
   o I forgive myself for thinking I could ever be anything less than love.
   o My true nature is that of light and love.

4. Recall something you feel you have already forgiven in yourself. In what ways did you grow from having had that experience? How did the experience of forgiving feel? How important are the details of the event now?

5. Choose an event you wish to forgive and set a sincere intention to forgive that event. As time passes, be open to what comes to you - memories of when you did something similar, opportunities to release aspects of the event, memories of when the perpetrator did something loving or kind, a softening of your own harshness about the event, ways you have magnified what actually occurred, etc.

6. Choose a painful event from your life, and write the story of what happened as if it had happened to someone else.

7. What upsets you the most in the world today? What stays with you and continues to bother you? Look at why you are emotionally attached to this particular thing or issue. In what way(s) does this require forgiveness within you? Is the attitude reflected by this behavior one you exhibit? If you had exhibited similar behavior, would you want to be forgiven?

8. As you go about your day, become aware of when your body tightens up. Dig deeper for the emotion that accompanies that contraction and work with it.

9. Get centered and ask that what still needs healing within be made known to you. Pay attention to what arises from the subconscious, whether it be a memory, a mental picture, a feeling, a thought, or a sensation in the body. Do not judge what arises, but rather choose to bless,

161

forgive, and release it. If you have difficulty forgiving a particular event, use the 40 day forgiveness prayer.

10. Choose any person and look at what you dislike about that person. Honestly look at yourself, and find where that resides within you.

11. Before falling asleep, release the day. Forgive any misgivings or transgressions, see it as perfect, and move it to the past.

Chapter 16 - Conclusion

He who gains victory over other men is strong; but he who gains victory over himself is all powerful.
— *Lao-Tzu*
*****

The Process

In the end, the process itself is simple and yet it is not easy. Sages have been telling us how to go about this for thousands of years and yet, for most, we have not come to the point where we consistently choose for what is life affirming. Basically, the process can be outlined as follows:

- Internal awareness
- Right intention
- A little willingness (choice)
- Surrender to a Higher Power

It always comes down to choice: Do you choose to give your allegiance to the ego or are you ready to set that aside? Are you willing to surrender control and give it to God? If we take the diagram reflecting our creative ability and modify it to reflect what we have discussed, it looks like this:

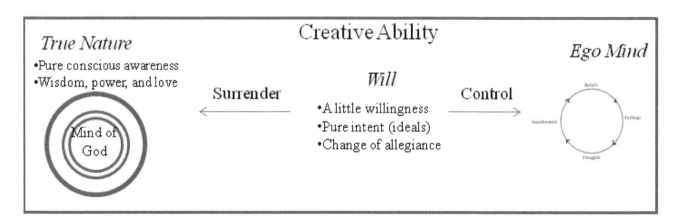

Diagram – Creative Ability (expanded)

We are creative beings and it is at the level of the soul, or what many call "mind," that energy is patterned for manifestation in the physical. It is the constant small moments of choice, where we choose to follow the ideal and to side with oneness over separation, that we build the will. Ultimately, the mist of the ego is dissipated and allegiance moves fully to our true nature as pure conscious awareness, where we are a beings of wisdom, power, and love fully aligned with the Mind of God.

It is inner awareness that positions us to make conscious choices. In coming to recognize and understand what raises or lowers our own energy level - in learning to detect that moment of choice - we are positioned to choose for our true nature rather than for the ego.

The process begins with the sincere desire to connect with the God within. That is what provides the strength to continue when things get tough. This process can be done as a secular practice, but it is still the love within that sustains. When God created souls, he imbued them with the seed of love within. Accessing this seed with sincere intent is what draws what is needed. It is the inherent nature of a seed to strive to grow and reach further out into the world, and so it is with the love within each of us. When a little light is allowed to shine within, the seed naturally takes hold and begins to grow. One way to think of this is that, when humanity was created, it was given the same capabilities as the Divine in terms of the ability to create or extend. In returning to our true nature as beings of love, we are able to extend that love as originally intended.

In misusing our power, humanity created imbalances that now must be brought back into alignment. We heal those imbalances by working with our thoughts, our feelings, and our limiting beliefs and choosing to let go of what no longer serves. That willingness to let go is what allows the wisdom, power, and love that are our true nature to be present. This is one large process of letting go - of thoughts, feelings, beliefs, and control - until finally we surrender all and become a clear channel for the Will of God.

In Edgar Cayce Reading 1904-2, he talks about why in recent times it has been rare to have direct communication with God.

In thy reading,...have ye not wondered why in the sacred writings it is said that God no longer spoke to man in visions or dreams? It is because man fed not his soul, his mind, upon things spiritual; thus closing the avenue or channel through which God might speak with the children of men. (Edgar Cayce Reading 1904-2)

In essence, by denying the spiritual within us, we have shut the door on direct communication with God. Conversely, it is by opening that door - through once again affirming the spiritual within - that we again have direct access to our Source.

One Relationship - One Goal

True love resides only within one's own heart and only within connection to our Creator. Looking to find love in the outside world is futile. It resides in the core of our being by the very nature of who we are. The only requirement then to fully experience love is to remember who we really are. In looking for love, approval, recognition, identity, and sense of self in the outside world, we are looking in all the wrong places, as those things can only be found within. That implies that the only relationship that really matters is the one between each of us and our Source. The ultimate goal of our existence is to be an extension of that love in the world.

Love is founded in oneness and unity. It assumes that we are all co-creators with the Divine, equally valued and equally gifted. In viewing another as inferior or superior, we create separation and thereby obscure the love that is our true nature. Conversely, in seeing others as equally valued co-creators, we move into connection and alignment with Source. Using the idea that others are a mirror, we realize that how we view others is simply a reflection of how we view the Self. In devaluing another, we are by definition devaluing the Self and thus cannot be in connection with Source. The Way of Mastery is helpful in understanding how to proceed in being this love to others: "We never withdraw our Love from you. We simply look through your story line because what we wish to Love is the Christ that dwells within you.." (p.79) It is when we treat others in the same manner that we awaken to the Christ within.

Importance of Mind

In many ways, this is about taking back ownership of one's own mind, where mind here is defined as creative ability and power of choice. We are by our very nature creative beings with the power to choose (free will) and it is what is patterned in the mind that manifests in the physical world. If all is energy, it is our mind that shapes that energy. The mind can be likened to fertile soil where we get to choose what we wish to grow.

It is awareness that enables the power of choice. Thus, there was an emphasis in the early part of the book on coming to know one's self and working with inner awareness. There is a direct relationship between level of awareness and the ability to make spiritual progress.

It takes effort to make spiritual progress. In his book, The Edgar Cayce Handbook for Creating Your Future[97], Mark Thurston says the time gap between what is patterned in the mind and what appears in the physical is a function of the scope of what is being built and the perseverance of those building it. We have looked at the will as a muscle that is strengthened through use. Resistance from the ego is simply a sign that further work is needed. It is important to persist in the face of that resistance. Forms of resistance might include: laziness, procrastination, frustration, doubt, and feeling stuck. When they occur, it is possible to see and own them, to choose to release them, and to surrender them also to a Higher Power.

One of the most helpful statements I have heard on this path is "you are doing this to yourself." This statement recognizes not only that we need to take ownership of what occurs inside (self-responsibility), but also that this is about change of perception. It encompasses the idea that what may have occurred once in the outside world, we continue to inflict on the self over and over again through continuing to bring it up from the past. It reflects the idea that others cannot change our thoughts, words, and actions; each of us has to do that of our own accord. It also reflects the idea that everything that happens is what we have called to the self. It might be said that enlightenment is a state of mind. In changing what we choose to perceive, the nature of our outer world also changes, as it has never been anything but the reflection of our own perception. Enlightenment, then, occurs through the unraveling of our own deception.

The Way of Mastery summarizes the importance of mind:

"...the very pathway of awakening...is always a retraining of the mind. It is a decision to choose to discipline the mind in each moment, to teach only Love, to hold only loving thoughts, and to recognize that there is no such thing as an idle thought, since each thought or perception held in the mind immediately generates your experience. " (p.239)

16 - Conclusion

Guidelines

Although the path to Self remembering is as unique as the individual, those who have preceded us have provided guidelines on how to move forward. The process begins with awareness and a willingness to question everything. It means being inner driven - giving up outside expectations and authority, and habitual responses. It involves relentless questioning, self observation and self honesty, allegiance to the inner world over the outer, and a tolerance for uncertainty. It means taking responsibility for what you have created and seeing the ego as illusion - as a mist that is standing in the way of your Self.

We looked at leaks to the energy body. It is negativity (judgment of self and others) that is the most harmful. It is identifying with judgmental thoughts, picking them up and treating them as valid, that reinforces the misperception that the ego is one's true identity. Avoidance behaviors - intellectual meanderings, idle talk, and busyness - are also distractions that keep one from the real inner work.

We looked at the importance of attitudes and ideals. Putting right attitudes in place has the potential to interrupt the ceaseless repetition of the egoic circle. An ideal is a personalized spiritual standard against which one can make decisions. In mapping the ideal from the spiritual, to the mental, to the physical via the ideals process, one puts in place a framework for a new way of being. The ideals process sets a powerful intention and begins to draw what is needed for growth. It is in acting from the ideal that one reinforces the new way of being.

We begin the letting go process by working with thoughts. It is not possible to directly stop thoughts, but it is possible to see them and to choose not to identify with them. Thoughts are sustained through attention and interest, identification, and acceptance of the belief that they are who we are. Thoughts are thus dissolved by seeing them as worthless, withdrawing interest from them, and recognizing the true nature of the mind. Deconstruction of the ego occurs by seeing it for what it is - a set of entrenched habits of thought.

We continue the process of letting go by working with feelings. As we disassemble our protective structure, we begin to get access to our own feelings. By keeping an open mind, and letting go of victim mentality and defense mechanisms, we begin to break down the wall around the heart that keeps us from feeling. As we learn to self-regulate, we are better able to recognize and direct emotional energy. It is at the emotional level that real progress can be made. Access to feelings sets the stage for Self remembering and it is Self remembering that is able to wake us up.

Emotions are a guide to what still needs to be addressed within. When they do arise, it is important to acknowledge them, to fully feel them while maintaining an observer perspective, and to choose to release them. There are multiple methods available for releasing attachment to an emotion, including a simple choice to release attachment, giving the situation to a higher power, and sending love to the self. Ideally, we would fully feel each emotion as it occurs and choose to release it. Suppressed emotions create energy blockages within the body and what arises as painful memories is an opportunity to release previously suppressed emotions.

Once the lower centers are in balance and we have learned to self-regulate, we are positioned to move allegiance from the head to the heart. The heart is the seat of the higher emotions of love, peace, and joy. The heart operates from a oneness perspective and a state of wholeness. The word discernment is often used to describe the ability to distinguish what comes from the heart versus what comes from the head. Coherence is defined as an optimal state in which the heart, mind, and emotions are operating in a manner that is synchronized and balanced. Benefits of operating in a coherent state are physical and psychological well-being, improved cognitive function, increased energy levels, drawing what we desire with grace and ease, resilience, greater access to universal consciousness via intuition, and access to the Divine within.

A Path to Self Remembering

We are here to remember who we really are and that means letting go of limiting beliefs that imply that we are anything less than co-creators with the Divine. There is comfort in the understanding that there is nothing we have to do to "earn" our way to connection with our Source; it is simply a matter of letting go of the illusions we created that obscure that truth and opening to the presence of the Self. In ACIM, a miracle is defined as a change of perception and that is what we have been working with in this book.

As we grow in consciousness, limiting beliefs begin to dissolve. Earlier, we talked about the increasing levels of understanding that occur as we move up the scale of consciousness. Each increase in understanding represents an increase in wholeness and the ability to take what was previously seen as separate and instead see its interconnectedness. Each step in the chain of being is an increase in unification of the self and a greater understanding of one's true identity. Eventually, there is the desired change of allegiance from the self to the Self - a full letting go of the limiting belief that we could ever be separate from All That Is. Life here is a precious gift, the opportunity to experience the contrast between light and dark, so we can realize that we are light.

The will is the least understood aspect of humanity and yet it is this power of choice that defines the world we live in. Unconscious choices are made from delusion, ignorance, fear, habit, and conditioning.

Development of the will is also a process. It is through making choices and experiencing the results of those choices that we gain or lose consciousness. It is in the constant small moments of life, where we choose for oneness over separation, that we build the platform for the change of allegiance from the self to the Self. Each moment is an opportunity to see what we have created, to take ownership of it, and to make a choice for the Higher Self or for continued separation.

Ultimately, it is surrender to the Higher Will within that allows us to act as Love incarnate. It is deep humility, letting go of all personal desires and expectations and the need for control, trust in that higher power, allowing the higher power to flow through, and giving all decisions to the higher power that foster surrender.

In the end, this is about forgiving the self. No one can forgive you but yourself, because this is all self-created. It is forgiveness of the self that releases the need to project onto another. Other people are simply a mirror for the imbalances within the self. Keys to forgiveness then are an openness and a willingness to work with everything that arises within, an awareness of how the forgiveness process works, and a willingness to forgive the self no matter what arises. It is the willingness to take personal responsibility that allows the change of perception from the self to the Self. True forgiveness stems from Self remembering, and reflects perception from a state of oneness.

We are caught in an endless circle of misperception, and it is through awareness and taking ownership of the power of choice that we find the way out. In addition to letting go of attachment to what stands in the way (misperceptions, limiting beliefs, fear-filled emotions, and negative thoughts), there are centering practices that can help us become more aware of the Truth within. These practices can be thought of as a turning toward the Higher Self or the God within.

Each day is an opportunity to grow in consciousness. It is never too late. One of the values of old age is that, once we are free of the need to make a living, it opens up a space for this inner work. At the time of death, our consciousness is all we have. This lifetime is our opportunity to grow that consciousness - and to release limiting habits, tendencies, attachments, and misperceptions - so we leave here that much closer to remembering who we really are.

All in This Together

We are all in this together. Each of us is a corpuscle in the Mind of God:

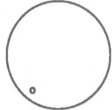

Diagram - Corpuscle in the Mind of God

While the larger circle portrays the oneness of all that is, the smaller circle represents the importance of each to the whole. In his book The Divine Matrix, Gregg Braden says, "the minimum number of people required to 'jump-start' a change in consciousness is the square root of 1% of a population."[98] This is a testimony to the power of light to dispel the darkness. As each soul grows in consciousness, it becomes a light to those around it and dispels a little darkness within the larger circle. A little light makes it much easier for others to awaken and find their way.

We have already looked at how thoughts are picked up by those around us and how we subconsciously influence each other with our thoughts, emotions, and beliefs. We are energy beings, and what we put out does affect the world around us. We are constantly shaping the world around us, individually and collectively. We can create heaven on earth or continue to create the world we currently have. What we can no longer do is pretend that what happens on the other side of the world does not affect us. The interconnectedness of the people of this planet is becoming clearer with each day that passes.

Philosopher, speaker, and writer Jiddu Krishnamurti expressed concern that reform impedes total transformation,[99] because it puts man to sleep by giving him temporary satisfaction. In other words, as soon as we become more comfortable - whether that be physically, emotionally, or mentally - complacency sets in and we give up the inner work needed to make further progress. Multiple sources have commented on how complacency is the real danger to society. This is about a fundamental change in perception, from a position of separation to a position of oneness on the part of humanity. Anything that impedes progress - whether that be complacency, busyness (doing rather than being), specialness, victim consciousness, etc. - is thus an impediment to further growth. Social change is a reflection of inner change in humanity's consciousness. As we move toward oneness consciousness, better social conditions will be the natural outcome of that change in consciousness.

We each bring a gift to the world. Being one does not negate the value of each of us and the unique gift we bring. In the circle above, we are each a small part of the whole, yet the whole is not complete without each of us. Another way to think of this is that we each pattern the Will of God in our own unique way; we bring God's presence into this world in our own unique manner. We are god beings manifesting uniquely in this earth plane. Simply by being, we leave our unique impression on this world.

It is our very nature to be in union with all that is around us all of the time. It is our own misperceptions that block recognition of that union. One way to view the changes occurring on the earth at this time is to see them as an opportunity to better understand our interdependency and oneness. Early in the book, we alluded to the idea that the history of humanity's growth in consciousness may not have been linear. We reach these points in time where we have an opportunity to move to a position of oneness and then we backslide into separation again in favor of power and greed. It is a fundamental change in perception, from separation to oneness, in the hearts and minds of enough people that can affect lasting change. We are meant to be co-creators with the Divine, an aspect of God working its way to full consciousness in the Earth plane. That is how God is made manifest in the world.

Happiness comes from recognition of our unity. The following excerpt from Pathwork® Guide Lecture No. 75 reflects this understanding:

"Truth — and you will experience it one day — is this: In the new state you will see that being no more and no less than a part of a whole, and sharing with so many others something that already exists, makes you a happier person. You have the right to happiness, and you have more rather than less dignity and individuality because of this fact. Your dignity will increase to the extent that your pride of separateness decreases. The fullness and richness of life will increase to the extent that you leave your state of separateness in which you assume that in order to have more for yourself you have to take away from others. That is the error and the conflict."[100]

Enlightened State

We are on the path to a state where mind chatter ceases completely, where knowing is the mode of operation, where peace, love, joy, and happiness are the natural state of being, and where allegiance has moved to the true Self, the spark of the Divine within. The following table summarizes some of the contrasts between the enlightened state and ordinary consciousness:

Enlightenment	Ego Consciousness
Allegiance to Self	Allegiance to self
Alignment of body, mind, and spirit	Separation of body, mind, and spirit
Present moment awareness	Past colors the future
Conscious intention and choice	Choice is unconscious
All is made known	Hidden aspects of the self
Knowing	Thinking
Acceptance	Judgment
Happiness	Suffering
Happiness is an inside job	Happiness depends on others doing what I want
Oneness	Aloneness, separation
Truth	Cultural mores
Inner-guided	Outer-directed
Trust in the Higher Self or Holy Spirit	Trust in the self
Act from what serves the greater good	Get my needs and expectations met
Self-acceptance	self-improvement
Ego dissolved - rational mind in service to the Higher Self	Ego in control
Spiritual intention and surrender to a Higher Power	Dominating and manipulating
Authentic power and strength of conviction	Control
Allowing	Control
Drawing to - visualization and attraction	Force and use of self will

In the end, we are one consciousness following a path of Self remembrance until, ultimately, we realize that we are one with All That Is (God).

Paths to God

There are as many paths to God as there are people on this planet. No one can tell you how to find your way back, because in the end - that is between you and God. All paths lead to God and none can be lost. It makes no sense to judge another's path or to believe that yours is inferior or superior. It is far better to recognize that the same Divine Intelligence is working with, and calling to, others just as it is calling to you. What is your choice, however, is how long you would like to remain in the present state of consciousness.

As I worked with the Cayce material and A Course in Miracles, I came to realize that they are psychological paths to God. Further reading of many authors confirmed that this is indeed inner work. The value of psychological work is that it directs people inward and familiarizes them with their own inner terrain. It raises awareness, looks at how to integrate aspects of the self, and explores other ways of knowing. It encourages directing attention inward in the form of self observation. It exposes the hidden so it may be made known - shining a light into the shadow side to dispel the darkness. It exposes aspects of the self so they can be integrated back into the whole. Since what is hidden unconsciously controls, reintegration of all aspects of the self enables conscious choice.

For each of us, this is about releasing our own self-created misperceptions. It is up to us to find the way to unravel what we mistakenly created and to find our way back to the Truth within. The timing and how that unraveling occurs are unique to the individual.

Again, it is not necessary to release every misperception. We are after a change of allegiance from the self to the Self. Eventually there comes a point where we see anything that comes from the ego as illusion and no longer pick it up and identify with it. Psychological work thus helps us see the ego as the cloud of illusion that it is.

The purpose of this book has been to summarize what sages say leads to growth in consciousness. There is really nothing new here. If anything, the book is an attempt to lend clarity to the Self remembering process. If it has done that, then it has served its purpose.

Mind Map

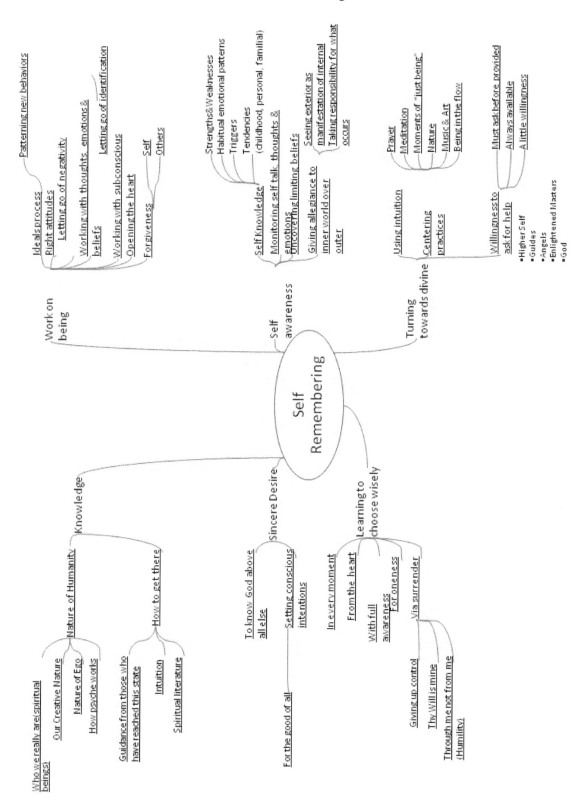

Index

References

Chapter 2

[1] Hicks, Esther and Jerry. *The Amazing Power of Deliberate Intent*, 90-91. Carlsbad, CA: Hay House, 2006.

[2] Hicks, Esther and Jerry. *The Amazing Power of Deliberate Intent*, 17. Carlsbad, CA: Hay House, 2006.

[3] Hicks, Esther and Jerry. *The Amazing Power of Deliberate Intent,* 37. Carlsbad, CA: Hay House, 2006.

[4] Hicks, Esther and Jerry. *The Amazing Power of Deliberate Intent*, 29. Carlsbad, CA: Hay House, 2006.

[5] Hawkins, Dr. David R. *Power vs. Force*, 238. Carlsbad, CA: Hay House, 2002.

[6] Chopra, Deepak. *How to Know God*, 180-186. New York: Harmony Books, 2000.

Chapter 3

[7] THE MANIFESTATIONS OF THE FATHER IN THE EARTH - We are each as a corpuscle in the body of God, performing our individual function. Just as the blood is the life flow in a physical body, so is the spirit the life flow of the universe and all that is in it. (Edgar Cayce Report of Reading 262-62)

[8] Sheldrake, Rupert. *Morphic Resonance: The Nature of Formative Causation*. Rochester, Vermont: Park Street Press, 2009.

Chapter 4

[9] Berns et al. "The price of your soul: neural evidence for the non-utilitarian representation of sacred values." https://www.ncbi.nlm.nih.gov/pmc/articles/PMC3260841/

[10] Tolle, Eckhart. *A New Earth: Awakening to Your Life's Purpose.* New York, NY: Penguin Group, 2006.

[11] Hicks, Esther and Jerry. *The Amazing Power of Deliberate Intent*, 228. Carlsbad, CA: Hay House, 2006.

Chapter 5

[12] Montessori, Maria. *The Absorbent Mind*, 112. New York: Henry Holt and Company, 1995.

Chapter 6

[13] Todeschi, Kevin J. "The Importance of Ideals." https://www.edgarcayce.org/about-us/blog/blog-posts/the-importance-of-ideals/

[14] Step by Step: A Guide to a Search for God Book 1, p.21. Virginia Beach, VA: A.R.E. Press, 2008. Also available in member's only section at:

https://www.edgarcayce.org/members-section/exclusive-member-section/member-virtual-library/member-literature-resource/

Chapter 7

[15] Hamilton, Craig. "The Mistake Most of us Make on the Spiritual Path."

https://integralenlightenment.com/home/the-biggest-mistake-most-of-us-make-on-the-spiritual-path-article/

Craig Hamilton is the founder of Integral Enlightenment and its Academy for Evolutionaries, which offers online courses on meditation and spiritual living to thousands of people in more than 100 countries worldwide. He is a pioneer in the emerging field of evolutionary spirituality who integrates decades of intensive spiritual practice with insights gleaned during his eight years as senior editor of *What Is Enlightenment?* magazine.

[16] Frazier, Jan. *When Fear Falls Away: The Story of a Sudden Awakening,* 4. San Francisco, CA: Red Wheel Weiser, LLC, 2007. Material excerpted from *When Fear Falls Away* © 2007 by Jan Frazier, used with permission from Red Wheel Weiser, LLC Newburyport, MA www.redwheelweiser.com.

[17] Frazier, Jan. "What You Can Do to Wake Up: Not This." https://janfrazierteachings.com/what-you-can-do-to-wake-up-not-this/ Permission to use excerpts from earlier version.

[18] Frazier, Jan. "What You Can Do to Wake Up: Not This." https://janfrazierteachings.com/what-you-can-do-to-wake-up-not-this/ Permission to use excerpts from earlier version.

[19] Parkyn, Chetan. *Human Design: Discover the Person You Were Born to Be*, 19. Novato, CA: New World Library, 2009.

[20] Parkyn, Chetan. *Human Design: Discover the Person You Were Born to Be*, 26. Novato, CA: New World Library, 2009.

[21] Eden, Donna & Feinstein, David. *the ENERGIES of LOVE*, 20. New York, NY: Penguin Group, 2014.

[22] Eden, Donna & Feinstein, David. *the ENERGIES of LOVE*, 21. New York, NY: Penguin Group, 2014.

Chapter 8

[23] Sen. "Calm Down Mind: The Brain, The Heart, and The Law of Attraction." http://www.calmdownmind.com/the-brain-the-heart-and-the-law-of-attraction/

[24] Larzelere, Bob. *The Harmony of Love*, 103. San Francisco, CA: Context Publications, 1982.

Chapter 9

[25] Johnson, Gregory. "Theories of Emotion." http://www.iep.utm.edu/emotion/

[26] Lieberman MD et al. "Putting feelings into words: affect labeling disrupts amygdala activity in response to affective stimuli." https://www.ncbi.nlm.nih.gov/pubmed/17576282

[27] Hawkins, Dr. David R. *Transcending the Levels of Consciousness*, 100. West Sedona, AZ: Veritas Publishing, 2012.

[28] Hawkins, Dr. David R. *Letting Go*, 37. Carlsbad, CA: Hay House, 2013.

[29] Hawkins, Dr. David R. *Letting Go*, 25. Carlsbad, CA: Hay House, 2013.

[30] Hawkins, Dr. David R. *Letting Go*, 39. Carlsbad, CA: Hay House, 2013.

[31] Dwoskin, Hale. *The Sedona Method*, 36-37. Sedona, AZ: Sedona Press, 2003.

[32] Dwoskin, Hale. *The Sedona Method*, 39-40, Sedona, AZ: Sedona Press, 2003.

[33] Kahn, Matt. *Whatever Arises Love That*, 7, Boulder, CO: Sounds True, 2016.

[34] Kahn, Matt. *Whatever Arises Love That*, 60, Boulder, CO: Sounds True, 2016.

[35] Feinstein, D. (2012). "Acupoint stimulation in treating psychological disorders: Evidence of efficacy." *Review of General Psychology*, 16, 364-380. doi:10.1037/a0028602
http://www.innersource.net/ep/images/stories/downloads/Acupoint_Stimulation_Research_Review.pdf

Chapter 11

[36] Jung, Carl. *Alchemical Studies CW 13*, 265. Princeton, NJ: Princeton University Press, 1967.

Chapter 12

[37] Perron, Mari. *A Course of Love*. Nevada City, CA: Take Heart Publications, 2014.

[38] Perron, Mari. *A Course of Love*, 132. Nevada City, CA: Take Heart Publications, 2014.

[39] Goleman, Daniel. *Emotional Intelligence*, 268. New York, NY: Bantam Books.

[40] Goleman, Daniel. *Emotional Intelligence*, 268. New York, NY: Bantam Books.

[41] Childre, Doc and Martin, Howard. *The Heart Math Solution*, 1. San Francisco, CA: HarperCollins, 2000.

[42] Bailey, Alice A. *Esoteric Psychology II*, 415. New York, NY: Lucis Publishing Company, first printing 1942, fifth printing 1970.

[43] Gross, Charles G. "Aristotle on the Brain." *Neuroscientist*, Volume 1, Number 4 (July 1995): 247-248.

[44] Gross, Charles G. "Aristotle on the Brain." *Neuroscientist*, Volume 1, Number 4 (July 1995): 245.

[45] Milner, Conan. "Understanding the Heart of Chinese Medicine." *Epoch Times*.
https://www.theepochtimes.com/understanding-the-heart-of-chinese-medicine_1944277.html

[46] Childre, Doc and Martin, Howard. *The Heart Math Solution*, 8. San Francisco, CA: HarperCollins, 2000.

[47] McCraty, Dr. Rollin. "The relationship between heart-brain dynamics, positive emotions, coherence, optimal health and cognitive function," 1. http://www.coherenceinhealth.nl/usr-data/general/verslagen/Verlsag_Rollin_McCraty.pdf

[48] Childre, Doc and Martin, Howard. *The Heart Math Solution*, 28. San Francisco, CA: HarperCollins, 2000.

[49] McCraty, Rollin et al. "The Coherent Heart: Heart-Brain Interactions, Psychophysiological Coherence, and the Emergence of System-Wide Order." 50. *Integral Review*, December 2009, Vol.5, No.2, (citing Armour, 2003, and Armour & Kember, 2004).

[50] Mercogliano et al. "Expressing Life's Wisdom: Nurturing Heart-Brain Development Starting with Infants." Interview with Joseph Chilton Pearce, *Journal of Family Life*, Volume 5, No.1 (1999): 1.

[51] Mercogliano et al. "Expressing Life's Wisdom: Nurturing Heart-Brain Development Starting with Infants." Interview with Joseph Chilton Pearce, *Journal of Family Life*, Volume 5, No.1 (1999): 1.

[52] McCraty, Dr. Rollin. "The relationship between heart-brain dynamics, positive emotions, coherence, optimal health and cognitive function," 2. http://www.coherenceinhealth.nl/usr-data/general/verslagen/Verlsag_Rollin_McCraty.pdf

[53] Childre, Doc and Martin, Howard. *The Heart Math Solution*, 35. San Francisco, CA: HarperCollins, 2000.

[54] McCraty, Dr. Rollin. "The relationship between heart-brain dynamics, positive emotions, coherence, optimal health and cognitive function," 5. http://www.coherenceinhealth.nl/usr-data/general/verslagen/Verlsag_Rollin_McCraty.pdf

[55] McCraty, Rollin et al. "The Coherent Heart: Heart-Brain Interactions, Psychophysiological Coherence, and the Emergence of System-Wide Order." *Integral Review*, Vol.5, No.2 (December 2009): 20.

[56] McCraty, Rollin et al. "The Coherent Heart: Heart-Brain Interactions, Psychophysiological Coherence, and the Emergence of System-Wide Order." *Integral Review*, Vol.5, No.2 (December 2009): 26.

[57] McCraty, Dr. Rollin, "The relationship between heart-brain dynamics, positive emotions, coherence, optimal health and cognitive function," 3. http://www.coherenceinhealth.nl/usr-data/general/verslagen/Verlsag_Rollin_McCraty.pdf

[58] McCraty, Rollin et al. "The Coherent Heart: Heart-Brain Interactions, Psychophysiological Coherence, and the Emergence of System-Wide Order." *Integral Review*, Vol.5, No.2 (December 2009): 56.

[59] Adapted from figure shown at McCraty, Rollin et al. "The Coherent Heart: Heart-Brain Interactions, Psychophysiological Coherence, and the Emergence of System-Wide Order." *Integral Review*, Vol.5, No.2 (December 2009): 22.

[60] McCraty, Dr. Rollin. "The relationship between heart-brain dynamics, positive emotions, coherence, optimal health and cognitive function," 3. http://www.coherenceinhealth.nl/usr-data/general/verslagen/Verlsag_Rollin_McCraty.pdf

[61] McCraty, Rollin et al. "The Coherent Heart: Heart-Brain Interactions, Psychophysiological Coherence, and the Emergence of System-Wide Order." *Integral Review*, Vol.5, No.2 (December 2009): 75.

[96] Tipping, Colin. *Radical Forgiveness*, 81. Boulder, CO: Sounds True, 2010 - "Radical Forgiveness" © 2009 Colin Tipping, excerpted with permission of publisher, Sounds True, Inc.

Chapter 16

[97] Thurston, Mark and Fazel, Christopher. *The Edgar Cayce Handbook For Creating Your Future*, 10. New York: Random House: Ballantine Books, 1992.

[98] Braden, Gregg. *The Divine Matrix*, 117. Carlsbad, CA: Hay House, 2007.

[99] Krishnamurti, Jiddu. *Commentaries on Living - Third Series*, 17. Wheaton, IL: The Theosophical Publishing House: Quest book edition, 1967. "This material was reproduced by permission of Quest Books, the imprint of The Theosophical Publishing House (www.questbooks.net)."

[100] Pierrakos, Eva, *Pathwork Guide Lecture No. 75*, https://pathwork.org/lectures/the-great-transition-in-human-development-from-isolation-to-union/ Quotation from the Pathwork® Guide Material ©(*1996)* the Pathwork Foundation. Reprinted by permission of the Pathwork Foundation www.pathwork.org.

Made in USA - North Chelmsford, MA
1041048_9781733693202
01.02.2020 1107